"Zweig's stint as a fact checker at a magazine no doubt inspired him to look closely at the unsung, behind-the-scenes workers he calls the invisibles. . . . [He] touches on philosophy, religion, and psychology in exploring the satisfaction derived from work exceptionally well done in contrast to the noisy self-promotion now prevalent . . . and uses the profiles to offer some quiet and thoughtful space to consider the inner value of high-quality work." —*Booklist*

"A fascinating tour of the hidden landscapes on which human society actually operates. This will change the way you see the world and, hopefully, your place within it."
—Douglas Rushkoff, bestselling author of *Present Shock*

"*Invisibles* is a one-book cultural revolution, fighting the current cultural tide toward narcissistic self-promotion with the truth that real satisfaction is often silent."
—Jean Twenge, bestselling coauthor of *The Narcissism Epidemic*

"A Top Business Book to Read in 2014: *Invisibles* explains why some of the world's most talented, accomplished people choose to fly under the radar. . . . It's a clarion call for work as a craft: for generously sharing knowledge without hogging credit and prizing meaningful work above public recognition. An excellent book."
—Adam Grant, Wharton professor and
bestselling author of *Give and Take*

"The genius at the top doesn't make his team look good. It's a great team that makes the guy at the top look like a genius . . . and *Invisibles* proves it."
—Simon Sinek, optimist and bestselling author
of *Start with Why* and *Leaders Eat Last*

"An interesting and important book. It takes us a step closer to understanding how we can be happier and lead more meaningful lives. We can all benefit from the examples of *Invisibles*." —*The Buffalo News*

"The Radical Power of David Zweig's *Invisibles* . . . precise and insightful. This year's smart business book." —*Flavorwire*

One of the "20 Best Books of June." —iTunes

"Invisibles perform key tasks without seeking credit. And they're in high demand." —*The New Republic*

"The great workers who get no credit in a self-promotion obsessed world." —*The Washington Post*

"There are high-functioning invisibles in all factions of the economy, and they operate almost in defiance of the prevailing wisdom that self-promotion and self-regard bordering on narcissism are the way to get noticed." —*Maclean's*

"Zweig challenges the pervasive notion that the people who spend the most time getting others to pay attention to them win." —*Fortune*

"A refreshing point of view, written with precision and detail . . . The values he champions are those that could surely benefit our society (and economy)." —*The Wall Street Journal*

"A fascinating new book." —*Strategy+Business*

"*Invisibles* is an important and timely book. It is also great fun to read. Not only does Zweig do a wonderful job of illustrating his thesis that invisible work is both more rewarding and usually more productive than work that is done for external recognition, we also learn a great deal about the worlds that these Invisibles inhabit." —*Inside Higher Ed*

"Why 'Invisible' people can be the most successful." —*Business Insider*

"Those who toot their own horn by nature get the most attention. But maybe those working hard at their jobs rather than working hard to raise their own profiles are the people who will get ahead." —*Fast Company*

INVISIBLES

"You've been obsessing over your likes and retweets way too much."
—*Wired*

"One of the best books on tech and society in 2014." —*Tech Republic*

"Life as an invisible isn't for everyone. But focus too much on the opposite, on making yourself seen, and you might wake one day to realise you're all visibility—with nothing important to be visible for."
—*The Guardian* (London)

"Unsung heroes understand what it means to live a rich life."
—*The Courier-Mail* (Australia)

"Invisibles are engaged in the most radical act of our era: not talking about themselves. . . . They have cracked the code for a satisfying life."
—*Los Angeles Times*

"Entertaining. The book's strength is in Zweig's portraits of those dedicated workers behind the scenes. . . . The author's genuine respect for his subjects shines through and keeps these stories lively."
—*Publishers Weekly*

"Zweig delivers an engaging read. . . . This well-researched and accessible title will be of high interest to business, psychology, and sociology students."
—*Library Journal*

"An encouraging salute to the world behind the scenes, where the "Invisibles" allow the show to go on. Journalist Zweig suggests, with considerable merit, that, in our culture of wanting it all, we have forgotten the hard work of getting there [and] that invisible work has its own beauty and meaning. The author points to people who take pride in elevating anything to an art, who lose and find themselves in projects that make a significant impact on our lives, leaving us happy while delivering the pleasure and self-respect from doing the job properly. . . . In Zweig's fascinating world, the limelight doesn't hold a candle to the satisfaction of hard work well done." —*Kirkus Reviews*

PORTFOLIO / PENGUIN

INVISIBLES

David Zweig has written for *The Atlantic*, *The New York Times*, and *The Wall Street Journal*, among other publications. His novel, *Swimming Inside the Sun*, was called a "terrific debut from a talented writer" by *Kirkus*. As a singer, guitar player, and producer, Zweig has released two albums, *All Now with Wings* and *Keep Going*, both of which charted on college radio and had the press calling him a "symphonic pop prodigy." Zweig has presented his research about how media and technology affect self-perception at academic conferences and universities around the United States and in Europe. *Invisibles*, his first nonfiction book, thus far has been translated into five languages. He lives in Brooklyn with his wife and two kids.

INVISIBLES

Celebrating the Unsung Heroes of
the Workplace

DAVID ZWEIG

PORTFOLIO / PENGUIN

PORTFOLIO / PENGUIN
Published by the Penguin Group
Penguin Group (USA) LLC
375 Hudson Street
New York, New York 10014

USA | Canada | UK | Ireland | Australia | New Zealand | India | South Africa | China
penguin.com
A Penguin Random House Company

First published in the United States of America by Portfolio / Penguin,
a member of Penguin Group (USA) LLC, 2014
This paperback edition with a new afterword published 2015

Illustration credits
Page 23: Courtesy of Entro Communications
31 (right): Mijksenaar Wayfinding Experts
48: David Apel
68: Courtesy Thornton Tomasetti
158: Pete Clements
188: David Zweig
201: © 2000 AIGA Design for Democracy

THE LIBRARY OF CONGRESS HAS CATALOGED THE HARDCOVER EDITION AS FOLLOWS:
Zweig, David.
Invisibles: the power of anonymous work in an age of relentless self-promotion / David Zweig.
pages cm
Includes bibliographic references and index.
ISBN 978-1-59184-634-1 (hc.)
ISBN 978-1-59184-790-8 (pbk.)
1. Career development.   2. Self-realization.   3. Success.   4. Motivational psychology.   I. Title.
HF5381.Z94 2014
650.1—dc23

Printed in the United States of America
3 5 7 9 10 8 6 4 2

Set in Sabon LT Std
Designed by Elyse Strongin

"The truth is that the heroism of your childhood entertainments was not true valor. It was theater. The grand gesture, the moment of choice, the mortal danger, the external foe, the climactic battle whose outcome resolves all—all designed to appear heroic, to excite and gratify an audience. Gentlemen, welcome to the world of reality—there is no audience. No one to applaud, to admire. No one to see you. Do you understand? Here is the truth—actual heroism receives no ovation, entertains no one. No one queues up to see it."

The Pale King, David Foster Wallace

"There is no limit to what can be accomplished if it doesn't matter who gets the credit."

Ralph Waldo Emerson

CONTENTS

INTRODUCTION

Led Zeppelin. The Rolling Stones. The Beatles. Eric Clapton. Van Halen.

Let's start off with a little quiz. Which one of the above doesn't belong?

Maybe you're thinking Eric Clapton because he's the only single artist, not a band, on the list. Or maybe Van Halen because their heyday was in the 1980s, and the others were a decade or two before. But you'd be wrong on both counts. The outlier in this list is actually the Beatles. All the rest of the artists are linked by one person: a man named Andy Johns.

Cavernous, thunderous, terrifying even, the opening bars of Led Zeppelin's "When the Levee Breaks" constitute possibly the most beloved drum intro of all time. The track, and especially that intro, is seminal, a sonic benchmark thousands of bands, including some of the most successful acts in rock history, aimed for or were inspired by. As the music recording magazine *Sound on Sound* noted in a piece on drum recording, it's "one of the most sought-after sounds in rock." The drum loop has also been widely sampled all over the musical map, from the Beastie Boys to Björk, Eminem to Enigma. Even if you don't know "When the Levee Breaks," you've heard these drums or their imitations.

Ubiquitous now, we take for granted how radical the sonics of (Zeppelin drummer) John Bonham's drums were in 1971, when the band's fourth album was released. As studio technologies were advancing at the time, the trend was toward more mics and more gear in general. On many recordings of the era bands were using multiple mics on the drum kit, usually with one near the bass drum. Also, for some time a more "deadened" and close drum sound, popularized by the Beatles' later recordings, had been gaining popularity. Yet Johns, as the album's recording engineer, the person responsible for getting the band's sounds on tape, tried something counterintuitive, and revolutionary in a way, to achieve such an exceptionally massive sound—he took just two microphones and hung them over a banister high above a staircase that was in the room where Bonham was pounding away. (The band recorded in an eighteenth-century country house rather than a traditional studio, enabling them to incorporate its varied acoustics, such as the stairwell, in the recordings.) He also compressed the signal and ran it through an echo unit, effects which, utilized together, made the overall performance sound simultaneously louder yet more distant, key to its mesmerizing quality.

When we think of our favorite songs, we think of the artists performing them. Perhaps if you're a serious music fan, you'll know who produced the tracks. But we never think of the engineer, which truly is an oversight. The unusual production on "When the Levee Breaks" is "arguably one of the most significant factors in its popularity and longevity," wrote Aaron Liu-Rosenbaum, now a professor of Music Technology at Laval University in Quebec, in the *Journal on the Art of Record Production.*

Johns didn't achieve this sound alone. Of course, Bonham's performance is what this all rests on, and Jimmy Page, the band's guitar player and producer, is widely credited, and rightfully so, as the mastermind behind much of Zeppelin's oeuvre. But it takes nothing away from Page and Bonham to acknowledge Johns's critical role. He was a highly skilled craftsman, who married a deep technical knowledge with an artistic gift for knowing how to get *that sound* on so many recordings. Beyond *Led Zeppelin IV*, Johns engineered nearly all of that band's most successful records, plus the Rolling Stones classics *Sticky Fingers* and *Exile on Main Street*, and numerous other acclaimed albums. This man's stamp is on some of the most widely shared cultural touchstones of a generation. Yet, other than a blip of recognition following his death in April 2013, he, and his work, have remained invisible.

▲

7:30 p.m. Peter Canby shuffles a stack of marked-up article proofs, flicks off his desk lamp, and finally shuts down his iMac for the day. He has pored over a journalist's notes for a particularly sensitive piece, double-checked quotes from a "blind" source formerly in the CIA, held a meeting with a writer and his magazine's attorney over concerns of libel, and instructed a new employee that she needed to be versed in the vocabulary of genetic coding before attending a screening of the sci-fi flick *Prometheus*, because its review, which she later had to check, had a line about a disintegrating humanoid's "DNA-laden chromosomes" sinking into water. No minutia is too minute for the fact-checkers Canby oversees at *The New Yorker*. The requirements to work in his department, beyond possessing a savant level of meticulousness, are stiff. More than half of the sixteen fact-checkers are fluent in a second language, among them Mandarin, Hebrew, Arabic, Urdu, and Russian, along with the usual French and Spanish; the majority have advanced degrees, including the expected Journalism and Comp. Lit. masters, plus an LSE grad, and the errant Oxford PhD program dropout; and "many stay only a few years before leaving because the pace is brutal," says Canby.

The fact-checking department's work is an unseen anchor to the celebrated writing that makes this august magazine's reputation. "We influence the way our journalists do their reporting and how editors edit their pieces," says Canby, who has led the department since 1994. And yet Canby and the fact-checkers at *The New Yorker* know you will not see their names in the magazine. No bylines, no biographical sketches that the authors enjoy. They are invisible to the reader. That is, unless they make a mistake.

Canby and his charges are by any account extremely bright, hardworking people whose traits could likely bring them success in myriad jobs, in journalism or elsewhere, that would gain them some recognition from the reader or other end user. But Canby relishes the behind-the-scenes work. "Even though our names aren't out there we take a great deal of pride in the final product, being part of a process that contributes to the way people think about issues of the day," he says. "That's our satisfaction."

Understandably, we forget that there are people like Peter Canby and Andy Johns making things happen for the stars out front. By the nature of their work, they don't make themselves known. And today, by many accounts, increasingly fewer people with the means to choose their career are pursuing paths like theirs, where they and the results of their labor are invisible. But Canby, Johns, and others like them know something that you will be surprised to learn: receiving outward credit for your work is overrated.

▲

How do you define success? If your search for prosperity is based on an arms race of external rewards and tireless self-promotion, of one-upmanship, the kind where frantic parents hold their kindergarteners back a year to theoretically give them a leg up over their younger peers—a trend known as "redshirting"—then you are free to pursue this too-often futile course toward alpha dog status. But if you come to define success, in both business and in life, as philosophers and religions have for millennia, by the satisfaction derived from work itself and not the degree of attention you receive for it, people like Johns and Canby—the Invisibles—offer a model you would do well to follow. Ask yourself: Do I want to be on a treadmill of competition with others, or do I want to find lasting reward by challenging myself?

I started exploring a group I've named the Invisibles because I was fascinated by people who chose to do work that required extensive training and expertise, that was critical to whatever enterprise they were a part of, yet knowingly and contentedly, they rarely, if ever, were known by, let alone received credit from, the outside world for their labor. What makes Invisibles so captivating is that they are achieving enviable levels of fulfillment from their work, yet their approach is near antithetical to that of our culture at large. What exactly are they doing, how are they *living* that brings them such attainment at the office and internal satisfaction?

The traits of Invisibles are not only consistent with classic tenets of a rich life, but also, as copious research attests, characteristics of business and leadership success. (And workers who embody Invisible traits not only elevate themselves, but improve whatever enterprise they are a part of.) People need to have a commitment to expertise, to find joy in the work itself, and have the will to place responsibility on their shoulders if they're going to excel in any endeavor. Indeed, even for the most visible among us—people like NFL quarterbacks, who spend countless private hours silently studying game film, or the overnight-sensation pop star who played dive bars for years honing her craft—invisible work is a critical element of their very noticeable success. The Invisibles are windows into a certain mentality. While this book offers a powerful example to learn from this quiet elite among us, ultimately, *Invisibles* offers an uplifting framework within which to view ourselves regardless of what we do or pursue.

As valuable as all of these takeaways and scholarly insights are, forget about them, if you will, on some level. The brazen lure of Invisibles is their stories. The major profiles that are the engine of this book are of people who are at the most elite levels in their fields. I was given highly unusual, sometimes the first-and-only access to their worlds. Join me as we: go backstage at a Radiohead concert with the band's legendary guitar tech; slide through highly restrictive security to go on-site with the lead engineer on the tallest skyscraper under construction in China; shadow a virtuoso cinematographer on a major film set; attend a closed meeting of the UN Disarmament Council with one of the world's top interpreters. Some Invisibles' worlds aren't restricted at all, though they are just as fascinating to learn about because we've never known of their existence before. Their work shapes our world—what we see, hear, smell, touch,

experience—yet to all but the few on the inside, is largely unknown . . . until now. I hope for this book to not only offer inspiration, but to help open your eyes, as it has done for me, to the unseen
expertise and passion that buttresses all that we do see.

▲

PERFECTION = INVISIBILITY

The premise of the Invisibles dates back a number of years to my
own stint as a magazine fact-checker. I worked meticulously for
long hours, under hard deadlines, yet never received notice for my
work . . . unless I made an error. (When's the last time you read a
great magazine article and thought, "Man, that must have been
fact-checked beautifully!") For most people, the better they do their
job, the more recognition they are likely to receive. Yet my situation
was the inverse. By design, the better I did my job, the more I disappeared. Yet despite my anonymity, I found the job immensely satisfying, and I began to wonder, as unique as the experience was, if
perhaps there are other professionals who share the attributes and
work conditions of a fact-checker.

As I researched an article for *The Atlantic* that served as a launch
point for this book, speaking to many people, characteristics of Invisibles began to crystallize. Fascinatingly, I found they all consistently embody Three Traits:

1) Ambivalence toward recognition
2) Meticulousness
3) Savoring of responsibility

Remarkably, the traits came to light organically as I spoke with
prospective Invisibles. To that point, almost every single person I
interviewed used that exact word—*meticulous*—to describe their
behavior at work, and sometimes in their personal life as well. After
I spoke with my first few subjects, the interviews took on an almost

comical "wait for it . . ." quality in my mind, as I knew all Three Traits would at some point come out. Working on the book, vastly expanding the number and variety of Invisibles I spoke with and met, only served to reinforce this magic triumvirate. The more I spent time with them, and witnessed how this silent yet steadfast group thrusts against our prevailing cultural current, the more I came to recognize that there is much we can learn from them, both as individuals and as a society. (The Three Traits will be present and discussed throughout the book, as all Invisibles embody all Three Traits, but like a trio of dancers on a stage, each trait will take a turn in the spotlight as the focus of each of the first three chapters. The remaining chapters illuminate secondary commonalities among Invisibles or offer broader perspectives.)

You may ask, given that the vast majority of us work in obscurity, wouldn't nearly all of us be considered Invisibles? But *Invisibles* is not about thankless, mundane jobs. Invisibles, as I define them (really, as they came to be defined through my research), are highly skilled, and people whose roles are critical to whatever enterprise they are a part of. And in contrast to America's working poor or the laborers of developing-world factory floors toiling in anonymity, Invisibles are often highly successful and recognized by, indeed deeply respected among their co-workers for their expertise and performance. What's remarkable is that, despite generally having had the means to pursue other careers, Invisibles have *chosen*, or fallen into and then decided to stay in, careers that accord them no outward recognition from the end user. This is defiantly in opposition to the accolades, or even just pats on the back, most of us so desire. And yet—Invisibles are an exceptionally satisfied lot.

AMERICAN SWING

Things seem to be getting louder. Whether it's an eardrum-punishing soundtrack in a movie theater, the relentless punditocracy shout-fests, or uncouth cell phone yammerers, it's noisy. (In fact, "there is plenty of evidence that the world, literally, is getting louder," Jesse Barber, a professor of biological sciences at Boise State University, who examines the effects of noise on the environment, told me as we discussed several recent studies his team conducted.) And yet perhaps the most blaring note in our zeitgeist is one we hardly notice—*the amplification of ourselves*. We are now a culture that can catalog our every thought and action on Facebook and Twitter. Online comment threads on provocative articles routinely run longer than the articles themselves. We celebrate mobile phone apps like Foursquare that encourage you to show where you are to everyone, all the time. No personal drama or trauma is too embarrassing or mundane to be broadcast on TV. Our ever-more-fragmented news and entertainment fosters an increasingly personalized experience, which research suggests implicitly reinforces a solipsistic attitude. Most of all, as we continue to develop and live through our online versions of ourselves—forever crafting our various social media profiles and avatars—there is the growing notion that we, as individuals, are actually brands to promote. This cacophony of self-importance, of personalized electronic vuvuzelas, has made us like that annoying kid in the front of the class who keeps raising his hand, moaning with distress as he over-tries for the teacher's attention. And it is tipping us dangerously out of balance.

The United States, as is broadly acknowledged, has always been a nation of strivers and ingenuity. Anyone who's made the effort to come here is a motivated individual. And for a long time this motivation gene has been in our cultural, perhaps even biological DNA, and still is in many respects. This American characteristic has two components. And just as the oars on both the starboard and port sides of a racing shell must move with equal force to propel the boat directly forward, the equilibrium of these two components has been crucial for the country's advancement.

Component #1, or let's call it the Port Side, is the Protestant work ethic of American lore, a nose-to-the-grindstone, silent determination. We saw it with the Puritans, the settlers out west, the stoical drive of our immigrant wave that bloomed in the decades around 1900 (by that time informed by more than Protestant traditions and heritage alone), and in the past century with the "company man" honorably satisfied with his role in the machine and the proverbial gold watch and pension at the end for a job well done. This "quiet dignity of the average American," as David Foster Wallace once referred to it, is essential not only to our business acumen, but I'd argue also to one's sense of self. Equally as important, however, is Component #2, the Starboard Side. This is our brashness, our Hollywood Klieg lights that reach to the world, our uniquely American *noise*. Not just the robber barons' gilded mansions, but Cornelius Vanderbilt's awesome sideburns. From Elvis's swinging hips to hip-hop's bling.

In the sport of rowing there's a revered, almost-mythic state when the crew operates as a unified front, the strokes of the oars on both sides matched in force and technique, the rowers in a kind of perfection, where time melts away as the shell glides across the water with majestic speed. Rowers call this state *swing*. And it's our American Swing, the equal force, the synchronicity of these two sides that has enabled our prosperity economically, culturally, individually. And yet it seems in recent years the oars on the Starboard Side alone are feverishly outpacing those on the Port Side, steering us perilously off course, risking our personal and collective potential.

We've been taught that the squeaky wheel gets the grease, that to not just get ahead, but to matter, to exist even, we must make ourselves seen and heard. But what if this is a vast myth? And, if you pull back even further, what if our very choice of fields to work in is affected by this overall ethos?

Deborah Rivera is the founder of the Succession Group, a New York executive search firm whose clients include some of the largest banks in the world. Her specialty is quantitative and analytical positions for global investment banks. "There aren't enough Americans who are prepared to compete for Wall Street's growing quantitative and technology roles that require degrees in math or engineering from top universities," Rivera told me. "It's really a cultural issue," she observed. "In the U.S. people want jobs that get recognition. All of my friends who are successful, hard workers in Wall Street or doctors, attorneys, many of their children are pursuing careers in the arts or entertainment (and thus far aren't able to support themselves)."

Even among the quantitative analysts, or "quants" as they're called in the industry, Rivera noted, too many of them were after "the fame, the fortune with the larger project but not the grunt work to get there. I see this in my own firm—people not willing to do the million cold calls, et cetera, to land a deal. They just want the glory when a big hit comes in."

Behind-the-scenes jobs where the worker gets little outside recognition (though is often highly respected among his peers), that require meticulousness and often have great responsibility—the Three Traits—such as computer coders* and technical analysts are in great

---

* Yes, some of the Internet's biggest players, like Facebook's CEO and founder, Mark Zuckerberg, are celebrated coders, but the vast majority of coders will always remain anonymous, grinding out code behind the scenes.

demand in an otherwise deflated employment environment. "The world is going digital, and software engineers who can help with that transformation are reaping the benefits. Their pay is great, hiring demand for their skills is through the roof, and working conditions have never been better," noted a report by Careercast.com on its most recent study. A *Wall Street Journal* article from late 2011 noted "demand for technical workers such as engineers continues to outpace supply at many companies."

While a variety of factors are leading to the demand for these types of unseen jobs, it is telling that the need is coinciding with our uptick in personal promotion. Through the Internet and its ancillary mobile apps, now more than ever, people are seeking, and have the means, to draw attention to their every thought and action. We are in the era of "microcelebrity." As Clive Thompson wrote about the phenomenon in *Wired,* if you have a blog or are on Facebook or Twitter (which recent studies show is the majority of us today), then "odds are there are complete strangers who know about you—and maybe even *talk* about you." Relatedly, the notion of the "branded self" is a growing phenomenon. As Peter Stromberg, professor of anthropology at the University of Tulsa, noted in a *Psychology Today* piece, branding coaches and business features today teach you to "figure out your strengths and then figure out how to market them, thereby creating a public relations image for yourself." Stromberg asks, "What is Facebook other than a vast platform for creating brand you? For the same reason that movies get louder and brighter and more violent each decade: there's a competition going on for people's attention."

What if the Invisibles' approach to work, which runs counter to this ethos of attention-seeking, not only is beneficial, indeed, critical for us on an individual level—both in our personal and business lives—but also economically essential on a societal level? The highly influential economist and sociologist Thorstein Veblen famously derided conspicuous consumption (a phrase he coined in his 1899 book *The Theory of the Leisure Class*) and displays of wealth and status; instead, he valorized the class of engineers and craftsmen, people with "artisanal instinct or workmanship, a taste for gratuitous curiosity"—essentially Invisibles—"as motors of economic, social, and scientific progress." Succinctly, what impacts on our economy and society as a whole could there be if more people embraced the values of Invisibles, rather than focusing on personal status and gaining notoriety, as is the dominant value today?

I reached out to the renowned economist James Galbraith, who, along with being a senior scholar at the Levy Economics Institute at Bard College and the chair of the Board of Economists for Peace and Security, is vice-chairman of the Veblen Institute in Paris. He remarked that "Veblen's concept of the instinct of workmanship is the right touchstone. We rely on it very heavily—on the simple fact that ordinary working people take pleasure in doing their jobs properly. And giving them the latitude to take that pleasure is a key to economic efficiency."

It's reassuring that Veblen also apparently lived by his philosophies. "Archival documents I have found suggest that Veblen always had a tendency to downplay his achievements," Francesca Viano, an associate at the Harvard Center for History and Economics, who has written extensively on Veblen, told me. "After completing a PhD in philosophy at Yale and when applying to Cornell to get a second PhD, he presented his philosophical studies and an important article on Kant as 'some work' in the field. He also wrote in his testament that nobody should ever raise a monument to his memory." Indeed, Viano noted, "Veblen fits into your definition of 'Invisible' as someone who derives 'satisfaction from the work itself, not recognition' and so did his ideal engineers and craftsmen."

In a case of "be careful what you wish for," it could be argued that a culture of recognition dovetails with a culture of excessive supervision. If the expectation of recognition for nearly everything we do becomes increasingly normalized, what affect does that attitude have on our relationship to privacy, in particular to employers, corporations, and governments overseeing much of what we do? Referencing our newly powerful digital tools, Galbraith said, "Universal monitoring is, it seems to me, corrosive, especially in office settings. One place you see the conflict very clearly is in teaching—the conflict between the autonomy of the teacher and the teach-to-test mentality which has so thoroughly invaded the public schools."

Our race for more attention has profound consequences, both

overt and indirect, societal and personal. There is, however, an antidote to this ever-escalating desire for acknowledgment.

▲

At first glance one wouldn't connect Andy Johns, a veteran insider of and participant in the most elite and decadent sanctums of rock (he was, after all, holed up with Keith Richards in the south of France for months on end), with Peter Canby, deskbound in a Midtown Manhattan office building, toiling amid high-achieving Ivy Leaguers, protector of facts at a prestigious magazine. But, in crucial ways, they are much the same. In fact, Invisibles are found in all walks of life. What binds them is their *approach*—deriving satisfaction from the value of their work, not the volume of their praise.

Like many of the most memorable characters in novels and on screen, we relate to Invisibles and at the same time see something in them that's better than ourselves. Nearly all of us are underappreciated for some aspect of our work (either in the office or at home); it's the Invisibles' pure satisfaction from the work itself, their lack of need for recognition, that is a powerfully grounded trait we all can aspire to. *The Invisibles are not an exclusive group*; they are simply at the far end of a spectrum we all live within. We are all Invisible to varying degrees, in different ways, and in different contexts. The elite professionals I will spotlight in this book, however, show that living at the apex of this continuum, that truly embodying these traits, directly links with success and fulfillment. This book is not a screed against notoriety or making a name for oneself. In fact, most of the Invisibles I've interviewed are well recognized within their fields. But, critically, being noticed was never their motivation.

AMBIVALENCE TO RECOGNITION

Finding Your Way

I am in a place filled with germs. Where people are often angry, tired, confused, and running late but forced to endure long lines and interminable walks. Where one is made to suffer indignities of invaded personal space and invasive bodily searches. And radiation. And overpriced food. Yes, I am in an airport. Atlanta's Hartsfield-Jackson, the world's busiest. And I plan to spend the day here. Why would anyone subject themselves to this environment if they're not going anywhere?

Jim Harding is in his early fifties, married with two daughters. He has thinning hair and a goatee. With an engaging warmth and a Nashville accent, he looks me in the eye and smiles broadly, then says, "No one grows up saying, 'I want to be in wayfinding!'"

When is the last time you've been to an airport, checked in, made your way through security, walked to your gate, used the restroom, bought a sandwich, then boarded your flight without getting confused, disoriented, or lost? For frequent travelers, hopefully this is the norm. Yet we don't think, "What great signs they have here! I found everything so easily." If Harding performs his job perfectly you will never think of him or his work. Its very success enables us to have our minds engaged elsewhere. In fact, the only time we tend to be aware of his craft is when it's done poorly—when we are frustrated because we can't find what we are looking for. Wayfinding, Harding's specialty, is the process of designing cues—from signage to lighting and color, even the architecture, anything at all—to help people navigate a built environment. I'm here to see the art and craft behind creating what is right in front of us but which we rarely notice.

We're riding the "Plane Train," officially an Automated People Mover (which looks like most airport monorails, though it's technically not a monorail), which shuttles between the domestic and international terminals, making stops at the various concourses along the way. Harding, a principal at the design firm Gresham, Smith and Partners, leads their environmental graphic design group, whose prime role is creating wayfinding systems for large, complex environments, including the recently completed Maynard H. Jackson Jr. International Terminal here at ATL (as I'll refer to the airport as a whole). I don't understand why he wants us to begin our day on the Plane Train rather than in the terminal he worked on. But Harding has a plan.

As we ride the train toward the international terminal we study a map posted on the interior wall of our car. "Why are we on the train instead of in the terminal I worked on? It's all about the Ripple Effect," says Harding. Wayfinding in one area of a large structure or environment always affects and is affected by the wayfinding in the rest of the complex. "It's like a spiderweb," he says. "You can't touch one spot without making the whole web move." For example, though the international terminal was the focus of Harding's team's work, every single one of the thousands of old maps of the airport throughout the complex, in the various concourses, the domestic terminal, the Plane Train (like the one we're looking at), the parking garages, the website, et cetera, all had to be redone to include the newly built concourse and terminal.

When undertaking a major wayfinding project like the one at the Maynard Jackson Terminal, as the ripple effect on the maps shows, everything outside the core area must be tied in to the master plan. On the roads encircling Maynard Jackson the top of every street sign related to the terminal has a slightly curved edge, echoing the gentle undulating aesthetics of the terminal's roofline. It's a subtle, likely subconscious wayfinding cue, letting you know you are in the vicinity of the international terminal. Many of the interior signs share this shape as well. This distinguishes the area from the domestic terminal and concourses, where all the signs are a standard rectilinear shape. If you are ever in an airport or campus or hospital or other complex environment and suddenly something feels off, you sense you are going the wrong way, there's a good chance it's not just magic or some brilliant internal directional sense, but rather you may be responding to a subconscious cue like the change of shape from one sign system to another. "Signage isn't only about consistency in terminology and typefaces," says Harding, but also about placing the overall ecosystem in a particular frame. It establishes a sense of place.

ATL has a layout like a fish skeleton, with the domestic terminal as its head, the new international terminal its tail, and a spine connecting the two, on which the Plane Train operates and seven concourses are laid perpendicular, like ribs. The concourses start with the letter T right at the domestic terminal, then run A through F, the newly built one next to the international terminal. The diagram of the airport we're looking at inside the train depicts Concourse F superimposed on the international terminal, a rib on top of the tail, as it were. The trouble is the F concourse is actually adjacent to but not inside the terminal, as it's depicted here. "This is a problem with retrofitting," Harding says. With limited space for signs inside the train, a decision was made to condense the map, even though it's not accurate. "The owners don't always follow our recommendations," he says. It's a minor miscue, and though I detect a wince on Harding's face, he takes it in stride. For all of the analysis, expense, and effort put into creating the ideal wayfinding system, inevitable compromises must be made.

We depart the train and arrive downstairs at the international terminal, as if we are travelers making a connecting flight. In the low-ceilinged claustrophobic space we're met by a large horizontal sign hanging from the ceiling. On a pewter background is bold white text listing concourses, gates, and other information. It has the same clean look of airport and highway signage everywhere. And that's not an accident.

As you walk around any large public environment—airports, museums, hospitals, cities—you'll notice that nearly every sign is written in a sans serif typeface. (Serifs are small lines sticking off the end of letters, like little tails. What you're reading right now is a serif font because it's believed that lengthy close text is easier to read with serifs.) But with near-absolute universality public signs are in sans serif. (The ubiquity of one sans serif font in particular, Helvetica, not just in signage but also corporate logos—employed by scores of global brands from BMW to American Apparel to 3M to, yes, airlines, including Lufthansa and the now-retired iconic American Airlines logotype—has been well documented and much discussed.*) Sans serif fonts' domination today in every environment other than long-form text has to do with a certain global aesthetic toward minimalism, and in the case of Helvetica, its supposed neutral character. But for wayfinding experts sans serif fonts prevail on every sign for one reason: They are easier to read, especially so at a distance. Innumerable studies support this notion. But degrees of legibility go beyond simply choosing sans serif. A lowercase letter "a" in the wrong font may look like an "o" from far away, for example. Within wayfinding, certain sans serif fonts, often specifically designed with distance viewing and legibility as their purpose, rule. Just three fonts, Helvetica, Frutiger, and Clearview, are used in more than three-quarters of airports. (Frutiger, which is the font on the sign in front of us and most of the signs at Maynard Jackson, in fact, was initially designed for Charles de Gaulle Airport in France in 1975.)

Aside from deciding which typeface to use, there's a seemingly endless list of other concerns regarding the presentation of text. Spacing between the letters, words, and lines on signs is also in-

---

* Amazingly, Helvetic Airways, a small airline out of Switzerland, the home of the typeface, does not use Helvetica for its logo. As the graphic designer Marc Levitt (whom you'll meet later in the book) told me when I sent him an image of the airline's logotype: "I can't tell if it's the biggest oversight in the history of design or if it's a bold decision to not go with the obvious."

tensely considered and tested for legibility. A study was even conducted to find the most legible style of arrow to use. Then one must
consider the size and placement of the arrows relative to the text . . .
Very, very little in the style of an airport sign is arbitrary.

And yet all of this attention to detail is in service of the work essentially passing unnoticed. We of course *see* Harding's signs, but
they often are most effective when they function as a kind of tran-
sient, touching just the most superficial (or perhaps, conversely, subconscious) part of our brains, conveying information without
drawing attention to the conveyer. "Ultimately," Harding says, "if
we do our job well, wayfinding enhances the customer experience
without them knowing why or how." For most of us, having our
work seen, or gaining recognition or a higher profile, is a key measure of success, yet for Harding invisibility is a mark of honor.

Harding puts the dizzying number of (often unnoticed) details that
his team must consider in a broader context by following the
Three Cs:

Connectivity—"Wayfinding is like links in a chain," he says. If
someone is walking and they follow a sign and they round a corner,
there should be another sign there to tell them what to do. "If you
miss a link then the chain is broken." This is a linear process.

Continuity—This is the spider's web Harding talked about. Many
airports make changes to one part of the web without taking into
account how those changes tie in to the rest of the system, resulting
in gaps in continuity. Further, on large projects you are confronted
with non-linear, non-intuitive circumstances. It's often not as simple
as "go here and turn left. And there is often more than one path to
a destination," he says.

An example of the challenge of nonlinear wayfinding can be
found in some work Harding's team is currently conducting for
Philadelphia's airport, which is composed of terminals A–F. US Airways has flights departing from A, B, C, and F. People assume that
if they fly into C they can walk to F for a connecting flight, but right
now E and F don't connect to A, B, and C. You have to walk out and

go back through security. US Air offers a shuttle bus so passengers can bypass going outside to connect to a different terminal, but not everyone knows about it. If this sounds like a setup for one of those mind-melt questions on a standardized test, you get a sense of Harding's challenge. As he says, "It's very difficult to communicate quickly and clearly to passengers that this shuttle exists, how to find it, and what it's going to do for them."

Consistency—"The backbone of airport wayfinding is consistency," says Harding. The terminology, typography, symbology, formats, and colors must be consistent for a traveler from the moment he enters the parking garage to when he boards the flight.

As one becomes aware of the extraordinary care taken in designing a successful wayfinding system, the miscues are all the more glaring. You may have noticed when I described ATL's layout the alphabetically dubious inclusion of a T concourse followed by the more logical sequence of A, B, C, D, E, and F. "It's a legacy thing," Harding says when I ask about the T, meaning it's an old, outdated component grandfathered into the new system. This usually happens for economic reasons. Since the costs of changing all the signage and literature can be exorbitant, ill-fitting components like this deviant letter T often are left as is if they're not deemed too critical. Except that all of the signs were being changed anyway after Harding's work on the new terminal, so why, when so much expense and effort had gone into getting things right, would this bizarrely out of place T continue? Harding admits that aside from economics the reasons can be political, and gives an apologetic smile that seems to say this was a lost battle he'd rather not relive.*

A slightly incorrect diagram, an inexplicable letter choice—these seem like minor issues, and they are for many travelers. But an aggregate of oddities like this, especially for less sophisticated travelers

---

* Unable to let it go, I later e-mailed multiple times with Jorge Cortes, assistant director of Design Planning and Development at ATL, to get an explanation for why 'T' was first used and why it's still in use now. Alas, the reasoning behind it is so layered and opaque, all I can say succinctly is that it's the result of repeated airport redesigns, additions, and renamings dating back to 1980 and "per the opinions of a formed focus group, the consensus was to name it 'Concourse T.'" I'm not satisfied, but I can see why Harding has a well-developed tolerance for aberrations to his otherwise logical systems.

or, frankly, anyone who has just stepped off a transatlantic flight, groggy and distracted, can add up to a disorienting environment even if you're not conscious of why you're feeling anxious. Harding's goal isn't so much to keep you from getting lost—that's a pretty low bar to set—but to get you where you need to go quickly, seamlessly, almost without having to think about it at all. And miscues aside, he's a master at it.

Why do a few of us like Harding perform our jobs at a masterly level while the rest of us fall short? Intriguingly, perhaps it's invisibility itself, the lack of promise of ever gaining recognition, that offers at least one answer. There's a host of research that suggests external factors such as reward systems or the opinion of others—what are known as "extrinsic" motivators—can actually decrease people's performance in sophisticated work. To pick one oft-cited experiment, the psychologist Sam Glucksberg, now at Princeton, found that when participants were incentivized with a monetary reward to complete a complex task that required creative thinking they actually executed the task slower than participants who were simply asked to complete the task without the cash enticement. It's theorized that external rewards can narrow people's focus, shutting down a wider view that's essential when tasks require creative thinking. Though money was used in the experiment, money and recognition both are considered key extrinsic motivators and one could reasonably be substituted for the other (research has shown that in numerous cultures money and status, along with appearance, tend to hang together as a single cluster as extrinsic motivators). If you want to perform difficult, creative work at a masterly level, one key could be to, at least some extent, disregard external motivators. In this respect perhaps Harding has an advantage because there is no promise of public recognition he needs to avoid thinking about. This isn't to say that Harding and the other Invisibles you will read about are indifferent to outside rewards, only that with near-unanimity they run second to rewards and motives derived from within.

Wayfinding as a distinct field is relatively new. The term itself was coined in 1960 by Kevin Lynch, a professor at MIT's School of

Architecture and Urban Planning, in his book *The Image of the City.* "To become completely lost is perhaps a rather rare experience for most people in the modern city," he wrote. "We are supported by the presence of others and by special way-finding devices: maps, street numbers, route signs, bus placards. But let the mishap of disorientation once occur, and the sense of anxiety and even terror that accompanies it reveals to us how closely it is linked to our sense of balance and well-being." Lynch understood and promoted the idea of how critical navigation is for people in complex environments like cities. Over time the concept advanced to include large, elaborate interior spaces like airports, hospitals, museums, and outdoor landscapes like corporate and college campuses. Today, a burgeoning subset of wayfinding is in virtual spaces like websites and videogames.

Large wayfinding programs today can have over 10,000 signs and environmental cues. So creating and implementing a highly organized system is critical. To that point Harding was the lead author on *Wayfinding and Signage Guidelines for Airport Terminals and Landside,* a 255-page guidebook for airports, complete with copious research studies, schematics, and diagrams. One typically thinks of designers as solely being artsy creative types, but to be really successful at this job one must possess a dichotomy of traits. "It's important for environmental graphic designers [the field under which wayfinding is typically assigned] to work with both sides of their brain," says Harding. "Many designers have a lot of creative talent," but because of the organizational complexity of large projects one must also possess "analytical problem-solving skills, the other side of the brain, so to speak." Not everyone can do both well.

This marriage of creativity and analysis is what's expected from great wayfinding. On large airport projects the data collected before design even begins is often extensive. Passenger surveys, testing of various pictograms, and studying and modeling the flow of people are just a few of the endless research tasks conducted. To give an idea of the minutiae considered, following are results of a test on understandability of different car rental signs.

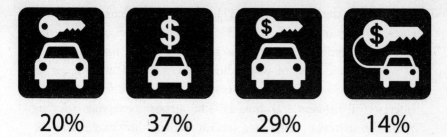

20%   37%   29%   14%

Even decisions that seemingly are whimsical are likely analytical at their core. I talked with Herbert Seevinck, a partner with the Dutch firm Mijksenaar, which has done wayfinding projects for numerous airports around the world, as well as long-running work for Amsterdam's Schiphol Airport. At Schiphol's parking lots, Mijksenaar replaced the standard letters and numbers (because who remembers they parked at B23 after a week in Paris?) with graphics of classic Dutch culture—a lighthouse, clogs, windmill, tulips, et cetera. "We studied the users of the car park and found most are Dutch so we used pictures they'd recognize." Not surprisingly, they found that travelers, especially children, find these far more memorable.

As we look at this same sign here in the subterranean level of the Maynard Jackson Terminal, I notice it reads: "Concourses T, A, B, C, D, E ↑" on one side and "Gates F1-F14 ←" on the other. Though "concourse" and "gate" technically refer to different things, in this instance for clarity and consistency they could have just written "Gates T, A, B, C, D, E" because that is the travelers' ultimate destination and better recognized term.

One of the basic problems with airport wayfinding is that the terminology is used differently and somewhat interchangeably depending where you are. Technically, the terminal is where you enter, get your boarding pass, check your bags, and go through security. Concourses are the long corridors, like docks, where gates sprout along the exterior like individual moorings. But some airports are small and have just one terminal which incorporates the concourse(s). Others interchange the terms *terminal* and *concourse*. And still others—like the sign in front of Harding and me here—essentially interchange *gate* and *concourse*. Harding's guidebook addresses this issue, but wayfinding experts don't always have the final say.

The platonic ideal of wayfinding, it seems, will likely never be found at a major airport. The costs associated with perfection and the interests of different stakeholders—the airport preferring a legacy term, the architect preferring a certain aesthetic that may not be the best functional choice, et cetera—will always prevent that. In the design phase of the project, representatives from the airlines, along with airport management, operations, security, architects, and wayfinding, all compete yet must work together. Harding's work, like all the others, inevitably must involve compromise, becoming somewhat invisible, merged with everyone else's ideas. But unlike the others, even when he does get to implement his plans, Harding's goal is for his work to disappear. Not to be buried under other stakeholders' interests or manipulated and lessened, but to be implemented in its most perfect form, its very success rendering it out of mind for the user.

We've grown to expect mediocre and even subpar service, products, and experiences in almost every aspect of our lives. And if any of them work out well we notice it—a great waiter receives a better tip, a powerful film gets rave reviews, a flight landing on time is met with relief and sometimes even applause from the passengers. Yet for Harding, flawlessness is expected. The beauty of his work, when done right, is its invisibility. No ones leaves a compliment about the wayfinding in an airport comments box. His work directly affects thousands upon thousands of people every day, yet they never know to appreciate when he's done an excellent job.

And yet silence as affirmation is essentially the opposite of what most of us are bred to desire and expect. (It starts young. As my two-year-old climbs a set of stairs I find myself absentmindedly saying "good job" with every step.) I ask Harding, when your end user expects perfection yet doesn't notice when it's been achieved, where is the reward? "There is a tremendous amount of satisfaction that comes from seeing a finished project, when you see it come to fruition. I still have a hard time explaining to my mom and dad what I do. So if I was in this work for accolades or public attention I would have gotten out a long time ago," he says. Beyond that, he relishes the "challenge of solving the wayfinding puzzle," he says. "All of these projects are the same but different. People getting lost is the same problem but the solution is always different. I like plowing new ground. Every project gives me something I've never seen before." Harding considers my question again for a moment. "There was a two-million-square-foot hospital in the Florida panhandle. They had great satisfaction scores on everything except the wayfinding. It was at twenty-six percent. A year after we did a redesign it jumped to eighty-four percent! That was great but getting that kind of feedback is rare." Considering the specificity of the percentages he's able to recall, one tends to believe him about the rarity of receiving a post assessment of the work. "What keeps me going is just knowing internally that a job was well done. And enjoying the process of the work itself."

Without exception, this is the unifying theme I encounter again and again with all my Invisibles—the first of the Three Traits—an ambivalence or even indifference toward recognition for their work. As I touched on earlier, this is a notion with deep roots in philosophy, religion, psychology. There's a part in most of us where we intuit this to be true, but the message is so easily drowned out by our insecurities and the larger ethos of the culture today as the conceptions of fame and celebrity evolve into ever-increasing prominence. (More on this in Chapter 5.) If there is one underlying message of this book, it is the value of reaping reward from the work itself, not recognition for it.

Dr. Sonja Lyubomirsky, a psychology professor at UC Riverside, and author of the bestseller *The How of Happiness*, affirms the power of not seeking outward recognition and connects it to a deeper point about how we live vis-à-vis one another. "This trait ties compellingly with a wealth of social comparison literature," she wrote in our e-mail correspondence, "which shows that happy people are less likely to compare themselves to others, instead they derive their sense of satisfaction from internal standards." Further, as Leroy Huizenga, a former Fulbright scholar who is a professor of scripture at the University of Mary in Bismarck, North Dakota, noted to me, the notion of "happiness coming from the internal sphere rather than from external accolades is a component of many religions. This is particularly so for certain Enlightenment thinkers who have reduced Christianity to a code of ethics. But," he continued, "Christianity [in a stricter interpretation as well] certainly does teach what psychology seems to support as true: The things of this world—the common triad is money, sex, and power—don't provide deep, lasting happiness even on earth, but rather finding oneself in serving others and through internal rewards, being happy with oneself, as is the Invisibles' way, does provide as such."

In research published in the *Journal of Research in Personality*, the psychologists Michael Steger, Todd Kashdan, and Shigehiro Oishi examined the psychological effects of eudaimonic behavior, a concept from ancient Greek philosophy that can be interpreted as a deeper and more sophisticated notion of happiness; the rich or flourishing life. "Eudaimonic theories of well-being assert the importance of achieving one's full potential through engaging in inherently meaningful endeavors," they write. Through two different studies the authors "examined whether eudaimonic behaviors were more strongly related to well-being than behaviors directed toward obtaining pleasure or material goods. In both studies, eudaimonic behaviors had consistently stronger relations to well-being than hedonic behaviors." Their research supports what Jim Harding already knows, that meaningful work, not material or external pleasures, provides true, lasting, and deep happiness.

My aim is that through their stories, the Invisibles, by example, will enable this message to penetrate us with a resonance that all but vanquishes the other noise. Most of us, of course, don't love every aspect of our work, therefore it's critical that we search for and focus on, and amplify if we are able, the elements of our work that do bring pride, that stimulate, that gratify. And if none of these aspects can be found in our work, then, as much as is feasible under the circumstances, we should pursue a job that does offer intrinsic reward. It's hard to overstate the benefits.

"These projects are all over the country, so we don't get to see them very long," Harding says. "It's like growing a flower—you water it, weed it, then see it bloom for a few days and that's it." While members of his team do on-site follow-ups after a job is completed, it's rare for Harding to come back after the fact. (After four years of construction the $1.4 billion terminal opened in the spring of 2012 and we are here late the following winter.) His tour of Maynard Jackson with me is an anomaly. He looks around, nodding with a small smile. "It's really nice to have an excuse to be here, to see the work."

"As a kid I always felt uncomfortable with getting praise," he tells me. He often received recognition for his artwork in school but abhorred the attention. "I didn't like the spotlight." But Harding had always been interested in design and wanted to be involved in communicating with others. Wayfinding has offered him a humble way to make a big impact communicating visually. Andy Johns, the recording engineer, too, found a way to directly affect countless people with his work—in his case, many tens of millions—without a desire for his name to be out front. Late one night during the recording of *Exile on Main Street* he actually refused an opaque offer from Mick Jagger to replace Bill Wyman on bass. "Look, you know, this probably wouldn't mean that much to you . . . but if you get rid of Bill Wyman I'm going home," he said to Jagger. Just imagine for a moment, it's 1970, you're a red-blooded male, and you turn down an offer to be in the Rolling Stones! That's like a mortal in *The Odyssey* passing up the opportunity to replace one of the gods on Mount Olympus. This is someone who clearly loved his work above all else.

Light! Sun! Air! Speaking of Greek mythology, it feels as though we've just ascended from the underworld on an escalator. We're in Concourse F, and for the first time the newness of the building is apparent. Extraordinary ceiling heights greet us as we enter a broad open area with long sight lines looking out at two levels of shops extending into the distance. Behind the escalators is an arresting near-sixty-foot wall of windows looking out at a parked plane. The stunning aesthetics are all the more impactful immediately following the dismal downstairs area we just left. Gazing out the magnificent windows at the nose of a jetliner, the grandeur of flight, just a touch of the storied romance of travel in days of yore is evoked. (With this backdrop I actually wouldn't mind if I got lost for a short while.)

Turning back from the windows it looks like an upscale mall (albeit with neon stripes running along the ceiling). The airport knows that people have to arrive very early for international flights, which means they're going to have a lot of time to kill once they get through security. Hence, the mall. This raises a critical component of way-finding we haven't discussed up to this point: money. It is notable that for the first time since I've arrived at ATL I have a clear, long, unobstructed view. They wanted to make sure travelers got to see as many storefronts as possible from one vantage point. For a certain traveler who has nagging thoughts about imminently sitting in an aluminum tube with dried-out recycled air for the next ten hours, once she sees the Kiehls sign the sale is essentially already made for a "Clearly Corrective hydrating moisture emulsion" pump.

Airports' interest is in keeping travelers happy, which means trying to avoid them getting lost or delayed. But the efficiency of good wayfinding also serves other purposes. While travelers in airports (and patients in hospitals, and visitors to museums) are Harding's customers, so are the owners. Sometimes their interests overlap with ours, other times they diverge. The Las Vegas airport has the fastest security throughput in the country. They want people on those slot machines in the terminal, not on a security line. Fast security (assuming it's no less effective) is good for everyone. On the other hand, I recount to Harding a recent trip to Florida's Fort Lauderdale airport. My wife had ordered a rental car from an off-site local outfit rather than one of the chains because it was inexpensive. Once we were in the car rental area, though there were clear, large signs for each of the major companies, which had desks and cars on site, information about how to connect with our company was nowhere to be found. We circled around and around the area with no luck. (You can imagine how fun this was with a two- and four-year-old in tow.) Finally we saw it. All the off-site car rental companies were lumped together on a small sign. The directions as to where to find the shuttle buses for their lots were vague and confusing. Outside we found two other families wandering around too, not sure where to get the shuttle. It was a total wayfinding failure. But why? "It's a money issue," Harding says. "The airport doesn't generate revenue from off-airport services." They have no incentive to publicize them; conversely, they *are* incentivized to make finding revenue generators easy.

Beyond economics, politics plays a role as well. On doors to the terminal it reads in giant letters MAYNARD HOLBROOK JACK-SON then in tiny letters INTERNATIONAL TERMINAL. This seems to be a clear violation of common wayfinding sense in that "International Terminal" is far more useful information than the name of the terminal. Clearly the branding of the terminal was more important to someone with decision-making authority. With a trained eye the push and pull between economic, political, and customer interests becomes more and more apparent. But, fortunately, the overwhelming majority of wayfinding is quite obviously geared toward the user's best interest (which isn't necessarily mutually exclusive to political and economic interests anyway).

Harding and I head out of the building to curbside at arrivals. There's a ground transportation sign with sections marked Taxis, Park-Ride Shuttles, Charter Buses, Hotel/Shared Ride Shuttles. Each of these are color coded: yellow for taxis, orange for park-ride, and so on. And as you peer down the sidewalk you see confirmation signs not only with the words but matching colors. So if the sign is too far away to read, just by seeing the color, which is discernable from a farther distance than the words, you know where to go. When outside interests are seemingly absent and various options are given equal billing, like they are here, the clarity and logic behind Harding's work is unassailable.

Back inside, with the day wearing on, Jim and I both take bathroom breaks. Not surprisingly, I had begun to think more and more about the symbols used in wayfinding, the ubiquitous images—a cross for first aid, a bold question mark for information, the skirted figure for ladies' room, the generic "human" on the men's door I'm looking at. The minimalist graphics all seem to look so similar no matter where you are. There's almost a tyranny of the aesthetic. So, how did we end up with essentially the same symbol—the disembodied orb for a head atop a figure without hands, feet, or a neck—outside every men's bathroom in the world? We're so used to it, it's essentially invisible, but the near-absolute universality of these images, and in particular this man on the bathroom door, is certainly one of the more remarkable examples of a global archetype. (This guy, by the way, is known in design circles as the "Helvetica Man" because of his and the font's "shared aesthetic look and ideology,"

Ellen Lupton, curator of contemporary design at Cooper-Hewitt, National Design Museum in New York City, told me.)

Pictograms and ideograms (symbols that represent ideas rather than objects) have been with us since the beginning of human history in some form going back to cave paintings some 30,000 years ago. But the minimalist graphical symbols as we know them today can be linked to a few milestones of just the last hundred or so years. As cars gained popularity at the beginning of the last century, the first internationally agreed-upon traffic signs came about in 1909 in Paris. Then, in the 1930s, an Austrian economist named Otto Neurath developed standardized charts and illustrations that were intended to be universally understood, and he pushed for an international pictographic system of these symbols. In a nod to Invisible values, Neurath "argued that, in contrast to the 19th century designer's urge to express his own personality, the modern graphic designer should sacrifice his own individuality in favor of the subject-matter he was trying to convey." In 1936, at the Berlin Olympic Games, the first Olympic pictograms were used. The Tokyo Olympics in 1964 took things a step further using abstract, geometrical images to "communicate facts to visitors, including different sports and general information." But the real launch point for our modern symbol systems can be traced to the 1972 Munich Olympics, where Otl Aicher's famous set of highly simplified and styled pictograms for the Games is widely seen as the model for the look of the symbols we see today. (A few years before, in 1968, an attempt had begun for a unified pictorial language to be used in all German airports. Germans do seem to have a disproportionate proclivity toward effective signage.) The actual symbols you see at airports today derive largely from a symbol library created in 1974 by the AIGA, an American graphic association. This library includes our pal the Helvetica Man. Another symbol library from the ISO, the International Organization for Standardization, is also widely used.

Of course, no signage is neutral. Some can see the global ubiquity of the Helvetica Man and his gang of related symbols as a form of cultural imperiousness. Without a doubt there is much gained by having universally recognized symbols. They facilitate an ease of travel, communication, commerce. And yet what is lost by the ubiquity? What message does it send when the "man" pictogram is the default symbol for "people"? How do societies where men wear skirts, and others where women don't, react to the images that don't reflect them? Herbert Seevinck, the partner at the Dutch firm Mijksenaar, told me that while his firm conducted wayfinding work for the Abu Dhabi airport, there was discussion about whether to use an image of a man in a dishdasha (the traditional Middle Eastern robe) for the men's room, but they advised the airport to stick with international standards because of international travelers. Considering that English is the default world language, and that the Western business suit is the near-universal attire of politics and finance, whether you're in Asia, Africa or the United States, it's not surprising that our pictograms, too, have become the global communication symbols.

There is, however, wiggle room within the confines of the international standards for these symbols. At the Naples airport the usual taxi icon has been altered to look like a Fiat. At Germany's Frankfurt airport, Mijksenaar was told that the skirt on the standard "woman" symbol was too high so they lowered it to a more conservative length. In Geneva they were instructed to make the woman symbol more shapely, curvy!

Everyday Lady   *Sexy Swiss*

Beyond cultural and political considerations, the graphical qualities of symbols have specific consequences. On a two-dimensional sign an upward-pointing arrow means "go straight ahead." Highways in the Netherlands used to have the arrows pointing downward to call attention to the lanes on the road. But they found that downward-facing arrows caused traffic to slow, and conversely, upward-facing arrows caused people to drive faster. They are now changing the arrows to point up to keep people moving, improve the flow. As Seevinck noted to me, this is an example of the sometimes unforeseen psychological effects of signs. Pointing down is about where you are, pointing up is about the destination.

When you couple the ubiquity of the same basic sets of pictograms with the dominance of just a few sans serif fonts (discussed earlier), the global homogenization of our public spaces seems inexorable, if not already complete. Just know, if you've had the sense for some time now that no matter where you are in the world the signs kind of look the same, you're not crazy. Most of the time they are. Ultimately, this points to the irony and power of Harding and his colleague's signage—its universality and omnipresence render it, in a figurative sense, invisible. "My wife jokes that I draw triangle dresses on stick figures for a living," Harding told me. "You tell people what you do and they cock their head." The only time one of these signs is memorable or registers on a cognitive level of any depth is if it veers from convention or isn't immediately decipherable.

Here's the thing, though: Signs are actually the last thing wayfinders want to use. The biggest misconception about wayfinding is that it is synonymous with signage. Signs are a key component of wayfinding, but they are just one element, and generally seen as the last resort. "The number one factor that influences wayfinding is the architecture," says Harding. Seevinck told me, "the less signs the better." The ethos of the field is that in an ideal wayfinding environment you won't need any signs at all. The need for "overt measures such as signage," wrote Enn Ots in *Decoding Theoryspeak: An Illustrated Guide to Architectural Theory*, signal "the failure of the architecture itself to assist the user in navigating the building or urban environment."

This is where wayfinding elevates from a science to an art. When wayfinding designers have the opportunity to get involved in the design phase of a building is when things get really interesting. Wayfinding signage is all about overtly providing information about where to go. However, in well-thought-out spaces we are being led in different directions without even realizing it. In this facet of Harding's work his goal truly is invisibility, at least to our conscious minds.

Harding and I are standing just inside the entrance of the international terminal. This is the starting point for most departing international travelers. Immediately, something strikes me as odd. I suspect I may have noticed this only because the terminal is nearly empty right now at midday, an off-time for international departures. The rows of ticket counters are positioned at a steep angle relative to the front and back walls of the terminal. Picture the letter "Z"—the front and back walls as the top and bottom horizontal lines, and the counters are at the pitch of the diagonal line. Typically, as you enter an airport terminal, often just beyond self-serve kiosks, you are met with a horizontal row of counters, or they are perpendicular, or in a hodgepodge arrangement as you make your way in. And yet the ticket counters here are in a uniform diagonal row after row. Why are they angled so unusually?

At the far right end of the massive terminal room is the security counter. "You ultimately need to go that way," Harding explains simply, "so the counters are angled to funnel you there." Human beings, like most animals, go with the geographic flow. As in most major international airports, miserable masses of humanity push through here, and anything to speed things along is beneficial. The last thing you need is a confused traveler—we've all seen this person, perhaps you've even *been* this person—blocking a crush of people as you're rushing to make a flight because he's spinning his head from side to side trying to figure out where to go next. Maybe he's asking other travelers where to go. Maybe he's taking up employees' time asking them. Or, as it seems is too often the case, he's just standing there, in the way. With the angled aisles, you have nowhere else to logically go other than straight to security. And if the pitch of the aisles isn't enough to flow you in the right direction, the angle also offers improved sight lines toward the security area so you can quickly see where you need to go. I've been in plenty of airports where I check in and then have to wander around a corner or trek unknowingly beyond a row of counters to find out where to go next.

A further ingenious nod toward efficiency in the ticketing area is that none of the check-in counters has static signage for individual airlines. Instead, above each counter is a large LCD monitor that allows any airline to work from any counter so there is maximum flexibility and efficiency. The idea is for any individual airline to be able to rotate to the counters closest to the entrance, with the proximity roughly aligned with departure times. With traditional counters, travelers find themselves, for example, walking by rows of empty Delta counters right in front of them, searching for the United counters they need, which are somewhere out of sight.

For the first time today I stop searching for signs and look around the room. Every detail of the space, always in front of me but heretofore unnoticed, now suddenly comes into view, as if a filter has been removed from a camera lens. The far right wall where security is located is painted a golden color, whereas the rest of the main room is steel gray. Harding says that this color change, what I assumed to be just a decorator's preference, is yet another subtle cue that that is where to go, and you will be entering a new zone. For nearly all of us in this type of environment, with our minds on the impending hassle of taking off our shoes or answering an e-mail on our phones, the color change on the far wall goes unnoticed. But subconsciously your brain is saying "that is different," signaling that you should head there for the next step.

Helping customers is of course a key goal of this surreptitious wayfinding. But so is efficiency and by extension economics. Good sight lines, being able to see as much as possible from any vantage, is perhaps the most effective form of wayfinding; it seems obvious but this consideration is not implemented often enough. The Hyatt Regency Atlanta, built in the 1970s, is widely regarded as the first true atrium hotel, what has since become a highly influential hotel design. "Large hotels have incredibly complex programs, and can be intimidating and confusing for guests," Martin Moeller, the senior Curator at the National Building Museum in Washington, D.C., told me. "An atrium-based design, if done well, can offer numerous wayfinding advantages, since, in effect, the hotel 'lobby' becomes a vast, open room affording views of key hotel elements. Some of the better designs allow the guest to stand in one place and see restaurants, meeting areas, the front desk, concierge desk, elevator core, and rooms," said Moeller.

Good wayfinding is also crafted for those with special needs. The St. Coletta School, in Washington, D.C., designed for children with learning disabilities, "consists of a series of almost cartoonish pavilions of different shapes and colors, linked by major circulation spines," explained Moeller. "The distinct shapes of the pavilions help the children to orient themselves and identify with various elements of the building that are significant to them."

Because people tend to flow with gravity, two-story shopping malls try to maximize the number of entrances on the second floor. Despite the fact that escalators and elevators do all the work for us, our innate tendencies rule our subconscious. Sight lines factor in with increasing the number of second-floor entrances as well, because it's easier to look out and down than to look up, so the likelihood of spotting a store you may want to patronize is better while on the second floor.

The Manhattan street grid system is perhaps the most famous example of wayfinding prominence in design. The streets intersect at 90-degree angles, are numbered in order, and the long sight lines down the canyons enable one to know (accounting for the island's tilt) which way is north, south, east, and west. Whereas in many other metropolises the streets run in concentric rings or other layouts, or no geometric layout at all, making it far easier to get lost.

And yet as convenient as the grid system is, it highlights that good wayfinding should also be cohesive with its environment. At the time of the grid's proposal, people lamented its departure from and destruction of the original topography of the land. And today its right angles and uniformity are still criticized by some. In *The*

Cruise, the award-winning biopic on him, Timothy "Speed" Levitch, a legendary New York City tour guide, remarks: "The grid plan emanates from our weaknesses." It's homogenizing and not in sync with the city's "flowing of human ethnicities and tribes and gradations of awareness and consciousness."

Jim Harding began his career in wayfinding as most people do, "through the back door." Wayfinding firms have any combination of graphic designers, industrial designers, architects, and interior designers. Mijksenaar even has a psychologist on staff. In college Harding worked for an architectural sign company that had just two partners. As the lone employee, he was the first person they hired. The job afforded him a lot of autonomy and varied experience and a small window into what was then just the burgeoning field of wayfinding. "I got to learn a little of everything. We were doing the fabrication and production of the signs, but not design itself. So I saw projects coming in from designers and I thought, 'I can do a better job than this!'" When he graduated from college in 1986 he became an entry-level designer at Gresham, Smith, and has been with the firm ever since. Back then, Harding says, "they didn't even call it wayfinding." Now the Society for Environmental Graphic Design (SEGD), the professional organization associated with wayfinding experts, has more than 1,600 members.

In its infancy Harding's field was largely associated with signage. It then progressed into a broader, more integrated pursuit. As Harding explained when talking about what I admiringly think of as "surreptitious wayfinding," "part of the reasoning behind the value of using as few signs as possible is economic. But more so it's about creating an intuitive experience for traveler. So they are just walking along, naturally flowing to where they are supposed to go. Good architecture makes for good wayfinding." Today, some wayfinding firms are even shying away from the term itself, seeing it as too limiting for their overall mission. The term is conspicuously absent from the SEGD's fifty-slide overview of the organization. Herbert Seevinck told me that his firm now tends to focus on "flow and routing," as the next two levels up from wayfinding and signage.

In an Amsterdam Metro station, Mijksenaar partners observed that the flow of people going down to the platforms was colliding with the flow of people coming up. When a train arrived, the people getting off were crossing on the platform and the stairs with the people coming down. They noticed, however, that with one minor alteration this "terrible clash" of people could be avoided: Change the direction of the escalators. This tiny modification, not even tangible or architectural, simply swapping the direction of the escalators, let the outdoor flow and indoor flow of pedestrian traffic move beyond each other without touching, bypassing each other's flow. When wayfinders get in early enough in the design process, their goal is to avoid even having to change the flow of people, and instead design the routes themselves architecturally for the best efficiency to begin with. In its utopian ideal wayfinding is utterly invisible, its functional aesthetic woven into the earliest overall layouts of the space. Alas, though people like Harding and Seevinck are continually pushing to make that more of a reality, that perfect scenario will likely remain mostly out of reach.

Not long ago, Herbert Seevinck had an appointment at the World Trade Center in Amsterdam. The parking garage is below ground, with low ceilings, and you need to take an elevator to get into the building. "People tend to walk toward light," Seevinck told me, noting that his firm often works with light architects, utilizing this element to help guide people. "I parked my car there for the first time and started looking for the elevator but the only thing I could find were the emergency exists," Seevinck said, as they were the only well-lit areas. "The elevator was in an area with an even lower ceiling, it had a dark blue door. It took me twenty minutes to find it."

▲

Jim Harding strives for excellence as its own reward and relishes the challenges his work presents, even though his work, when it's at its best, goes by unnoticed. Whereas most of us, at least in part, are spurred by external metrics, primarily money and recognition. And, intriguingly, it's the people who've achieved both at the highest levels, some of the most visible among us, who, at their core, have the most in common with Invisibles. They vividly show that one need not be an Invisible to benefit from the Invisible mind-set. It's paradoxical, but seemingly the way to achieve external rewards like money and recognition at the highest level is to not be focused on them but rather to be driven toward intrinsic goals.

When we think of elite athletes, we often hear platitudes about the thrill of competition. But the winningest coaches and players are apt to be motivated by something internal. This is particularly evident for athletes in sports that don't carry the cultural cachet of mainstream fare such as basketball or tennis and the like.

In the mid-1970s through early '80s, Bill Rodgers scored numerous record-setting wins at the Boston and New York City Marathons, landed on the cover of *Sports Illustrated* twice, was christened "Boston Billy" by his hometown, and was one of the leaders of the running boom that still rules American streets thirty-plus years later. (In some families, like mine, where my dad was running marathons regularly himself, Rodgers was very much the proverbial "household name.") Yet in the early 1970s, while Rodgers embarked on a grueling training regimen, long-distance running was still a fringe activity. As he ran the streets of Boston, guys would heckle him, shouting "Who are you running from?" or "Where's the fire?" or "Hey, fruitcake! Nice underwear!" He even had beer cans thrown at him. In his memoir *Marathon Man,* Rodgers summed up the attitude at the time thus: "Football was a real sport; running was for freaks and fairies." With little promise of fame or fortune, what drove Rodgers?

> Of course, most people back then had an easy time criticizing me for spending as much time as I did running. 'Why do it?' they would ask. 'You're not making money at it?' [But] I didn't share the common viewpoint that an activity had little value if it didn't result in some financial gain. I championed the idea of doing things just for the sake of doing them . . . Here's what you have to understand: For runners, progress is the root of pleasure.

Though Rodgers went on to great renown, in his early years what kept him going was his passion for the task, the mission. The occasional crumpled can of Schlitz hurled his way notwithstanding, he too may as well have been invisible.

But even for people who have entered and conquered fields very much in the celebrated mainstream, garnering the related praise and money were rarely a prime motivation. Daniel Paisner, a veteran co-author and ghost writer, has published scores of books with some of the most highly accomplished athletes, politicians, and entertainers of our time. Having spent over twenty-five years helping enormously successful and famous people like Denzel Washington, Ed Koch, Serena Williams, and the like tell their stories, he's uniquely positioned to speak to their motives and rewards. Paisner told me that across their disparate professions, almost uniformly these people "pursued excellence itself, not fame. It wasn't the title, the ring, or the contract—those were not the goals of most of the people I've worked with."

Ostensibly, Jim Harding and the other Invisibles you will read about are worlds apart from the celebrities and power brokers whose stories Paisner so intimately knows. Yet to achieve the success they all have—in endeavors both invisible and not—their motivation and fulfillment is tied to the value they derive from their work. Paisner, both affable and thoughtful about his work process, engaged me in a long talk about the premise of this book. As a writer myself, where getting a byline or credit on a book cover is expected, I was especially curious about his unique niche in the field. After all, even when Paisner is given a co-author credit, readers undoubtedly gloss over his name to home in on "Williams" or "Koch." Nevertheless, I assumed at the outset of every project that he tried to negotiate for co-author credit on his books and was "ghosted" only when he lost the debate. Surely, some credit is better than none. But Paisner sees no difference. "It's all ghostwriting," he told me. "It's the same muscle whether you get credit or not." Whether official credit is awarded is often just a marketing decision. "Whoopi Goldberg thanked me heavily, but the publisher felt the book would brand better with just her name on the cover, and I was fine with that. To me it doesn't matter. It's the joy of the work and the accomplishment that rewards me. I don't need to be on *The Daily Show* or see my name in the bookstore."

Even Paisner's ideal scenario is simply to be able to confirm that his work is being enjoyed while still remaining unacknowledged. "My fantasy is to sit down on a plane next to someone reading one of my books and not say anything to him or her the whole flight," he said. "I just want to watch them read it, take in their body language and see what parts they're enjoying. I've seen people with my books before, on the beach, other places," he continued, "but my wife or friends who are with me have always blown my cover. My dream is to just soak it in. Anonymously."

DEVOTION TO METICULOUSNESS

Blue Sky Days

There was a girl named Amy whom I dated briefly my senior year of high school. I had had a crush on her for some time and after I got up the nerve to ask her out, to my amazement she said yes. We only lasted a few weeks. It turned out, as these things so often do, that I liked the idea of her more than the reality (and, to be fair, I suspect the same for her). But there was one thing about her that was outside my imagination.

Over twenty years later, I can still picture standing in the foyer of her house on our first date, drunk with excitement and possibility, as she strode up to me. I'd always coveted her from afar, but now, here we were just inches apart and she had the most painfully lovely scent. It came from her like heat from glowing coals. I was entranced. I didn't think of it as her perfume, it was just *her*. The amazing thing about fragrance, perhaps more so than clothing or any other accessory, is that it fuses with the wearer in our minds, rendering the scent and the person one. That's why it's so disorienting when my wife wears something different than her normal perfumes, and so comforting when she wears what she had on when we first met.

Crafting a magical scent requires a peculiar combination of disciplined hard science and an artistic gift for converting metaphor into aroma. As I luxuriated in Amy's floral cloud the only person I thought of, of course, was her. The perfumer, the master behind my teenage swoon, was not part of the equation. And to know the name of a fragrance just distances us even further from its creator, as the name or attached celebrity then becomes inextricably linked to the scent in our minds. "I made fragrances for Elizabeth Taylor and my own mother was like, 'But Elizabeth Taylor makes her own fragrances!' I had to convince her," David Apel said, laughing, recalling the conversation. Apel is a perfumer, or "nose" as they're called in the business, for Symrise, one of five global companies that dominate the fragrance industry. Along with creating "fine fragrances" (the perfumes and colognes that are Apel's specialty), the companies also make the scents in basically every consumer product on shelves today—from laundry detergent to aerosol cleaners to candles to "unscented" lotions (yes, "unscented" is a crafted scent).

I'm in Apel's office, high in a Park Avenue skyscraper, wisps of cirrus clouds drifting in the Manhattan sky behind him. On his desk a computer and various papers desperately compete for space with scores of tinted glass vials and bottles containing his latest formulas in development. With a head of stylishly coifed thick silver hair, and sporting dark jeans and a crisp white dress shirt, Apel speaks softly and clearly. His relaxed yet precise manner befits someone whose professional success depends on a marriage of scientific exactitude and artistic insouciance. Apel has created some of the most successful fragrances of the past two decades, blockbusters like Calvin Klein's Escape for Men, Hugo by Hugo Boss, Sunflowers by Elizabeth Arden, and multiple hits for Tom Ford, including Black Orchid, among many others. I'm fascinated about Apel's craft, but also by his role as a hidden artisan behind such iconic brands, designers, and celebrities. There's a story behind every one of Apel's fragrances, but I want to hear about one in particular.

By late 2004, Puff Daddy, aka P. Diddy, aka Diddy, aka Sean Combs, had made a name for himself not only as a hip-hop producer, executive, and performer, but also as a heavyweight in the fashion world with his label Sean John. As the owner and design director of the company, which had grossed in the hundreds of millions of dollars, Combs was named Menswear Designer of the Year by the CFDA, a leading fashion organization. He was poised to expand into the lucrative but ultracompetitive world of fine fragrance, and to become the first male celebrity with a prestige cologne. And David Apel joined the scrum of perfumers vying to be his invisible nose. Expensive perfumes and colognes call to mind a gentility and refined luxuriance. But the behind-the-scenes, niche world of creating them, in actuality, is a brutish competition, a head game, where you never know where you stand among your foes until the end, and your artillery is as intangible as the clouds high above the New York skyline. The fragrance is to be called Unforgivable.

Despite what Apel's mom thinks, designers like Calvin Klein or Gucci, let alone celebrities like J Lo or Lady Gaga, do not make the fragrances that bear their names. They team up with companies like Estée Lauder, Coty, Procter & Gamble, and Elizabeth Arden, which, acting as intermediaries, then contract with the fragrance houses like Symrise to create the product. The fragrance houses first compete to be on the "core" lists for Coty et al. to then have the opportunity to compete against each other for new business. The process starts with a "brief" given to the members of the core list that outlines the idea behind the new fragrance being considered for launch. "I've gotten incredibly long, complex briefs. We've gotten videos. If it's an established artist we'll get CDs of their music," says Apel. "And I've gotten a single page with just text, not even a photo."

"I remember thinking about his famous white parties in San Tropez, a Mediterranean freshness. That's what stuck with me from the Sean John brief," recalls Apel. "Others may have had different elements jump out at them." They had about three weeks to flesh out ideas for the first round of submissions to Estée Lauder, who had partnered with Sean John. Typically, each house sends in multiple samples, sometimes by different perfumers from the same house, so there is internal as well as external competition for each nose. As a company, Givaudan (where Apel worked at the time) submitted about a half-dozen samples. "Lauder narrows down all the submissions to about a dozen, from probably around thirty or so, and makes recommendations for modifications on the ones that made the cut. Of those dozen, mine was the only one that made it from Givauden," says Apel. "I remember the Lauder guy saying kind of negatively, 'You only have one in.' But I was totally pumped. I told him, 'It only takes one.'" Apel was on a corporate trip when he got the word and immediately flew back to New York to get to work on the next round.

Over the course of the next two weeks Apel creates around six to eight new variations of his initial fragrance based on Lauder's recommendations. Like a chef concocting a dish in his mind, Apel creates the fragrance in his head first then writes out the formula for what he believes will create the scent in his imagination. He gives the formula to a lab tech and he or she creates it and around an hour later gives it to him. "I keep modifying until I reach what I'm happy with," he says. "I probably made thirty different modifications a day, *hundreds* total over the two weeks." Apel explains, "Once it's in your nose, not just your mind, you either get another idea for a new direction or you realize you really love a certain piece in the formula and you want to pump that up. Or you get new information from the client—maybe at this stage they talked more about the Mediterranean, or something similar—and you make changes based on that." With his new variations finished Apel hasn't yet met with Diddy. Some celebrities have virtually no direct contact with the perfumer. Everything goes through the intermediary firm. Others get way more involved in the process, communicating directly. With his second round of fragrances ready to be presented, Apel doesn't know where Diddy falls on the spectrum.

What exactly does Mediterranean freshness mean to Apel? How does the image of Diddy in a white suit drinking Champagne on a yacht in the French Riviera translate into a fragrance? "You have to start with the history of perfumery," Apel says. "Modern perfumery revolves around the Mediterranean basin. That's where all the original sources of perfume raw materials came from in some sense. Bitter orange. Bergamot." More personally, he adds, "Also, my wife is French. We spend a lot of time in the Mediterranean. I have traveled a lot in the region. All of those things are impressions that are in you as a perfumer. For Escape for Men, and Hugo [two of his past successes], I brought in elements of the sea, ozonic freshness, the feeling you get when at the beach. It triggers something unique. I love those notes."

In the Sean John fragrance Apel utilized bitter orange tree, and plants and herbs like cistus, immortelle, lentisque, and thyme found in maquis (a type of brush in the Mediterranean area). Plus he needed to incorporate the all-important salty sea air "where this ozonic feeling comes into play." With ozone, Apel says, "there's almost a burnt electrical effect, like a stinging. To create the effect I use a variety of different raw materials depending on what I'm going for. Calone," a synthetic molecule discovered by Pfizer in the 1960s that has a similar structure to pheromones secreted by some forms of algae, "is incredibly powerful. For me, it smells like a freshly shucked oyster." Florazone, which as the name suggests has a floral ozonic note, is also important. "I use that sensation and tie other ingredients to it, like bitter orange, to create a Mediterranean feel." If Apel is trying to create a feeling of the countryside he might use ozone with fresh grass. For an earthy feeling he adds geosmin, an organic compound that gives beets what my wife refers to as the taste of dirt. "There's almost a textural note," he says, as if there's a physicality to it.

Like any artist, a perfumer's life informs his creativity. For Apel travel is especially important. Years ago he camped for a month in Madagascar. He shows me a photo of a blimp over the rain forest canopy. "We'd float above the jungle in that and we'd find flowers," he says. Perfumers aren't allowed to take anything from remote regions like the jungle. Instead, to bring home the aroma of a flower or other botanical, they must capture its gases in a trap, usually a glass cloche held over it. "The plant is emitting its scent over a period of time and you're sucking that air out of the vessel and putting it into a little carbon trap. You seal the trap, bring it home, then analyze it." But technical analysis is just one part of trying to re-create the scent. Just as important are the field notes Apel makes. Sitting next to the flower, he writes down the formula of raw materials he imagines would re-create its scent. Partly, this is as a failsafe because sometimes the cloche doesn't work, so he could end up with nothing without his notes. But it's also because knowing the scientific components of a raw material doesn't always translate to being able to re-create its scent. His impressions are critical. It's this matching of science and artistry that brings about the ultimate result.

"But those trips are not usual," says Apel. "It's everyday life— every time I'm on vacation, or a great beach or something like that, you're kind of bringing it back with you." Apel now lives in the Hudson Valley but for many years resided on Manhattan's Upper West Side and would pass through Central Park every day on his way to his office. "You'd be amazed at how beautiful Central Park smells almost any time of the year," he says. I sense some hyperbole and ask if winter in the park has a smell. "Absolutely! That frozen smell is what everyone always tries to capture. It's this crisp metallic kind of brightness that hurts your nose, kind of. Those are the things you try to capture."

A call comes in—Diddy will be coming to the office personally to test the new samples. He shows up with a modest entourage, a personal assistant, a liaison from Lauder, and a two-person camera crew, because during that period of time he was being filmed everywhere he went. Hip-hop moguls tend to function as one-person conglomerates, their fingers in many pots at any given time. Apel notes that Diddy is rarely doing one thing. "It took me a while to get used to." A source I spoke with (who wishes to remain anonymous to not jeopardize the relationship) who has done business with Russell Simmons, a fellow hip-hop mogul, attests to staring at the top of his head for half of their meetings because he was consumed with his Blackberry, working on other deals. But Diddy does something unexpected as the parties settle around the conference table and he realizes he missed some introductions because he was on his phone. He preemptively offers a sort of apology, saying, "I've got a lot of things going on." Ironically, after that statement, Apel says, Diddy stays entirely engaged for the rest of the meeting.

A Givaudan employee offers her arm as the canvas. "You always smell on skin, not a blotter," Apel says. She goes through several rounds of being spritzed in different locations, walking over to Diddy for his assessment. "He tells us a few versions he likes and after he leaves we get started on the modifications," which will again total in the hundreds, says Apel. While Apel is working around the clock trying to create that Mediterranean freshness, Diddy is going to the other fragrance houses that have made it to the second round, testing all of their samples as well. "It's intense," Apel says. At this point, since he is the only perfumer from Givaudan with a fragrance still in the game, he's now working in teams with his colleagues. "Everyone is helping. We all [the noses] smell things differently, with different palates," he says. One of them might notice a special note that Apel has missed and explore it further.

Over the course of the next few weeks Apel has third and fourth meetings with Lauder, presenting newly modified versions each time. "The client might like the 'freshness' of this and the 'warmth' of that, and you figure out ways of merging them together," Apel says. "Or you take one scent and split it off into two, three, or more versions, taking specific elements and building around them." As he goes through each variation Apel keeps meticulous notes keeping track of each formulation, which typically run around fifty or more ingredients each.

In the early years before computers dominated the modern office, Apel handwrote every ingredient in spreadsheets. He takes out a binder filled with them and shows me a formula he worked on years ago as an example. It includes black currant buds, a peach note, a prune note, clove buds, carnation, chamomile, narcisse. "These are all different individual raw materials but in each case what you do is you balance them one at time, one at a time, one at a time"—Apel points at each column—"so every formulation is meticulous, each new column with a different balance of the raw ingredients." There are hundreds upon hundreds of pages of these charts as he fastidiously, element by element, tweaked the formulas. His old employer, where he spent nearly his whole career prior to Symrise, generously let him bring the binders with him.

An excerpt of one of Apel's old spreadsheets:

FASHION

	CONSTITUANTS 104	F-13	G-1	G-2	G-3	G-4	G-5	G-6	G-7	G-8
GC-1022-A 'RUGGED' MENS COLOGNE 10%. DATE 9-24-86 FDR. NO. 0668 0747

	CONSTITUANTS	F-13	G-1	G-2	G-3	G-4	G-5	G-6	G-7	G-8
2016.36	Base 104 F 1 G	626	605	605	605	605	605	605	605	605
200.75	IPA 1%	15	10	10	10	10	20	20	20	20
303.06	IBQ 10%	10	10	10	10	25	15	15	15	15
716.77	Rosemary Pure	10	10	10	10		10	10	10	10
1019.05	Mandarin Oil Yellow	5	/	/	/	/	/	5	5	5
7046.76	MD Origanum Abs 2x BV501	30	40	40	30	20	25	25	25	25
1649.01	Vetiver Bourbon	15	15	15	15	10	15	15	15	15
247.23	Tabac Supra Abs 10%	15	/	/	/	10	/	10	10	10
107.18	Ambanoms Abs 16%.	15	/	/	15	/	/	15	/	/
204.82	Mandarinal 3204501 10%	5	/	/	/	/	/	15	10	10
3024.00	Sarb Dalmatian	5	5	5	5	/	5	5	5	5
5031.85	Tabac Anhydrol Jmc 55	5	/	/	/	/	/	/	5	5
1112.71	Ciste Labdanum Verte	5	10	10	5	/	7	7	8	8
6166.02	Civet Abs 10%	2	/	/	/	/	2	2	10	10
7021.00	Armoise O	3	3	3	3	/	3	3	3	3
807.45	Costus Pur 10%	5	5	/	5	5	/	/	/	/
907.90	Heliotropin	40	/	/	5	/	/	/	/	/
711.23	Phenyl Acetic Acid 10%	2	2	2	2	/	/	/	/	/
261.55	Amyl Salicylate	65	/	/	5	/	/	/	/	/
5042.26	Estragon Oil	5	/	/	/	5	/	/	/	/
808.96	Lavandin Commune	40	20	20	20	20	/	20	5	5
751.00	Lavandin Abs	5	5	5	5	/	/	/	/	/
1158.20	Amara 162 B	3	4	4	3	3	/	3	/	/
	Cistemthor Abs Pure 10%	20	20	20	20	30	/	/	/	/

"They say you were either born into it," Apel says of being a perfumer, "or you stumble into it. My wife is French, and she's also a perfumer. She was born into it—her father is a perfumer, they own a perfume company, so it's sort of in the blood." Apel stumbled. While in college studying environmental chemistry—"I wanted to be an environmentalist, work for the EPA or the DEP"—Apel took a day job at Givaudan in its environmental department. When he arrived for work, though, that job had been filled and they offered him a job in the lab bulk-compounding fragrance instead. The job, which required constant precision, didn't offer creative opportunities but Apel used his newfound knowledge and circumstances to that advantage. "I started making little blends of my own just to bring home because I thought they smelled nice," he says. Like Jim

Harding, who started by doing production work for designers before becoming one himself, Apel, too, had the desire and, critically, the initiative to move to the "other side." "You see people doing it every day and you start to realize what this whole thing is about," he explains. But it would be years before Apel segued into the more creative role in perfumery that he had begun exploring on personal time for his own satisfaction. Early on, Apel "had no idea what perfumery even was." His aspiration for years was simply to work hard in the lab and to craft fragrances for his own enjoyment.

After a year and a half of compounding, an analytical perfumer, whose job is to analyze fragrances on the market to help identify trends for the creative perfumers, saw that Apel was a diligent worker and took him on as an apprentice. In that position he used gas chromatography–mass spectrometry (GC-MS), which analyzes the individual components of anything. It's a complex process that Apel breezily describes in great detail.

> You take the oil and inject it into the machine - it basically vaporizes the liquid at the injection port because it's a high temperature, and a mix of materials go through this very fine tube with a substrate on the inside that is either polar or non polar . . . what happens then is it goes into an oven which ramps up at a very, very consistent and accurate rate and each one of these things separates out from the others to individual chemical components and at the end of it you've got a chart . . . and what our GC-MS does is analyzes that by its mass spec. So basically it takes a look at the ions, their basic structure . . . just to back track for one sec, so as it goes through this very thin tube it comes out at the end in a puff of visible smoke or invisible smoke and where it comes out is right at the detector area because there was a flame detector. So it goes through a flame and the flame basically burns more. You get a peak on the chart with a graph and what you do is actually you calculate the area under each one of these peaks . . . as it comes out we would sit at the machine for about an hour and a half for each analysis and you would smell constantly and write your notes on that chart that came out. I'd say, 'oh this smells like linalool, this is whatever . . .

Note all the ellipses—trust me, those are just some highlights of his description. It was but one of many circumstances where Apel started by apologizing that he's "not a chemist" then proceeded to go on an encyclopedic tear on the chemistry and hard science of his craft. For example: What if you shot a droplet of orange juice into the machine? Does it tell you the chemicals within?

Apel:

It tells you completely the individual components that make up that juice and there would probably be sixty of them—limonene, Gamma-Terpinene, just on and on and on. But where it gets very tricky is that in one fragrance compound you may have six things that will give you a peak of limonene, which is the terpene which most represents natural citrus oils, bergamot has it, mandarin, orange, lemon, tangerine, grapefruit, they all contain predominantly limonene as their main component . . .

Eventually, Apel's mentor moved into being a creative perfumer and Apel took over her lead position in the lab. Only then did he begin to think about moving into creative perfumery himself, which he shortly did thereafter, and hasn't left the role for twenty-five years. There's a naïveté and humility in Apel's path. For years, with no motive beyond his own fulfillment, he created fragrance blends on the side as he mastered the science behind his craft. While almost all noses start in the lab, it's likely that Apel's tenure there, and his not seeing it as an obligatory stepping stone but rather reveling in the scientific details of the job, has given him the foundational mastery that has enabled his elite stature as a creative perfumer today. In fact, research shows that Apel's respect for and tendency toward meticulousness has a direct tie with his success.

As you enter the studio of the New York graphic design firm MSLK, the first thing you notice is a sort of airlock feeling of futurism, as though a *swooomp* of depressurization occurs upon opening the door. There's a hospital-like abundance of white and an eerie sense of silence even though the indie-folk darlings Fleet Foxes are softly drifting from unseen speakers. It makes one wonder whether this hyper-clean aesthetic sanctified by Apple's retail stores is not a trend but a near-permanent shift in what we consider to be a modern interior. Surely typesetters and designers of yore, with their presses and inks and multitudinous papers, wouldn't recognize these people or this studio as their own. What few objects that are around beyond the wide-screen Macs feel strategically whimsical and brightly colored, bringing humor and personality to the otherwise sterile confines—a set of ceramic wedge-shaped mugs fitted together like a pie, an illustrated poster of a cartoon mouse digesting cheese with PacMan-like pellets exiting its bottom in a swirl, a collection of classic cameras painted in highlighter fluorescents. Everything is neat, just so. And that's the way Marc Levitt, the creative director and co-founder of the firm, likes it.

The surprising thing about Levitt, however, is that he's not intrinsically neat or organized. Sure, he has the obligatory black-framed glasses and sharp sartorial eye one expects of a designer, but outside the studio he confesses he's a "pretty messy guy." This admission reminded me of a *New Yorker* cartoon where below the image of an obese man in an ill-fitted and stained tank top, tufts of hair poking out the neckline and sprouting off his shoulders like poison shrubs, discarded beer cans littering the floor around him as he's slouched in a beat-up La-Z-Boy holding a TV remote, the caption reads *Giorgio Armani at home*. What's instrumental about Levitt for us to pick up on is that his *meticulousness*—the second of the Invisibles' Three Traits—was learned, and that he turns it on when he needs to, and turns it off when he's off the clock. We too often assume certain traits like meticulousness are innate, but much more of them can be learned than we realize. Apel, too, with his years in the lab, trained to be meticulous. Even his extraordinary olfactory abilities aren't innate. "Unless you have an anatomical problem, anyone can train their nose," he says, citing the Jean Carles method, an analytical way to look at the raw materials of perfumery, as the most recognized in the field. Apel says most perfumers can recognize in the neighborhood of 1,200 single components.

"The truth is I never had any real inclination toward precision until I started studying graphic design," Levitt told me. "It wasn't until college when I studied the craft, where teachers made us do these OCD-level exercises, that I began to even understand what's required of becoming a great designer. We'd do things like spend half a semester drawing the same four letters over and over, getting the spacing perfect, using just black ink, no computers," Levitt said, marveling at the memory. "We were required as designers to take black-and-white photography. We had to make sure our gray scales were calibrated correctly, we had to do complex exposure tests, mix the chemicals properly. It was so detailed, laborious. We'd be working on these tasks forever. Even in the darkroom you could see the photography students rolling their eyes at us. But we were trying to capture the technical. Emotion is critical for us too, but in order to achieve it we had to have a technical foundation first." The echoes of Levitt's experience in Apel's, the mastery of the technical in order to excel at the creative, resound.

The value of meticulousness is well acknowledged from grammar school writing teachers to astrophysicists. What may come as a surprise, though, is that this specific trait is also directly tied to business leadership. Several meta-analyses of studies on personality and job performance conducted by the Notre Dame business professor Timothy Judge, along with others, show that conscientiousness—which in the studies is defined as being "cautious, deliberate, self-disciplined, and neat and well-organized," in other words meticulous—is a core predictive trait for successful businesspeople. To emphasize the power of this data, Judge's meta-analysis was of twenty-six independent studies. He later (again, with colleagues) conducted a meta-analytic study of fifteen prior meta-analyses on the same subject, further cementing this conclusion. The data shows that "overall, conscientiousness was the most consistent predictor of leadership effectiveness." As Bret Simmons, a professor at the business school at the University of Nevada, and who provides corporate training on leadership and management, puts it bluntly to his clients, "Hire the most conscientious people you can find."

When meticulousness and seeking no outward recognition—two of the Three Traits—are combined, their effectiveness toward advancement and personal fulfillment is even more powerful. Stephen Sauer is a professor at Cornell's Johnson School of Management and at the School of Business at Clarkson University, with a specialty in Leadership and Influence in Management Teams. Prior to his career in academia he served as an armored cavalry officer, a background that has influenced his thinking on his current work. "A lot of people find satisfaction in being the 'unsung hero' in an organization," he told me. "In my military experience, these people were often serving in a support role in one way or another—tank mechanic, cook, fuel truck driver—and they took great pride in filling their role in a highly conscientious manner. We often had younger or lower-ranking soldiers who were widely recognized as being 'the glue' that held the whole outfit together." So, not only did these lower-rung workers take enormous pride in being silent heroes, it's their conscientiousness that kept them in such high esteem by their peers and superiors.

After the several rounds with Lauder, Apel and his team are green-lit to meet with Combs again. At this point Diddy's involvement escalates dramatically. While much of the story behind Unforgivable is typical of the process, his accessibility and repeated direct involvement with the perfumer was unique. "He made himself incredibly available," Apel says. "He would just pop over and smell a few things. And we would also go to his offices, and his recording studio here in New York."* Combs was also becoming more intense at the meetings, his growing knowledge of ingredients and formulations feeding his passion for the process. "He was extremely excited but also nervous," says Apel, "because this was an area he was new to. He knew if people didn't like his fragrance he'd be embarrassed." Aside from the NYC drop-ins, Apel also hopped a plane to Toronto, a suitcase of samples in tow, to meet with Combs while he was filming the movie *A Raisin in the Sun*.

A few months have gone by at this time. Apel knows that two

___

* An aside: Despite our ever-increasing digital interconnectedness, this strikes me as a powerful example of the importance and advantages of physical proximity. If one of Apel's competitors was in Columbus or Little Rock they wouldn't have been able to have these frequent, brief visits that became routine for him during the Unforgivable creation process.

other houses are still in the game, though when he and Combs meet there is never any discussion of them. Givaudan is investing an extraordinary amount of time and money without knowing if it will ever make a dime. If you don't get picked, that's it. Nothing. But this is how the business works, and the proceeds from one win hopefully will exceed the expense of all the lost pitches. "We're given the go-ahead to start meeting with package designers, which changes some olfactive components," Apel says. "We feel like we're getting closer but still don't know if we're going to win or not at this point."

It's amazing how much Combs is juggling—he's not only thinking about the different versions that Apel is bringing to him and judging them against each other, but also judging them against whatever scents the other two houses are bringing to him as well. Not to mention all his other businesses. "We leave samples with him each time so he can test them himself and with others around him he trusts." The opinion of some dude in the studio who smells it sometimes is "how fragrances are won and lost."

They learn that Combs is going to be at his estate on Star Island in Miami for a few weeks. The process had been moving along quickly and intensely with regular contact; they weren't sure what to make of the news, fearing perhaps that Combs was checking out of the process or maybe they were out. Then Apel gets a call: Diddy wants him to come to Miami.

"**W**e were told he was going to be doing a lot of decision making over the next week," Apel says, "and to be ready to work down there." Apel puts together a mobile lab for the trip. As he gathers raw materials, each carefully metered out in individual vials, he slowly runs through in his mind again the initial brief, and Diddy's subsequent comments over all of their meetings, and tries to imagine what direction the fragrance could go from here. What is the fragrance missing? What is *Mediterranean freshness*? What does a client *mean* when they ask for something lighter or cleaner or brighter? How will he translate metaphor into reality?

When I worked as a magazine fact-checker you would think we didn't have to worry about esoteric considerations like these. But the job's number one role was to be meticulous with the facts, which meant everything, *everything*—including olfactory claims—had to be checked before an issue went to press. Better to be persnickety and have an editor say "Don't worry about it" on a particular point, than let something slide through only to catch hell for it later. If a travel writer said it took her two hours to drive from Florence to Genoa, I'd consult a map.* Is *Dr. Feelgood* really Mötley Crüe's best-selling album? (And does the band really have an umlaut over the "o" too, not just the "u"?)** Was Gary Kasparov the world champion of chess from 1985 to 1993?***

Among several magazines, I spent my longest tenure at the venerable fashion bible *Vogue*. While there, a manuscript landed on my desk one day for a short piece on a new fragrance launch, Vera Wang's Princess. In addition to various floral components, the company listed "pink frosting" as one of the fragrance's notes. I remember thinking, *This is unacceptable, pink frosting does not have an aroma* (or at least not one any different from white frosting; the pink is just a result of food coloring). You can't claim something smells like pink frosting, damn it! I was pretty indignant. Sarah Brown, the beauty editor at *Vogue*, is a no-nonsense type. She expected anyone working with her to perform, but accorded respect in return. She considered my case for a moment. Then we got on the phone with someone from Vera Wang and debated the point.****

But in David Apel's world the "fact" of pink frosting and the like having an aroma is not to be debated. It's to be interpreted. "You have to have a trick to do it," he says. "In some cases it really still is simple. You can do a couple little subliminal things. Years ago when you wanted to make something smell pink you would add methyl salicylate, which is like a wintergreen, because Pepto-Bismol was

---

* It's actually closer to 2½ hours.

** Yes, and yes.

*** Technically, yes, because he left the main international chess organization that year and started his own organization but many chess followers considered him number one until 2000. (This is the tough thing about fact-checking. Facts can often be debatable.)

**** Alas, pink frosting stayed in the final text. My memory of why it did escapes me.

big then. Now it's a very different thing you would add. If you want something to smell purple you'll add something like grape notes. If you wanted red you used to add cinnamon because of Red Hots."

Beyond sensing which cultural touchstones a client might sub-consciously be thinking of when he speaks in abstractions, a larger part of translating this metaphorical language—which, considering many of the briefs can run for many pages and rely on photographs, videos, and more, is often much more nebulous than "pink"—is to know your raw materials. You have to have a list of a thousand-odd components in your head, though Apel says he uses "only" around five hundred regularly, and a command of how they may interact with one another. Some fragrances have hundreds of raw materials in them. On the other end, some prestige fine fragrances have just sixteen ingredients. Apel's Warm Vanilla Sugar, a huge seller for Bath & Body Works, has just eight raw materials. Apel estimates around fifty to sixty ingredients were in each formulation of Unfor-givable.

To get an idea of what Apel faced when he put together his mobile lab for the trip to Florida, I popped into the Symrise lab in New York, which is down the hall from the perfumers' offices. Techni-cians in long white lab coats stood at various desks, five-foot-high shelves of vials and canisters separating them from each other. I expected an off-putting olfactory cacophony, but instead the aroma was complex but pleasant. Potpourri meets medicinal meets earthy? Sadly, I lack Apel's tools to describe it. Cindy, the tech I met with, said the overall aroma in there changes depending on what they're working on.

The sheer number of containers on the shelves filled with raw materials is overwhelming. It's essentially a library of ingredients. Most are contained in small brown glass bottles, reminiscent of old-timey prescription bottles. I pick one up at random—lemon. "So this is the lemon bottle?" I ask. "It's *one* lemon. We have probably over ten different types of lemon. Lemons from each region of the world smell different," she says. One quickly gets a sense of why the quantity of bottles is so voluminous. If there was an earthquake I don't know which would be more dangerous, the shattered glass from all of the bottles or the scent cloud.

Each tech's section has duplicates of the most popular ingredients, much like a long bar has duplicate speed racks for multiple bartending stations, and single bottles of the more unusual stuff along the back wall. For temperature-sensitive materials there's also a large walk-in refrigerator, that as I entered instantly brought back the fear of being trapped I used to experience as a waiter when I had to grab something for a chef. Ingredients are never measured by eye. They use a pipette and weigh each ingredient based on the specifications laid out in the perfumer's formula.

Some ingredients, usually ones that are extraordinarily powerful, are measured down to .005 of a gram. In rare circumstances Cindy has used just .001 of a gram. Those materials are housed in the Stink Box, a specially vented chamber resting atop an explosion-proof refrigerator. One of this motley crew of nose disintegrators, more odiferous than Tommy Lee's armpit after a two-hour performance, is the musk secretion from a civet, a small cat-like creature. (The species is known for helping to create the world's most expensive coffee, which is prepared from partially digested coffee beans in their poop. I'll take a venti of that, please.)

Some of the raw materials are natural, made directly from the source material, others are synthetic. Most fragrances are composed of both. Synthetics are often used when a natural material is of limited supply or banned from use. They're not necessarily considered inferior. "There are some synthetic chemicals that are exquisitely beautiful and absolutely ridiculously expensive," Apel says. A coveted one is ambroxan. It represents an amber note from ambergris, an excretion from a sperm whale, and can cost around $700 a kilo.

"**W**e set up the lab in the kitchen. His mother is there. There is a buffet," says Apel, who's accompanied on the trip by a salesperson on the account. "He's got a huge workspace there, very free-flowing, gorgeous home. It used to be Mariah Carey's." While Apel is working a stream of people are rotating through the house, being interviewed by Combs for a fashion show he's overseeing. Package designers for the fragrance, who also are presenting, are set up nearby. Over the course of the day Combs pops in and out of the kitchen, testing Apel's modifications. The sprawling tropical manse was a state of rarified chaos set in languid luxury. "He's seeing us, the package people, he's reviewing mock-ups for advertising," Apel says. I ask him if he knows if other houses are still competing with him at this time. "I don't know for sure but I know *we're the only perfumers on Star Island!* At this point we sense 'it's ours to lose.'"

Late in the day Combs enters the kitchen to test yet another preparation. For this one Apel has tried something a little drastic. He went in unusually big on "some extraordinarily pure product of bergamot." The package people are futzing with their wares in the corner. The chilled fruit on the buffet, long ago gone tepid, sits half-eaten. Combs sniffs the latest formulation. The central air softly whirs above them as Apel silently waits for a response. With his eyes closed, a smile blooms on Combs's face. "Give me more of that!" he says. "I love it!" Apel has unlocked the mystery. "I knew that was the key," he tells me.

As Apel gets ready to leave he notes that Combs "*still* hasn't said 'you got it.' But we had gotten over a hump, an impasse. He understood what he wanted with such precision that I have a good idea of how to finish it off back in New York in like two moves. I describe to my colleague in the office this piece, this sparkle in the top that I think it needs. And she crafts the sparkle for it. When I come back in the office I know we're there. I am like, 'YES!' [pumps his fist] to everyone. There are high fives all around."

A couple weeks later in New York, Apel gives Combs the final formula. "Bang! It was done." The colleague who crafted the sparkle? She is Apel's wife today.

By this time around six months have passed from the initial brief. After stability testing, production, packaging, and shipping, another six months or so will pass before Unforgivable hits the shelves. It is the first-ever male celebrity prestige fragrance. The first formulation, a couture, limited-edition $300 bottle, sells out immediately. A national launch of a more affordable mainstream version of the original comes two months later. In record-breaking time it becomes the number-one-selling men's fragrance in department stores. Combs and executives from Estée Lauder and Federated Department Stores ring the opening bell at the New York Stock Exchange to celebrate the success. Apel goes on to create five Sean John fragrances in total.

Apel leaned back in his chair as he recalled the finale to the Sean John story. On the wall next to his desk are ads for some of his greatest hits, Escape for Men, Sunflowers, Hugo, Black Orchid. His pride in his success is evident. Yet Apel is equally charged simply by the creative process. He's unknown to the millions who have purchased his perfumes and colognes over the years. Some, like his mother once did, even think the designers and celebrities themselves concoct the fragrances. But he's fulfilled doing his work behind the scenes. "We are commercial artists," he says. "We are not writing our own story. I get plenty of chances to do that—we call them Blue Sky Days," when the perfumer is free to create anything he wants, for his pleasure and inspiration. But most of the time, "it's their brief, it's their project, so I am kind of a ghostwriter, crafting someone else's story."

3.

SAVORING RESPONSIBILITY

Raising the Roof

At over 2,000 feet above the ground wind can behave in peculiar and often violent ways. Whatever speed a gust blows on the street, up there it's 100 percent stronger. When it confronts an obstacle, like a tall structure, effects like buffeting can occur, the vibrations of which can be severe enough to topple a building if it's not designed properly. I've spent a fair amount of time worrying about wind at unnatural heights because, with any luck, I'm going to be on the roof of an unfinished skyscraper. Not just any skyscraper but what will become the tallest building in China, and the second-tallest in the world, when it's complete. At its final height of 632 meters (or 2,073 feet) the Shanghai Tower will have 124 floors, 20 percent more than New York's One World Trade Center.

Someone else who worries about wind at these heights is Dennis Poon, the lead structural engineer on the Shanghai Tower. Poon led the engineering on Kuala Lumpur's Petronas Towers, the tallest buildings in the world for some time until they were replaced by

Taiwan's Taipei 101 in 2004, also a Poon building. The engineering on three of the five tallest buildings in the world currently under construction is under his direction—two of which will ultimately surpass the Shanghai Tower in height. By 2020 he will have had a hand in ten of the twenty tallest buildings in the world. Yet outside his insular field Poon is unknown. When people see an iconic building like a skyscraper, if they think of the structure at all, they think of the architect. (It's not for nothing that use of the term *starchitect* has exploded in the past decade.) And yet it's the structural engineers who enable these buildings to stand. Without them the architect's vision cannot be realized.

I'm flying to China because I want see Poon's work firsthand. To better understand and appreciate what he does, I want to witness the vast complexity of the beams, columns, trusses, framings, and untold other structural members that mostly are hidden once a building is complete. From the mechanical and electrical engineers to the glass fabricators, crane operators, and welders there are of course myriad invisible specialists involved in creating a massive structure like a modern skyscraper. But none have more responsibility for the overall integrity of the building—its longevity, safety, and efficiency—than the structural engineers. And second only to the architect, none impact the overall design of the building more than they do. As Poon told me, "When you get to the pinnacle, the very high end of things, you cannot separate art from engineering and engineering from art. A good engineer must be creative. He must have an artistic mind."

As much as an iconic building may be intended for good business, as Jun Xia, a design director and principal at Gensler, the architectural firm behind the Shanghai Tower, said in a presentation he gave about the Tower, it also is seen as "a symbol of modernity, and a metaphor that China has arrived." The city as a whole is working quite hard on the idea behind the metaphor. From Shanghai Pudong International Airport I take the Maglev (short for "magnetic levitation") train, what has become a rite of passage of sorts for travelers to the city since its debut nearly a decade ago. That the $1.25 billion project has been noted for its questionable economics is no matter. A surrealistic rocket on rails, as the world's fastest train in commercial operation it reached 431 km/hr (268 mph) on my trip and conspicuously let riders know it with its speed clocked on digital displays in our car for us to marvel at. (The speedometers were a shrewd decision, as my fellow passengers and I spent as much time looking at, and in most cases filming, the numbers flash upward as we did the blurred landscape out the windows.)

The striking wealth disparity in Shanghai, with its innumerable sinuous alleyways of tragically dilapidated two-story domiciles in the shadows of gleaming high-rises, functioning almost as an alternate city within the city, makes New York City by contrast look egalitarian. But like governments everywhere, presumably this is not what the municipality wants its better-off inhabitants and visitors to focus on. Instead, attention must be paid to the trappings of economic progress. While America and much of Europe are in the midst of a long-term recession, I wandered from one overpacked mall to the next, Chinese shoppers jamming L'Occitanes and Gaps as if it were Black Friday. There's incessant music pumping in the elevators of my sleek high-rise hotel, and the building across the street has hundreds, maybe thousands, of Dan Flavin–esque fluorescent lights changing colors above every window. Why? Why not!

In this seemingly unstoppable chimera of communistic capitalism, the Shanghai Tower already holds a position of honor and great import. Touring the Shanghai Urban Planning and Exhibition Center, I went straight for its vaunted, massive scale model of the city. Like a room-sized, 3D tilt-shift photograph, it already incorporated the Shanghai Tower rendered in its finished state.

It's no surprise that the Lujiazui Finance & Trade Zone in the Pudong district, where the Shanghai Tower is being constructed next to two other recently built preeminent skyscrapers, is part of China's "ambitious strategy to create an international financial center on a par with the cities of London and Manhattan," as Jun Xio, the Gensler architect, said. When you're in charge of engineering a landmark skyscraper your responsibility extends far beyond the stability of the structure itself to the aspirations and integrity of the city, even the nation, where it will stand.

It's still a bit of a mystery what's going to happen when I arrive on site at the Tower. Though I'd made arrangements with Poon and his firm, Thornton Tomasetti, for the visit I wasn't able to confirm how long I'd be there, how much of the building I could see, and most important to me, whether I'd get to the top. I have a healthy fear of heights but the prospect of being on top of a building so tall, and still under construction, was exhilarating. Great views can be had on observation decks elsewhere, but being in the sky on the roof of a tower still reaching upward would offer a unique sense of the grandiosity of the endeavor. And, without the requisite safety measures and formalities, the prospect of a subversive thrill. Though Poon is a senior figure on the project, even he wasn't exactly sure how the visit was going to play out. Building sites of this magnitude are extremely restricted. Frankly, they're dangerous. In the litigious United States, with liability and whatnot, getting on site at a building like One World Trade Center is near-impossible. Yet where China perhaps lacks some of America's legal and insurance obstacles, as an American journalist I wouldn't exactly be a welcome visitor either.

Poon meets me in the lobby of the Jin Mao Tower, which along with the Shanghai World Financial Center comprises the two completed skyscrapers of the tri-towered district. We walk a block over to the Shanghai Tower's adjacent low-rise building, functioning as administration offices for the site, as well as a showplace for potential tenants. In a large backroom in the lobby is an extravagant promotional installation of sorts. Numerous framed diagrams and blueprints of the Tower line the walls. 3D computer animated videos with moving diagrams play on a quartet of vertical video screens with a choreographed interplay between them. A very large, maybe thirty-foot-tall, model of the Tower, complete with neon blue lighting, looms over me on a pedestal in front of the monitors.

The section of floor I'm standing on is clear glass encasing an illuminated map of the city. It's rendered two-dimensionally with simplistic lines representing roads and a large glowing blue swatch for the Huangpu River. The World Financial Center and Jin Mao and Shanghai Towers, crafted in frosted glass miniature, are the lone three-dimensional objects on the map. The whole room is kind of like a dazzling, private museum exhibit.

Poon is a small and slight man, vibrating with energy. (One of his colleagues suggested his demeanor is a result of being in a permanent state of jet lag from constantly traveling to and from Asia. He's based in New York.) He has the air of someone always in a rush, making it hard to feel comfortable asking him questions. I'm still wondering exactly what the plan is but I'm reluctant to ask. Will my visit amount to a twenty-minute gloss-over at the foot of the Tower, or will it be a penetrating three-hour tour? Watching Poon and an employee in dress slacks and a windbreaker converse in Chinese, it's not clear if Poon knows the answer right now, or if he's going to decide as we go, or if it's not even up to him. The employee, who turns out to be our guide and handler, dispenses hard hats to us. Poon and he continue talking in Chinese and I trail behind, tightening the strap on my helmet as we head outside toward the Tower.

Dennis Poon grew up in Hong Kong, where learning English as a second language was common. Seeking opportunity, as a nineteen-year-old he came to the United States as a student in 1974. "I was always fond of the U.S. for its freedom in thinking, freedom in writing, freedom of expression and democracy. And," he added, "it was very advanced in technology at that time." He attended the University of Texas at El Paso, supporting himself through college, earning a degree in science and civil engineering in six semesters. After a bachelor's degree at "UTEP," he went on to Columbia University to get a master's in civil engineering.

During his first year at Columbia, in 1977, he began working with Thornton Tomasetti (then called Lev Zetlin & Associates). As a junior engineer he was the number sixteen employee. The firm now has over seven hundred employees and more than twenty branch offices worldwide. Poon, having been "fortunate to grow with the firm over the last thirty-five years," today is a vice chairman and member of the board of directors. Though Tomasetti provides engineering services for a gamut of structures—arenas, stadiums, hotels, airports, and more—the firm's growth, to a degree, has mirrored the rise in prevalence of what are known as "supertalls," buildings that are 300 meters (roughly 1,000 feet) or higher. (Floor heights vary but this usually translates to seventy-plus stories.) Just six years ago, in 2008, there were roughly thirty-six supertalls. Today there are seventy-two. The ability and desire to build to the sky has become so heated that a new categorization, "megatall," is now in use for buildings 600 meters and higher.

"Basically, there were no supertall buildings in the old days," Poon told me. "In 1977 they were quite rare." So, in the beginning, the first projects the firm worked on were schools, hospitals, malls, and warehouses. "Most were around twenty stories, thirty tops," said Poon. "But then, suddenly, we were doing more and more investigation projects." This investigative work, often called forensics, has developed into its own subfield of structural engineering, and is a specialty of Tomasetti. Among early forensic projects, the firm investigated why windows were falling from the John Hancock Tower in Boston (quite a scandal at the time), and how to remedy excessive swaying and cracks in New York's Gulf & Western Building. Understanding buildings' failures, in part, facilitated Poon's knowledge about how to engineer supertalls from scratch.

Today it's typical for Poon to be brought in during the earliest stages of design, working with architects as a team before they've even been awarded business. For the Shanghai Tower the owner held a design competition, which is typical for large-scale projects like supertalls. While the architects who enter these competitions tend to make the news, and have their designs shown in the media— as was the case with the One World Trade Center competition, which was breathlessly reported on—what we don't hear about are the engineering firms the architects have already teamed up with to help create these designs. Prior to the Shanghai Tower, Gensler had never built a supertall, so presenting as a team with Thornton Tomasetti, a firm, under Poon's direction, that had already built many of the tallest buildings in the world, gave the owners a degree of confidence in their plans they wouldn't otherwise have had.

For many buildings today the engineer follows the architect. Yet with more complex, challenging structures like supertalls and long-spans (airplane hangers, bridges, arena roofs), the form and function unite, making the work more collaborative. A great example where you can see this marriage is the fantastical CCTV skyscraper in Beijing, where two leaning buildings bend at right angles at the top and bottom creating one continuous structure. The engineering supporting this strange building is immediately visible in the highly irregular steel grid on its façade which "forms the stability system and reflects the distribution of forces that the structure experiences under different load conditions." For elite structural engineers like Poon, bearing an outsized amount of authorship for the aesthetics of architecturally ambitious projects is part of their burden and distinction. "If you are a good engineer," Poon told me, "you must design your engineering elements with art in your mind."

And yet, even when the engineering is overtly woven into the form of the structure, the professionals behind those plans remain invisible. Or even maligned. "An engineer is only a rudimentary, undeveloped architect . . . The engineer is a book man, as a rule . . . [they] know all about everything and understand nothing." That this sentiment was expressed by Frank Lloyd Wright is particularly galling because the engineering schemes (at his insistence) on a number of his most famed works, in fact, have not stood the test of time. But structural engineers, as a norm, care so deeply about the responsibility of their craft that they've been known to surreptitiously "correct" architects' plans. At Fallingwater, one of Wright's most celebrated buildings, the flaws in the design were so obvious to the engineers on the project that beams were secretly reinforced well beyond what Wright's plans called for. (Wright was so notoriously stubborn that he never would have agreed to the alterations, so carrying out the work, initially without his knowledge, was the only way to ensure the safety of the building. In fact, when Wright found out he went ballistic, threatening to walk away from the project.) But they were right. If that hadn't been done, said Robert Silman, an engineer who has repaired numerous Wright buildings over the years, "the building would have collapsed."

We intuit a brass-bound link between authorship and responsibility. After all, attaching one's name to a product or project is seen as the ultimate sign of "taking responsibility" for it. But what if genuine responsibility is often obscured? There's an interesting interplay between responsibility and anonymity. Though their names are but a footnote in the public consciousness for his acclaimed house, had the engineers on Fallingwater not embraced their unseen responsibility it would have, well, fallen into the water it so spectacularly overlooks. Similarly, though he is the chief engineer on the Tower, and personally behind the design of the structural scheme, Poon repeatedly took great pains to emphasize to me that "engineering is always a team effort." Further, he often talked about the collaboration between his specialty and the rest of the trades at work on the project, how working together to achieve the best result is his prime motivation. Whether you literally perform work that is hidden, like the engineers on Fallingwater, or you openly view your authority as part of a communal process, taking responsibility doesn't necessarily mean writing your name in neon. In fact, it may often mean the opposite. It may be counterintuitive, but true leadership and responsibility perhaps come from viewing oneself as part of a team, viewing your work as always in service of the endeavor.

Despite his humility, as the chief engineer, Poon is the ultimate accountable party for the soundness of the Tower. And to truly appreciate his role and responsibility on an undertaking as grandiose as a 2,073-foot-tall skyscraper, perhaps the most sensible place to start is by understanding the structure itself. And the building we are touring today is a marvel. In one respect the Shanghai Tower can be thought of as two buildings in one—the main building, which rises cylindrically, and a triangular outer skin that spirals upward.

If you were to look down on a two-dimensional cross-section of the Tower you'd see a circle inside a soft-edged triangle, almost like a guitar pick. Now imagine this guitar pick rotating, one tick each floor, around the circle. In another respect, the Tower can be thought of as nine separate twelve-to-fifteen-story buildings stacked on top of each other, each stepped back a little more, like a wedding cake.

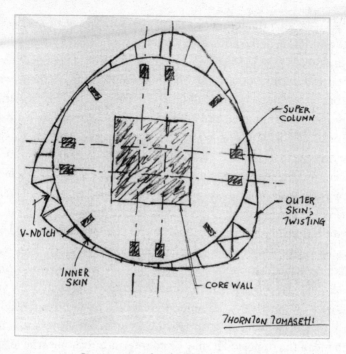

Cross-section sketch of Shanghai Tower

In between each section are concrete slabs, the world's largest guitar picks, extending to the outer skin, upon which the next twelve-plus cylindrical floors rest. The outer skin smoothly tapers inward while it twists toward the top, kissing the inner building at each of the slab floors where the circle and triangle intersect.

These multiple buildings in one—both the exterior skin and inner building, and the nine stacked buildings—and how they work together are the genius of the design. In the space between the circular central tower, which is fully enclosed with its own glass façade, and the triangular outer façade are a series of atriums for each fourteen-story section. On the slab floors will be food and shops, services and amenities, and parklike areas complete with fully grown trees in the atriums. Workers and inhabitants need not travel all the way down to the ground for lunch or errands, or even some greenery. The slab floors also serve as a safety refuge and for mechanical equipment.

Because only the slabs extend to the outer skin, the atriums feature extraordinary fourteen-story ceiling heights. While there are a few other buildings with this outer skin design, the Tower is the first skyscraper in the world to feature usable public space like these multi-zoned atriums. "It is difficult enough to design a double-skin building, but one that requires the outer skin to be constructed at continuously varying distances from the inner curtain wall has never been done before," said Daniel Winey, a principal at Gensler.

Standing at the foot of the Tower, with its massive supercolumns exposed, and the maximum neck-crane necessary for the straight vertical sight line to the top, one is confronted by the sheer magnitude of the structure. Above the first five floors or so, which are open, the next twenty-odd floors of the outer skin are already sheathed in glass. Above that the building is in various states of completion, enabling one to see the interaction of all its elements, the twisting curtain wall (as the outer skin is technically called), the sheer glass façade, the interior cylinder, the guitar-pick slabs. I spent extensive time reviewing materials on the building and meeting with Poon in New York prior to my trip, but seeing the Tower now, in person, especially in its unfinished state, brings all the descriptions to life in a way one can't fully mentally prepare for. There's an image-to-reality buzz like finally meeting a spouse's college friend you'd heard so much about.

As we enter the site, walking along temporary metal catwalks, I peer down into the five-story basement. Bundles of rebar sprout out the sides of concrete columns like Play-Doh pushed through a spaghetti filter. A steel beam on the ground is slowly being raised by a distant crane all the way up on the roof. As I watch this impossibly heavy thing dangling by a wire I reactively pat my hard hat, not that it would help. I follow Poon and the handler, who never is named for me, deeper into the structure. Everything is loud, slightly wet, and supersized-feeling since it's all support beams and columns without any of the interior walls to bring things to human scale. We get locked into a cage and slowly ascend.

It's a tight fit with me, Poon, the handler, the female elevator operator, and five construction workers. We get off at the eleventh floor. Everything is smooth concrete and wide open. I walk to the edge of the interior space and peer into the atrium. Looking down, giant ovoid shapes are cut into the slab floor, with deep squares embedded in the lemon cutouts. These will be for the mature trees that will live inside the atriums (with fourteen floors of height, there will be plenty of room). Even in its unfinished state the atrium is quite extraordinary.

We walk down a dark staircase two flights to a partially finished floor, presumably a model for potential business tenants. After a few floors of retail on the bottom of the building, the next eighty-odd stories will be for office space, followed by another thirty-odd stories for the highest hotel in the world. Topping off the building is another 35 meters for an observation floor and crown. Here in the model office space, a raised floor and dropped ceiling are already in place. The lights are strips of pinpoint LEDs. Yet, interestingly, they still have the stark white cast of hated fluorescents. After the wow factor of the Tower's unique overall design, the standardized office interior is a letdown. Poon and I leave the model office and head toward an unfinished part of the floor, which looks like the space we were in two flights up. I feel at home, back in the engineer's skeleton.

"What are these beams, here?" I ask Poon, pointing to the vertical posts in between the panes of glass. "Those are vertical mullions," he says. "What's this beam, here?" I tap a large pole next to me. "That's a secondary steel post with spray-on fireproofing." "OK, so it's a steel I-beam underneath the fireproofing," I confirm. "No, it's a steel *column*," he patiently corrects me. (Hearing me refer to everything I see as a beam must have felt to Poon like Jonathan Franzen teaching an intro creative writing class, temples throbbing as a student calls *run* and *talk* nouns.) Every single member (a catchall term I should have been using for any individual piece of a structure) is made out of either steel or reinforced concrete. Poon's team runs tests and analyses to determine not only the shape and size of each member but also the best mix of concrete and the optimum amalgam of steel, with different tensile strengths and properties based on what the member is used for. They even specify to the ironworkers what type of member-to-member connections to use. Recalling the hybrid of science and art aptitudes needed for Harding's wayfinding and Apel's fragrance work, the engineering on a supertall requires an extreme dichotomy of the mind—the broad creativity for the macro plan of the building's overall structural system but also the micro attention to detail for the proper design of every post, beam, mullion, column, truss, metal deck, rebar, and so on.

It's an almost unfathomable quantity and complexity of work and materials to be accountable for. But Poon seems to revel in it. "I think I fell in love with tall buildings because I'm short," he said once by way of introducing himself in a lecture. By his résumé of skyscrapers he should be a dwarf. This love of overseeing the engineering on such exceptional buildings necessitates a healthy ego to holster so much responsibility. It also requires a certain humility. "When you have enough experience, you are allowed to take on more responsibility. So responsibility grows hand in hand with your experience," he told me. Through Poon's slow ascent to the top of his field, one begins to understand how important patience is in taking on responsibility. "Once you have so much experience, you can handle a lot of difficulties, challenges in the engineering design, challenges in construction. How to handle different situations with business," he said. It's only through experience that Poon became ready and qualified to take on so much responsibility. But once you're ready for it, the rewards are immense. "The challenge should not be stressful to you. It should be an excitement and an honor."

That Dennis Poon is now in a position of such power is not a surprise. Cameron Anderson, a professor of psychology in the Haas School of Business at UC Berkeley, pointed me to research he conducted that "shows desire for authority—which corresponds with desire for responsibility—is predictive of attaining power." He explained, simply enough, that people who want responsibility, who truly revel in it, are more likely to move into leadership roles within an organization. This desire for and even *savoring of responsibility*— the third of the Invisibles' Three Traits—is apparent in nearly every Invisible I interviewed.

"We are the San Andreas specialty—no matter what happens it's always going to be my fault," said Albert Scarmato, an anesthesiologist at the CentraState Medical Center in Freehold, N.J. While the surgeons get the accolades and "fruit baskets," as Dr. Joseph Meltzer, an anesthesiologist at UCLA Medical Center, told me, it's the anesthesiologists who run the operating room. "It's funny how on TV the surgeon is the leader of the OR, but in reality, during an emergency they're often the ones freaking out, looking to me for assurance. Whatever happens it is my job to be the leader and maintain calm in the OR," Scarmato said. "But I love the responsibility; I'm a bit of a control freak," he said, exemplifying the trait.

"There are a number of adverse events and scenarios that arise not every procedure, or every day, but happen often enough that you need to become familiar with them so you know how to deal with emergencies while staying focused and calm," said Meltzer. "We had a patient the other day who we had a problem intubating [putting the breathing tube in]. I began to run down the line of ways to handle airway management. When several standard methods didn't work, I then headed toward less-common maneuvers. All the while, bear in mind if the patient doesn't get oxygen he's dead," he said. "Ultimately, I used a small fiber optic camera to insert the tube and the patient was fine. You stay calm and make it happen."

While different fields, or different people, by their nature may elevate one of the Three Traits over the others, every Invisible embodies all three of them. To that point, anesthesiologists also embody meticulousness and training at a level not easily surpassed. "I can tell just by the tone of the different beeps of the machines hooked up to the patient what is happening," Dr. Scarmato said. "I can hear a certain heart rate on the monitor and can tell what it is without even looking at the number." And this meticulousness brings them satisfaction. "Many of us relish the precision and detail," said Dr. Meltzer.

And while anesthesia is hardly an unknown specialty, because the practitioners have a very temporary relationship with the patient they rarely receive the accolades (or fruit baskets, as Meltzer noted) after a successful operation. Indeed, they generally are only thought of if something goes horribly wrong. One can only thrive working with this inverse formula for acknowledgement if he embodies the first of the Three Traits—ambivalence toward recognition. "Even though we are critical to the patient's survival, we have an understated role with the patient," Meltzer said. But that doesn't bother him. As all Invisibles demonstrate, the reward is in the work itself, he says. Prior to being an anesthesiologist, Dr. Scarmato was a fireman and an EMT, two jobs where he not infrequently was thanked firsthand by the people he helped, and when he told people of his job he had a sort of societal gratitude that is absent in his current work. Yet, he says, "I love what I do, now more than ever. The paycheck isn't as rewarding as people think. The joy I get is from the power and responsibility of my role, and the pride of helping people, even though I don't have the long-term post-op relationship they have with their surgeons."

I follow Dennis back to the cage, not knowing what's next. Are we visiting more floors? Are we done? Will we get to the roof? Poon knows I want to go to the top, but I now sense that this is a bit of an unusual VIP tour for him as well. While he travels to job sites often, it's more for high-level meetings with the other principals on the projects, and not necessarily to personally inspect the construction. Not knowing Chinese, and because their default brusque tone won't allow me to make out the tenor of their exchanges, I'm not sure what Poon and the handler are arranging next.

We join a different group of workers already in the elevator. They all have on hard hats and the same dust-, paint-, grease-, and grit-stained work clothes of construction workers anywhere, though theirs are windbreakers and thin pants, not the rugged Carhartt jackets and Dickies coveralls standard for American construction workers. More worrisome, their feet are clad in sneakers or casual street shoes, a far sartorial cry from the steel-toed work boots that surely are expected on job sites in the States. I hope this lack of safety norms for attire doesn't extend to the construction and maintenance of the elevator. Sitting on a stool, a woman with glazed eyes and a face mask manually operates the lever, and the cage climbs slowly. Very slowly. Numbers painted on the walls pass us by—18, 19, 20. With each floor I'm a little more excited and a little more apprehensive about the whole endeavor. 31, 32, 33 . . .

At 47 the cage stops and the workers get out. We stay on another two floors and wander out into the Mars-scape of the forty-ninth floor. As we walk from the elevator we're met with a roar of wind, enough to ripple the bottom of my pants. The same beautifully smooth concrete surfaces as on the lower floors abound, but there are seemingly fewer secondary beams and posts. And no windows. Without any glass, the elegance of the skeleton of both the inner building and the outer curtain wall are on full display now. Poon and I stop a foot shy of the edge, where a loose netting dangles from a waist-high bar. It feels as though I can reach out and touch the Jin Mao Tower, while the street and cars below recall the miniaturized model of the city from the Exhibition Center. I lean just a bit to get a better view of the ground and my foot grazes the netting. A flash of vertigo lights up my spine to the top of my head. I live in New York City, and have spent years working in high-rises, but I assure you the sensation of being forty-nine stories up in an unfinished skyscraper without walls or windows is not something one can be prepared for. I take a step back and notice Poon is several paces behind me, looking askance.

Directly above us is one of the slab refuge floors, extending beyond our own. The giant cantilevered trusses it rests on are visible underneath. The clean geometry of the massive steel members interlinked with assorted columns and beams is like a mathematical proof; there's an aesthetic beauty in witnessing the simplicity of refined engineering. While the design of the Shanghai Tower seems fanciful, there are sound structural reasons behind it. The developer was initially wary of the double skin and twisting façade, Poon told me. "Too fancy equals too expensive," he recalled being told. But Poon convinced him that the form actually followed the function and that the design was not only logical but economical.

Supertalls in general have unique challenges, and the Shanghai Tower in particular has its share. Shanghai is in an active earthquake zone. To make matters worse, the ground beneath the building is soft, made of silty and sandy clay and soil. Even a half-mile down they couldn't find rock. Because the water table is so high—just three feet below grade—there is 5,000 pounds per square foot of hydrostatic pressure trying to uplift the slab at the bottom of the foundation. They had to use over eight hundred reinforced concrete anchor piles, each pounded 60 meters down, to prevent the slab (and the building) from being pushed out of the ground. Bear in mind the slab itself is made of 61,000 cubic meters of concrete, enough to fill roughly twenty-five Olympic swimming pools. To keep the water at bay a slurry wall (a protective barrier underground) over one meter thick was constructed. The histories of 132 earthquakes were studied to run tests. (At the Thornton Tomasetti offices in New York I viewed a computer simulation, with the effects magnified many times, where the building wiggled and swayed like a dancing windsock in front of a car dealership.) As a result, the Tower is now designed to withstand a 2,500-year earthquake.

Holding the whole building together are eight "super columns," in pairs on the north, south, east, and west sides of the cylindrical inner building. They run from the ground straight to the roof unabated, in smooth arcs tapering inward as the Tower narrows. At their base, each is 5 by 4 meters (over 16 by 13 feet) reinforced with 145-metric-ton steel plates. Through the center of the building runs a 30-by-30-meter stabilizing reinforced concrete core, where elevator shafts, mechanical ducts and pipes, and stairwells are housed. The scale and detail of it all is hard to fathom. At its essence, though, the cross-section of the building depicted in a hand-drawn diagram framed on the wall in the administration building lobby (akin to the image printed near the beginning of the chapter) is a square inside a circle inside a triangle.

Everything must be accounted for. Alas, this includes terrorism as well. For all supertall buildings the firm is currently designing there is a system to prevent progressive collapse. In the Shanghai Tower, "we checked the structure by assuming some secondary columns (between the supercolumns) are knocked down in a particular floor," Poon told me. "To offset this there will be an alternate load path to transfer the column load to other locations."

But in extremely tall buildings, the wind can be the most challenging element to manage. This is where the outer curtain wall's utility really comes into full relief. The outer skin serves multiple purposes. By creating atriums it allows for the unique resting areas in each of the segments of the Tower. The space also acts as an environmental buffer, like a vestibule. It helps control the amount of sun that enters the building, reducing electrical loads for air-conditioning, and reduces the cold directly impacting the building in the winter. But perhaps most important, the outer curtain wall is a critical component in managing the wind's effect on the building. It can be twisted and contorted to reduce the wind load while allowing the interior space of the building to remain normalized, with straight vertical glass walls.

Hundreds of thousands of dollars were spent conducting extensive wind studies in conjunction with RWDI, wind consultant experts. They utilized a special wind tunnel similar to the ones used for rockets and missiles, and a giant 16-meter-tall scale model of the Tower. In their wind tunnel testing they even incorporated models of the Jin Mao Tower and the World Financial Center to ascertain how the wind would interplay between the three buildings. It all comes down to "how do we cheat the wind," said Poon. "Because the taller you make a building, the higher the wind. If you build in the typical way, the width of the building at the bottom is X and all the way at the top of the building it's X; basically you're putting a big sail on top. Because the wind load at the bottom can be 20 pounds per square foot, but at the top the windows might have to bear 100 pounds per square foot, 200 pounds per square foot." One of the ways to cut down on the wind is to taper a building from a wide bottom to a narrow top, as many skyscrapers do. But the other way to cheat the wind is "to cut the building into different aerodynamic shapes."

Ultimately, the extensive testing engendered two key design elements, that in turn are unique aesthetic components of the building. They found that by rotating the curtain wall 1 degree every floor, this cut down the vortex shedding effect (a type of wind flow disturbance) by 25 percent. In total, the building rotates 120 degrees. There is also a notch (or what Arthur Gensler, the head of the architecture firm, calls a "zipper") like a "V" chipped out of the tip of the guitar pick, which spirals up the full height of the building following the twist of the curtain wall. The reduced wind load saved over $50 million in normal structural costs, Gensler has said. The building is also designed to withstand the wind forces of a hundred-year storm. Nevertheless, of course, all of this only minimizes, but does not eliminate, the effects of wind. To counteract the inevitable sway of the Tower, a 1,500-ton pendulum—called a Tuned Mass Damper—hangs in the top of the building; whichever way the building sways it swings in the opposite direction, offsetting the motion and keeping the building more still.

Standing here, open to the elements on the forty-ninth floor, I can see up close the system Poon designed to connect the outer curtain wall to the building. A low-rise building only needs a trunk or core to stand up safely. But when you get up to 2,000 feet the core by itself is not sturdy enough to withstand the winds. "So we did an outrigger truss system," explains Poon. "When you're skiing, your body is the core, just like the concrete core of the building. Every fourteen floors of the building is an outrigger truss." He sticks his arms out straight and stiff. "At the end of each truss is a post. These are the supercolumns. These are the ski poles. When the wind blows"—he tilts his body but shows that the imaginary ski pole is preventing him from tipping over—"I'm still standing! But instead of two poles there are four sets of twin supercolumns. We hide the trusses every fourteen floors within the mechanical zone. That's how we achieve simplicity and efficiency and leave plenty of floor space for offices."

Amazingly, the curtain wall, which extends the full height of the building, has its name because it actually hangs just like a curtain. Every fourteen floors, trusses are cantilevered out where steel rods are then hung to support a ring for the curtain wall. This is called a radial truss. Poon points out beyond the netting to one of the many giant, curved steel pipes that encircle the building like costume jewelry bracelets. In essence, the whole outer skin, 120-plus stories of it, is just hanging from these steel rings.

This system is good enough for the wind, Poon says, "but not good enough for earthquakes. Because if there's an earthquake we also want some elasticity." For this they devised a second system of defense. "We also have a ring of bell trusses two stories deep, every fourteen stories. This forms a mega-frame," he says. "We try to fit all of the components together like a Swiss watch." With the trusses reaching from the core out to the rings, it looks very much like a bicycle wheel, with spokes radiating from the center outward, as

Dan Winey, a principal at Gensler, referred to the system. All of this somehow seems both impossibly complex yet, at its essence, utterly simple.

As we head toward the elevator I finally get up the nerve to ask Poon if we're going to the top. "Yes, yes, that's where we're going," he says impatiently, as if I should have known that all along. This is a different elevator from before, since the first one doesn't go above our floor. A different group of workers cram in with us. No one talks. The elevator seems louder than the other. Is it laboring more? There's a lot of rattling. The female operator sits motionless, head down, with a mask on her face and hand on the lever, guiding us upward. There's a metal box on the cage wall with a giant lightning bolt on it. I don't need to know Chinese to not go near it. Because less of the building has been constructed on the higher floors, we're not as enclosed. Splinters of light strobe through the cage walls. The clacking of the motor, like a weak jackhammer, is both disconcerting yet reassuring in its steady rhythm. The building stands at eighty-seven stories tall today, around 407 meters, roughly just a hundred feet shy of the top of the Empire State Building. I really shouldn't be here. I shouldn't be doing this.

The door opens. We're met with a burst of white light. The workers file out first and are cast in silhouette, black figures against a glowing sky. Poon warns unnecessarily, "Now, you have to be super, super careful!" Immediately in front of the cage is a sheet metal floor, which is wet. About five feet beyond this metal plate that I'm standing on the floor effectively disappears. It's just a mishmash of rebar and sporadic planks, and beams jutting upward. A riot of different materials litter the unfinished floor, with piles and piles of what appears to be rebar or steel rods all over the place. Several one-foot squares are cut into the unfinished floor. Where they lead down to isn't clear. Some have safety bars around them, some don't. Foolishly, until now I had been imagining standing on a somewhat regular roof, just with workers building upward from it. It didn't occur to me when you're on the very top there of course is no floor, they have to build it.

And then I realize something: There's no wind. It's some sort of weather anomaly. It's very quiet, almost serene. Or perhaps there were jackhammers and drills but, like a movie where they drop out the sound at that key moment, my mind went silent. Poon and I hover together, marooned at the core. Because I can't go out toward the edge there's no view of the ground. Just sky. Up here, with no ceiling, no walls, and very little floor to speak of, it's just Poon, me, a handler whose name I don't know, and a dozen fearless Chinese construction workers just going about their business 1,300 feet above the world. Poon and I stand silently for a long moment and I watch him look around with pride.

Imagine standing eighty-seven stories up on a roof that, aside from a tiny patch in the center, is essentially nothing but rebar and planks. In this precarious position, it's hard to overestimate the importance of the engineering having been done right. I ask Poon if he normally would go up to the top on a site visit and he grimaced the universal *Are you kidding?* It's an extraordinary place for a regular person to be. Other than these workers, *no one* has business being up here, not even the lead structural engineer.

▲

"We coordinate with all the various trades—wind, mechanical, electrical, elevators, plumbing, architectural, on and on," Poon had told me when we had met in New York. "We need to work together as a team, to make things fit, and to avoid crashing effect." I don't know if the phrase was an English-as-second-language miscue, or a purposeful euphemism, but I couldn't help but laugh. In the end, though, this enormous responsibility is the essence of Dennis Poon's job—to *avoid crashing effect*. When we rode down the elevator at the Tower he said, "This is what I love to do," and repeated what he had told me earlier: "It's an honor."

Though many of us instinctively try to avoid much responsibility, research shows there is a strong correlation with relishing responsibility, or learning to do so, and personal fulfillment. Dr. Sonja Lyubomirsky, the psychology professor and author of *The How of Happiness*, explained that traits like goal pursuit and commitment, both of which are tied to responsibility, have powerful connections to well-being. "People are happier when they are pursuing significant goals (such as career advancement) and are making progress toward them," Lyubomirsky told me. "Taking responsibility is part of the commitment and effort that meaningful career goal pursuit requires." "And," Robb Willer, a sociologist at Stanford University, added, "there is a robust link between feelings of control and positive emotions."

Though the stakes aren't always life and death, as they can be with anesthesia and with the engineering of supertall buildings, this desire for responsibility in whatever field one is in—and the benefits of this attitude—runs through all Invisibles. Pam Vu, a fact-checker I worked with at *Vogue*, and who went on to head the fact-checking departments at *Shape* and *Marie Claire*, noted to me, "Part of the thrill of the job is sometimes being able to control the direction of a big piece, which is fun because there is such a machine—esteemed editors, famous writer, big-shot photographer—behind an article and lil' ol' fact-checker gets to alter the piece."

While modern psychology and sociology offer much to verify the rewards of responsibility, perhaps it's philosophy that best explains why savoring responsibility leads to fulfillment. The model of happiness perpetuated by the cultural juggernauts of Hollywood, Madison Avenue, and Disneyesque fairy tales of everyday effervescence, broad-smiled contentedness, and perfect relationships is a historically anomalous, and for most, unachievable state. In contrast, we shall return to eudaimonia, the classical Greek concept of happiness that essentially means the "flourishing" or "rich" life. With their devotion to training, meticulousness, and desire for quiet power and accountability, Invisibles understand the value of a life not necessarily of the moment-to-moment happiness that many mistakenly strive for, but of an overall *richness* of experience, a life grounded in eudaimonic values.

This approach to happiness begins to get at why a *New York* magazine feature from 2010 on the joys (or lack thereof) of parenting—to which, as a frequently frustrated yet occasionally elated father of two children under age five I all too well related—ends with a compelling and instructive point about the rewards of responsibility: "Tom

Gilovich, a psychologist at Cornell, made a striking contribution to the field of psychology, showing that people are far more apt to regret things they *haven't* done than things they have," the piece noted, specifically such as having children. Gilovich then recalled watching TV with his children at three in the morning when they were sick. "'I wouldn't have said it was too fun at the time,' he says. 'But now I look back on it and say, Ah, remember the time we used to wake up and watch cartoons?' The very things that in the moment dampen our moods can later be sources of intense gratification, nostalgia, delight." I can attest that kids, at least in the early years, are a nightmarish grind of responsibility. But at times, especially in reflective moments, they also bring an unrivaled deep, soulful type of happiness. Responsibility, be it with parenting or with our work, is not easy but Invisibles intuit its lasting reward.

Like ambivalence to recognition and meticulousness, the first two of the Invisibles' Three Traits, the third trait—savoring responsibility— also runs counter to our prevailing cultural ethos. Who can forget after 9/11, when instead of the citizenry being encouraged to collectively sacrifice for the impending "war on terror," we were instead told by President Bush simply to continue our "participation and confidence in the American economy." It's a fairly apolitical statement to acknowledge that our wars are no longer about shared sacrifice; rather, today, they largely directly engage only those in the military (and its subcontractors) and their loved ones. Whereas in generations past the country as a whole was involved in some fashion or another during wartime. Factories producing consumer goods were mandated to switch over to production of munitions and military equipment. Food was rationed. There was a collective responsibility for such a grave undertaking as a war. I'm not advocating the righteousness or value of certain wars over others, nor of war as a practice in general—this book certainly is not the place for that— but I *am* arguing that there has been a clear reduction in collective responsibility in our wars, and that lack of involvement by the citizenry adversely affects our ability to gain perspective on the impacts of military action.

And like the first two traits, technology again can be seen as fostering an environment that runs counter to the Invisibles' values. Of course, anonymity is a hallmark of Invisibles' circumstance, but for them not being noticed is a directive to work even harder, to be even more responsible for the outcome. Whereas some have argued, as the *New Yorker* writer David Denby did in his book *Snark*, that the anonymity the Internet can offer encourages incivility and a lack of seriousness. Interestingly, some research has shown that using real names doesn't decrease trolling (as poor behavior online is called). So it may not be anonymity that reduces responsibility, but the mediation of the Web. Unless someone is in front of you, you are less likely to have empathy or embarrassment, research shows. For example, it's easier to break up with a girlfriend over the phone (or by texting or Facebook or whatever it is that people under thirty do today) than it is in person. It's worth noting that making the effort to do something unpleasant, such as ending a relationship, in person is pretty much universally considered the high road. And that's the point—taking responsibility requires effort. But as the psychology and philosophy literature suggests, and the example of Invisibles demonstrates, the rewards for this effort are manifest.

Jim Harding thrives on the notion that he's responsible for getting hundreds of thousands of travelers where they need to go, and not noticing his work is its sign of success. David Apel's sensibilities can make or break millions of dollars in business for his employer and for the brands, designers, and celebrities who rely on him to craft their fragrances. But he's not an isolated, effete artist; rather he revels in the competition with his rivals for the "win" and in the process of divining what will enchant his clients. While he's part of a team of specialists, ultimately, as the lead structural engineer, the safety of some of the world's tallest buildings rests largely on Dennis Poon's designs and calculations. Anesthesiologists run the OR, and in the inevitable moments of terror that can arise during surgery, they keep us alive. And yet it's the surgeon who gets the kudos from the patient. We too often associate power, and the responsibility that goes along with it, with visibility. But as Invisibles exemplify, unseen power and responsibility, which is perhaps its purest form, excites, emboldens, and fulfills.

4.

FLOW AND THE POWER OF EXPERTISE WITH EFFORT

The Unlikely Adrenaline Junkie

As you walk east on 45th Street in Manhattan, passing Third Avenue, you begin to notice something about the people around you. Specifically, the range of foreign languages spoken by men and women in suits escalates dramatically. And the intonations sound different from the languages heard on the subway and most other streets; even without understanding them, there's an apparent eloquence and businesslike concision. The sensation of being a stranger in your own city only deepens as you continue. By the time you hit the block between Second and First Avenues, vehicles with New York plates are almost nonexistent, having been overtaken by SUVs and dark sedans with diplomatic plates parked or idling curbside. And you may not hear English at all.

When the term *adrenaline junkie* is mentioned, it's usually in relation to a rugged NASCAR driver. Or perhaps a nineteen-year-old X Games skateboarder launching himself off the lip of a half pipe. Or habitual skydivers. And yet adrenaline junkies come in more forms than you might think. Perhaps the most unlikely, though, is

Giulia Wilkins Ary. A cardigan draped over the shoulders of her tall, thin frame, her black hair with hints of gray parted on the side and falling just to her chin, she wears elegant wireless glasses and is soft-spoken and warm. Like a sophisticated yet caring aunt, she projects an urbane yet unassuming demeanor, smiling easily as we meet then firmly directing me where to go for my press pass.

As a member of the elite Interpretation Service at the United Nations, Wilkins Ary works here, at the UN Headquarters on First Avenue, for those people on 45th Street, or more likely, their bosses. Without her and her colleagues, diplomats from around the world would not be able to communicate with each other. It's not hyperbole to say that the gears of international diplomacy, to a large degree, would seize without the IS (as the service is called in shorthand). And yet its offices are in the basement of the UN. This placement could be taken as a slight. Or it can be taken as an appropriate, even respectful nod to their invisible role at the institution. For as critical as they are to the proceedings, they must remain essentially unnoticed. If all work is performed perfectly, they will function as mere conduits for one nation to converse with the next.

From grand speeches at the General Assembly to the year-round quotidian interchanges of diplomacy, Wilkins Ary hears one language, interprets it into another language in her head, then speaks the new language *while at the same time continuing to listen to and interpret the next lines of the original language,* a practice known as simultaneous interpretation. (And don't confuse it with translating. Translators work with written text and can take as long as they need. Interpreters, on the other hand, work with spoken language, and "just have to jump on the train," as Wilkins Ary says.) There are no pauses, no taking turns. As long as the speaker is talking, she is interpreting. And research shows this to be one of the most unique and taxing cognitive activities a mind can undertake.

Wilkins Ary and I are quickly heading down a labyrinth of hallways, winding our way toward one of five large meeting rooms. We're in a huge temporary structure on the UN site that serves the organization while the main building undergoes a multiyear renovation. Each meeting room has an adjacent "interpreters row"—a long hallway with six booths on one side and a couple tech rooms for AV people and the like on the other. There is no outside light, the walls are gray, and it's quiet. The décor and architecture could be described as bleak institutional, but presumably that will change when they're back in the main building. As we turn from one endless, windowless corridor to yet another, the monotony and lack of any distinguishing landmarks has me totally disoriented. Jim Harding would not be pleased here. Finally, we make it to interpreters row for Meeting Room 1, the very last hallway.

We enter the second-to-last booth. FRENCH is written on a plaque next to the door. There is charcoal gray foam soundproofing material on the walls, dark gray carpet, light gray paint on the door. A gray desk, gray chairs, and, clearly the result of an insane error, the chairs have blue cushions. Because of the soundproofing there is no echo in the booth. I clap my hands to demonstrate the dead sound and I remark that this is just like an "iso booth" at a recording studio, where you do vocal takes. Wilkins Ary is amused that this is the very first thing I comment on.

There are three large double-paned soundproof windows looking out onto the conference room. The booths in interpreters row are roughly a flight up from the main floor of the meeting room, looking down on the proceedings, simultaneously giving the feeling of authority yet the physical distance implying you are observer more than participant. The architecture reflects the interpreters' importance and their intended heard-but-not-seen neutrality. Each booth, interestingly, also has double-paned side windows so all the interpreters can see one another. I look to the left and peer into booth after booth, the figures inside each one successively more opaque with distance and the additional layers of glass. Alone in their silent pods yet connected through sight, the interpreters function in a strange kind of communal isolation. As maligned as cube farms and open office layouts are, the interpreters' row plan won't likely supplant either as the next office design trend.

We're here for the 333rd Plenary Meeting of the United Nations Disarmament Commission. It's a closed meeting and ostensibly off-limits to the press. There will be no official transcript released to the public. It's not entirely clear how I've made it in, other than I'm not a political reporter and I'm a guest of the IS. This is not the only time an Invisible has gained me access to an otherwise restricted environment; one starts to realize how much power certain behind-the-scenes people have.

We're joined by Myriam, Wilkins Ary's French booth colleague. Because the work is so taxing, UN interpreters always work in pairs, taking half-hour turns. It's extraordinarily unusual to have a visitor in the booth, and though Myriam earlier agreed that my presence would be okay, she seems slightly uneasy now. That we're in a gray, echoless booth probably doesn't help. I feel for Myriam. I'm not surprised why, as policy, outsiders aren't allowed in here. It's a sacred work space. And these people, whose stress load has been compared to that of air traffic controllers, need to concentrate. *Hard.* I'm a distraction. Wilkins Ary, though, is relaxed, and offers me a glass of ice water. I decline and wish I could melt into the chair she's brought in for me as they settle in for the meeting, which is about to start.

A microphone and small audio mixing unit is in front of each interpreter in the booth. Wilkins Ary and Myriam both are wearing headphones now and rapidly pass back and forth papers on the desk that give the schedule of the conference overall and of the speakers at this meeting. "Okay," Wilkins Ary says quickly, "we're about to begin." She takes a big breath and hits a button on her mixing unit. A red light goes on and a torrent of French flows out her mouth. Since I don't have headphones I can't hear the speaker, and since delegates speak from their seats in the meeting I can't tell who is talking by sight either.

UN speeches (outside the high-profile ones at the General Assembly) tend to have a style. The speech, often read from prepared text, is accelerated and just north of monotone, as if they're all in a rush to say what they have to say and then get out. Though I don't know French, it's clear she is speaking very, very fast. Languages, of course, rarely have one-to-one translations. For example, French tends to not use acronyms, so a one-second utterance of "ICBM" in English by the speaker requires a lengthy interpretation in French. For the French booth this means an acceleration of the already fast pace; this is especially problematic because acronyms are a mainstay of UN-speak. (Russian, which is wordier than French, is even more challenging in regard to word-to-word ratios.) This differential has become a trope of comedies—Google "Japanese photographer in *Lost in Translation*"—but it's based in reality. Feeling lost amid Wilkins Ary's indecipherable flood of Français, I console myself by making out "nuclear" quite a few times.

As time passes I continue to marvel at the cognitive churn that is taking place in her brain. English is going in, French is going out. At the same time. Without stopping.

Giulia Wilkins Ary was born in Connecticut but moved to the French-speaking part of Switzerland when she was five. She quickly learned French there by immersion and in school. Her father was a British biochemist with a wanderlust, transferring to different research labs around the world. This would be the first of several moves for Wilkins Ary during her childhood. Her Italian mother spoke Italian with her at home, but she learned that language mainly by spending time with cousins in Italy every summer. Still in grade school, she was now fluent in three languages. "Languages came easily to me," she says. When she was around eight her family moved to France. While there, at age thirteen she started learning Spanish "because I wanted a language my parents wouldn't understand, just so I could have my own private thing." Two years later she spent a summer in Madrid with a Spanish pen pal and came back fluent. Let me get this straight, I say to Wilkins Ary. By the time you are thirteen you're speaking English, Italian, and French, and then you add Spanish just for fun? "I also could read and translate Latin and Ancient Greek." Of course.

In college, Wilkins Ary spent a year in the UK, a year in Spain, and two in France. She started by majoring in ancient languages, but wanted skills and knowledge more applicable to modern-day life and switched to double majors in Spanish and English. After college she completed a one-year training program in interpretation at a school in London. (Completing a training program, however, does not equal being a proficient interpreter. One study showed that interpreters don't feel they've reached their peak performance until they've worked professionally for ten years.) At this point Wilkins Ary was fluent in four languages. And should she stumble across a copy of *The Republic* on papyrus in the original Greek, she could read that, too. After the program in the UK she moved straight to . . . Portugal?

"I didn't know the language at all. On the plane there I was like, 'My God, what am doing!' But I wanted to add another language," she tells me, and she knew there was a need for French interpreters there. Upon arrival, Wilkins Ary started studying Portuguese on the side while doing interpretation work for English and Spanish into French. Between governments and ministries and also finance, the medical community, global business, and international conferences of every type there is a great need for interpreters, even if they don't work in the language of the country they are residing in.

Wilkins Ary recalls one of her first jobs. She was quite nervous because most of her colleagues had been to school for up to four years, usually two years of interpretation and two years of translation. And after just a year of training she was now working in the field. She was in a hotel room with the president of Mexico, Carlos Salinas de Gortari, and a journalist from the French daily *Le Figaro*. "It was just the three of us," she says. "The president was on his way to Davos and had stopped off in Portugal for some reason. I remember there was a lot of concern about the contents and timing of the interview because he didn't want the article published before his big speech at Davos." It was her first time going through all the security related to top-level politicians and it was exciting.

Wilkins Ary found Portuguese difficult to master because of interferences with Spanish. "It took a little longer than I wanted," she says, "before I started doing Portuguese interpretation work." What's "longer" than she wanted, you ask? "Four years."

So along with Spanish and English into French, she added Portuguese into French interpretation. She also did French into English. Since Wilkins Ary considers French her mother tongue (with English as a very close second), this last relation—French into English—is an important distinction, as neuroscientific research suggests it is harder to interpret into a secondary language. To that point, the UN only allows interpreters to work one way—into their mother tongues. (The Chinese and Arabic booths are exceptions to this rule.) "I knew the closer I got to Portuguese the more I'd have to let go of Spanish," she says. "The pronunciation is totally different." Fearing the loss of Spanish mastery and more so wanting a change, Wilkins Ary decided to take a test for the UN in 2000.

While many highly skilled interpreters work outside the UN, as Wilkins Ary's career in Portugal bears out, the IS interpreters are generally considered the best in the business. "A simultaneous interpreter who works for the United Nations has reached what is very much one of the pinnacles of the profession," Barry Olsen, Professor of Simultaneous and Consecutive Interpreting at the Monterey Institute, a graduate school of Middlebury College, said in an interview. "It's the gold standard." Very few spots open up for the IS each year, and not surprisingly, the competition is keen. The exams are offered only intermittently as needed for each booth, around every two years, Kate Young, the IS program officer told me. Every UN interpreter is expected to be fluent in three languages—the mother tongue, plus two others. (The interpreters in the Chinese and Arabic booths just have to know their mother tongue plus English.) To even be allowed to take the exam, which is all oral and in which you have to interpret three speeches of varying difficulty in each language, you must first fill out an application and make it through initial filtering. A recent search for a Russian interpreter for the English booth drew just twelve candidates deemed qualified to take the exam. And even if you pass, that doesn't mean you get a position. You are then put on a roster and if a slot opens up you then have to make it through an intensive interview process.

Wilkins Ary passed the exam and was immediately offered a job in Nairobi but couldn't accept for personal reasons. A year later the UN offered her a job in New York but again she passed for personal reasons. Finally, in 2007 she was offered a position in New York yet again and this time accepted. Her now-husband, a journalist, whom she met in Portugal, moved with her.

Though unusually skilled from the beginning, over time Wilkins Ary learned the nuances of the trade during her eighteen years in Portugal. Once, during a dinner following a two-day conference, one of the speakers stood up to thank the Portuguese authorities and she got ready with her notepad to do a consecutive interpretation (unlike simultaneous, this is when the speaker and interpreter go one after the other). "But the amount of alcohol he had ingested during the meal made his speech utterly incomprehensible," she tells me, laughing. After he finished talking, she looked around and understood what everyone else in the room knew. She made up a short, generic thank-you speech and all parties were relieved.

Simultaneous interpreting, which is now over 90 percent of the IS's work at the UN, was invented in the late 1920s. Prior to that time all interpreting was consecutive. But the practice really came into its own during the Nuremberg Trials, when the demands of multiple language interpretation in the courtroom were simply too much for the inefficiency of stopping every few moments for interpreters and speakers to alternate talking. Some of the people who helped develop the practice were the first people in the Service at the UN. Today the UN has around 150 interpreters, with another 50 to 60 freelancers who are used as needed in New York and around the world.

The UN has six official languages: English (which is first among equals), French, Spanish, Russian, Chinese, and Arabic. This means that official documents can be written only in one of these languages and speeches can only be given in one of them. (The politics behind how and why it's these six are hairy and best left for another discussion.) Most nations have delegates who speak in one of the official languages. If they don't, they will bring their own interpreter who interprets into one of the six languages.

Each language has its own "booth," which at the IS refers to both the literal room they work in but also the team or division for that language. The English, French, Spanish, and Russian booths generally interpret from any of these languages into their booth's language. The Arabic and Chinese booths function differently. They interpret in both directions, and almost exclusively interpret from English into their target languages and from their target languages into English.

Wilkins Ary works from English and Spanish into French. She typically will be paired in the booth with an interpreter who does Russian into French, so they cover all the bases. To her chagrin her Portuguese and Italian are now relegated to personal use only. Like Wilkins Ary, many of the UN interpreters have some degree of fluency in additional languages beyond the ones they use professionally. At one point, after we had talked for a long time, I jokingly ask Wilkins Ary if she knows any other languages. "They offer classes here at the UN in the six official languages so I said I'd give Russian a try," she says. "I reached a reasonable level but then it was too much work and I didn't have time. I could get around in Russia though." I find this oddly comforting, that there seems to be a limit to Wilkins Ary's multilingualism.*

As she speaks, leaning toward the microphone, Wilkins Ary is moving her hands around and motioning with her head. The Russian interpreter in the booth next door is leaning back in his chair, looking at the ceiling while he talks, as if he's musing about something. It's amazing that humans continue to use body language even if it's unseen. Myriam has a Web page open on her laptop to the "UN Term" portal, to use as a sort of "cheat sheet" that she's reviewing to prepare for her turn. Giulia has her own sheet of acronyms and obscure terms written in pencil she made earlier based on notes she was given on the meeting. Each conference and meeting has its own specific argot, often including a library of acronyms, and a big part of an interpreter's job is studying the particular subject matter ahead of time. Sometimes they're even given the text of a speech, usually just minutes beforehand, that they follow along with as the person speaks. But the text is just a guide, as the speakers often veer from what's written.

---

* This isn't entirely true. In a subsequent conversation I ask about Wilkins Ary's family and she mentions a sister in Germany. (Just like Giulia learned Spanish to have her own thing, her sister learned German.) Wilkins Ary then admits that she did "study German for two years." For a normal person this wouldn't amount to much, but for Wilkins Ary, I believe her when she says she understands basic German.

Wilkins Ary continues with the stream of French. *Blah blah blah nuclear, blah blah nuclear blah blah.* I feel like the dog in the famous Gary Larson comic imagining what dogs hear—"Blah blah blah blah GINGER. Blah blah blah GINGER. Blah blah." During the course of the afternoon she will translate from both Spanish and English into French, depending on which country is speaking. Among others, representatives from Moldova, Ecuador, Norway, Bangladesh are all set to speak at the meeting, though it's not known yet what language they'll speak in. The Russian next door now has his eyes closed, still leaning back. He looks like he's in a therapy session, thoughtfully discussing something. Wilkins Ary and the other interpreters I can see down the row all are sitting erect or hunched over their microphones.

Myriam hastily jots down a word and passes the paper to Wilkins Ary. Since the mic is hot and we can't talk in the booth, Myriam pantomimes to me that she thought Giulia may have missed a word. Because they're essentially alone in their work, the interpreters all are quick to help each other. It's surprising that a job so solitary actually has a degree of team effort behind it. To the right I notice that the men in the English booth aren't interpreting. "The English booth statistically works less because more speeches are in English than any other language," Kate Young, the IS program officer, later explained to me. "However, when they do interpretation there is more pressure because all the news outlets, CNN, et cetera, take the news from their interpretation. The interpreter's voice will be on radio." "Annoyingly," she adds, "they incorrectly call us 'voice of translator.'"

But perhaps the misnomer is just as well. Wilkins Ary thrives on the anonymity of her work, and the responsibility that goes along with it. Shortly after I met with her she traveled to Turkey to work at a satellite UN conference (a sporadic opportunity she enjoys). In the huge assembly hall, a cameraman, who had been filming delegates, swung around and zoomed in on Wilkins Ary. "I suddenly appear on two giant screens before all the audience!" she e-mailed me from Istanbul. Cameramen never film the IS booths, and it was "unsettling but fun. I carried on interpreting without losing a beat. I wouldn't want it to become a habit, though!" Ultimately, she said, "not being in the limelight suits me." Rather, she prefers to be ensconced in her booth, doing her work knowing that "people depend on our perfect understanding and transmission of the message. It's stressful but immensely rewarding."

Wilkins Ary never has a break during her turn. Even if a speech isn't given in English or Spanish, she will interpret the "relay" of the English interpretation, done by either the English booth or the Chinese or Arabic booths, into French. The relay system means that every one of the six languages will always be covered, interpreted from the English interpretation as a default if the person in the booth doesn't interpret the language of the speaker. After a particularly long and fast passage ends, Wilkins Ary turns off her mic for a moment, lets out a "phew!" and smiles at me, then flicks it back on and jumps back in.

To give some perspective on the extraordinary strain Wilkins Ary and her colleagues are under, and why the half-hour break rule is in place, we turn to Muammar Gaddafi. In 2009 he gave an infamous, rambling ninety-five-minute speech to the General Assembly. He brought his own interpreter for the job, who, after seventy-five minutes without a break cried into the microphone, "I can't take it anymore!" and then collapsed. Horrified yet still under obligation to interpret, one of the IS staff in the Arabic booth picked up where he left off and finished the speech.

Vous êtes une très jolie fille.

I have a confession to make. Above is the grand total of my foreign-language knowledge.* Despite years of Spanish and French in school, I never could get the hang of it. I've spent much of my life trying to better master English, and other than the "baños," "mi amigos," and the like that every American knows, I seem to have a mental block on allowing another language in my brain. That's why I've long been fascinated by bilingual and multilingual people. I'm

---

* I only had the fortitude to memorize this phrase because I was trying to impress the French au pair I dated while studying abroad in London my junior year of college.

quite in awe of how they do it. But interpreting is magnitudes more complex than mere multilingualism. As Wilkins Ary told me, "Contrary to what people may think, being able to speak several languages does not make you an interpreter."

The more time I spent with Wilkins Ary watching her work, and doing subsequent research, the more difficulty I had wrapping my head around the basics of what she does. How does someone hear one language, interpret it, and speak a different language *simultaneously* as long as the speaker continues to talk? I don't think I could even simultaneously "interpret" English to English. The best analogy I can think of is the circular breathing technique that wind instrument players use where they breathe in and blow out at the same time. And yet that's just a pulmonary acrobatics of sorts, it doesn't involve the cognitive dissonance of one language in and another out *at the same time.*

"Interpreters are made, not born, although there are basic aptitudes that a successful interpreter must have, beyond just speaking two or more languages," Barry Olsen, the interpretation professor, told me. Some people aren't cut out for it. There is a methodical process most schools follow, that slowly builds up the technique. As Kate Young explained, an early exercise has the instructor "read a sentence in French or Russian then stop and have the students say it back in English. There were many in class who couldn't even do that." Another early technique is "shadowing," basically just repeating back what you hear while the speaker is still talking (akin to my English-to-English interpreting joke).

A key component of interpreting is "deverbalizing the message," Olsen explained. Essentially, this means instead of trying to convert word for word as the person speaks, being able to listen to a stretch of speech and conveying the message of a sentence, phrase, or even paragraph as a whole into the target language. The hard part, of course, is being able to 1) very quickly convert the source language message into the target language, and more so 2) speaking this message while simultaneously listening to and converting the next phrase of the speech. Interpreter training utilizes a variety of multitasking exercises to develop this very challenging skill.

But these are learned techniques to accomplish the task. What, uniquely, is happening in multilinguals' brains versus us monolingual folk, and even more extraordinarily, what is happening in the brains of simultaneous interpreters versus mere multilinguals?

Numerable scholarly fields—linguistics, neuroscience, psychology, and various cognitive sciences, to name just a few—study how we process language. And bear in mind, among and within the different fields there is some dispute about what is, quote, actually happening in our brains with language production. But, in essence, "research suggests that it is a multistage process," Janet Nicol, an associate professor of linguistics and psychology at the University of Arizona, told me. We move from thoughts, to thoughts into language, to selecting specific words and tenses, and positioning the thoughts and words into the grammatical structure of a given language. After all that, Nicol continued, "The next stage involves articulating the utterance." With just monolingual language production requiring this much cognitive action, it's quickly apparent how taxing interpretation is on the brain. There's a lot going on!

"For the bilingual," Nicol says, "the steps are similar except that the first stage will also involve language selection." For simultaneous interpreters, like a fidgety five-year-old on a light switch, they're essentially hyper-toggling between two languages—and, wearyingly, all the dominoed steps required for each. Just *thinking* about what Wilkins Ary has trained her brain to do, let alone actually doing it, is a hornet's stinger to the temple.

Indeed, all of this intensive mental activity has serious effects on the minds and bodies of interpreters. At its worst you end up with an incident like Gaddafi's interpreter being driven to collapse. But even the regular workday with its breaks is exceptionally draining. "Levels of mental and physical exhaustion, cognitive fatigue, and mental stress are higher for interpreters than for hi-tech workers, and similar to those of senior officers in the Israeli army," a 2001 study showed. The constant information load and tremendous amount of concentration required were cited as lead stressors for expert interpreters. Wilkins Ary told me that sometimes after her shift her head hurts so much that she has to go outside and not see or talk to anyone for a half hour until it's her turn again. "Simultaneous interpreting is a highly complex discourse performance where language perception, comprehension, translation, and production operations are carried out virtually in parallel and under severe time pressure," noted a study conducted in 1990. The task "is likely to create a heavy processing load." The mental firepower required, like redlining a car's RPMs, produces exhaustion over time. But in the moment it's pure exhilaration.

Back in the booth, Wilkins Ary is churning. The meeting has been under way for several hours, and though she has been alternating with Myriam every half hour, she seems to have built up a stride. Perhaps her posture is different or there is a more intense look in her eyes, it's hard to articulate how exactly, but her manner is more focused. On the agenda for the meeting, several countries, notably Iran and North Korea, are listed as being given a "right of reply." The following account of what happens next is based on an official UN summary of the meeting (as I noted earlier, actual transcripts were not released).

As the North Korean representative spoke, I subsequently learned, the proceedings quickly reached a level only elite interpreters could handle. Wilkins Ary later confessed, with some understatement, that this was a particularly difficult interpretation. The representative spoke in heavily accented English, making it formidable to discern his words, especially with the required speed. Now couple that demand with combustible rhetoric and emotion from the speaker. Wilkins Ary does not turn to smile at me during this session. Her focus is palpable, yet almost paradoxically, like an elite golfer just before her swing, she appears serene.

The representative begins by saying that "the [nuclear] situation is becoming very dangerous, reaching an irreversible point." He then goes on to defend his country's satellite launch and condemn the United States for "distorting" the reason for the launch for political gain. Things only get worse from here. He complains that the United States is "misleading the international community and misusing its permanent seat on the Security Council." He goes on to say, "The United States is the 'champion' of launching satellites and having excessive stockpiles and missiles and threatening international peace and security." Further, his country "has no choice but to test its weapons in self-defense. The people of the Democratic People's Republic of Korea have been living for sixty years under 'nuclear blackmail' since 1957, when the United States planted the first nuclear weapon in South Korea." As the intensity of the rhetoric increases, Wilkins Ary remains in her same focused state yet mirrors the rise in cadence of the speaker. As Kate Young told me, interpreters try to match the emotion of the speakers. They even will try "to inject some inflection if there is a boring speaker."

The North Korean representative is not boring. Think about the following rhetoric and imagine Wilkins Ary in the zone, her eyes closed, intensely listening to extremely accented English and simultaneously interpreting into and speaking French, as the speech builds to a terrifying crescendo: "Current escalation is reaching the possibility of nuclear war," he warns. The United States had, three days ago, made a "historic deployment" when a fighter plane flew over the Pacific Ocean, and CNN broadcast bombs dropping. "The danger level is increasing beyond control," he says. It is not a question of whether war will break out or not, but when. His country has no option but to consider a preemptive strike, which is not a "monopoly" of the United States!

Afterward, as we step outside the booth for tea, Wilkins Ary looks depleted, but has a glow about her, the way one does after an intensive workout. "I believe in the mission of the UN," she says, as one of her motivations for the work. But what really drives her is the challenge. "I seek some degree of perfection," she says. And working toward that goal, first through preparation, and then through the heightened state she must enter while interpreting, is the reward.

There is almost something athletic about it, the speed and difficulty of the task. "If I were to compare it to translation," she says, "that person can look at the text at leisure, but I don't know what's going to come out of my speaker's mouth. It's a total surprise and that's what thrilling about it. There is something very artificial that we're doing—speaking and listening at the same time. Sometimes you don't get into it immediately. But once you get going, after a while, it comes so naturally. There are certain moments, where you're in a rhythm and you reach a point of super-concentration, you're not actively thinking, and it just feels that everything will be done brilliantly. Sometimes I reach the end of the half hour but I want to go on because I feel so connected with the speaker." She continues, "It's like a muscle exercise. There is a feeling of euphoria, a zone. I go through that often. That's what makes the job worth it." As Hossam Fahr, the head of the IS, said in a BBC interview, "They have to be addicted to their own adrenaline." It would come as no surprise to Wilkins Ary to learn that there is compelling psychological literature linking focused, challenging work with deep personal satisfaction.

Flow is a trancelike mental state that occurs when a person is completely immersed in an activity, where "the ego falls away, time flies, and every action, movement, and thought follows inevitably from the previous one," stated Mihály Csíkszentmihályi, the psychologist who proposed this renowned concept. Colloquial phrases for this state are being "in the zone" or "in the moment." Not only does flow produce "intense feelings of enjoyment" and satisfaction, it also improves performance. There are several factors that can lead to and be part of the experience of flow. A key component is intense concentration. Another factor is working on challenging yet attainable, or just-beyond attainable goals. Csíkszentmihályi has suggested that achieving flow can happen by working hard to "overlearn" a skill. These two factors get to the core of what elite Invisibles do—a dedication to the task at hand that "overlearning" or persistent practice requires, and a focused attention, often manifested as meticulousness, as they immerse themselves in their work. I found that most of the Invisibles I talked with have some element of flow in their work.

As someone who spent many years playing music professionally, I've had countless experiences of flow. In the midst of a great jam, my band members and I wouldn't even need to look at one another, and I would be in a Zen-like state, one with my guitar yet simultaneously hearing all the other parts gelling together—*that* was flow. Time disappeared, and I was oddly at once elated and at peace. The afterglow from a great show would stay with me for days, and on a certain level has stayed with me forever. But reaping the benefits of flow need not require the (naturally) narcotic experience of rocking out on stage. In my years as a fact-checker there were many times when I would meticulously comb through a complex article, and the soft machine-gun clatter of typing fingers, the discordant chorus of ringing phones, the low hum of office chatter surrounding me would disappear like a slow fade at the end of a long song. And, at some point, finally exhausted, I'd look up and notice it was dark out as I eyed a wrapper from a half-eaten lunch still on my desk. Meticulous, focused work, even in a gray-lit office cubicle, can elicit flow and its resulting positive feelings. At the end of certain grueling days in the office—the ones when I wasn't popping Advil like popcorn—I was tired, but satisfied in a way that surfing the Web during temp jobs never provided.

This reward of hard work, the flow experience it can elicit, can be achieved only through first building a foundation of skill and knowledge. It took years of relentless practicing and playing with others before I got good enough at guitar to experience flow. And as gifted as Wilkins Ary is, she repeatedly emphasized to me the studying and preparatory work that is an obligatory part of her job. "I love doing the research," she tells me. "It's critical. There is a lot of preparation." This is especially so for when the Security Council meets. "You have to know all the names of the people, the acronyms, who the leaders of the rebels are, and have a strong grasp of the overall issues at hand so you can follow exactly and won't get thrown off by a name you don't know, so you can just keep going fast," she says. "Since you never know what's going to be said, there's a built-in level of surprise. But we try to reduce all of the surprises that are within our control."

Top interpreters are like the best actors and elite athletes in this regard—to watch them work, it appears it's just innate talent. But it's the early work, the practicing, the studying beforehand that allows their gifts to flourish. Even for an invisible job, there is often an even deeper layer of invisibility, if you will, with preparation. It's not surprising that Wilkins Ary relishes this behind-the-scenes work, as her devotion to details and dedication to mastering a craft, characteristics deeply aligned with *meticulousness*, are a commonality among Invisibles. In the broadest sense, meticulousness is really just work ethic. And this attitude runs in direct contrast, is a rebuke, almost, of larger trends today.

While the primary, and most obvious, characteristic that sets Invisibles apart from our prevailing culture is their ambivalence toward recognition, the Invisibles' other traits run counter to the culture at large as well. While certain innate talents help, Invisibles show that to get to an elite level of your field you must devote yourself to learning, then mastering, the techniques of your craft. If you want to achieve flow, "pretty good" won't get you there.

And yet "pretty good" appears to be an increasingly shared value today.

For all of history there have always been varying degrees of divisions of labor within societies. Yet over the millennia, even with these divisions, most citizens were still generalists in many regards. Whether you were a blacksmith or a baker, to function you still chopped your own firewood, tended to your crops, managed your money. Thinkers across the ages, from Plato to Hume, Smith, and Marx have delved into the economic and philosophical aspects of the division of labor. But as disparate as their approaches were, the consensus is that the more advanced we are, the more specialized our labor has become. This particularly holds true after the dawn of industrialization in the eighteenth century. This extreme division of labor and of expertise, of highly specialized employment, is how advanced economies and cultures function now. (How many people chop their own wood today? You call the gas company and hit a switch on a thermostat.) And yet, with the aid of recent technologies, in our creative leisure pursuits many of us are generalists again, but we operate under an illusion of expertise. We've become a nation of dabblers.

For the photo enthusiast today, who fires off hundreds of shots with her DSLR on a weekend trip, and utilizes apps like Instagram that do the creative "developing" for you, and then posts them all online, there can be a creeping illusion that we are more skilled than we actually are. The same holds true for the common teenager or twenty-something who, with the aid of home editing software like iMovie, makes and uploads videos on a regular basis. Our ability to do this is in many respects empowering, satisfying, and just plain fun. And that's hugely important. But it also can lead to a misperception of what true expertise in photography or filmmaking requires.

While many have suggested, such as Paul Levinson, professor of media studies at Fordham University, that the Web has beneficially helped increase writing among the population, it also has increased a sloppiness in the craft. The distance between a hastily written blog post, tweet, or Facebook update and a carefully researched article that's been vetted by fact-checkers and refined by editors in a well-regarded magazine is always just a click away. The democratization of areas that were once left to experts, or at least amateurs with great dedication, has left many of us experiencing and creating much that is mediocre. Why learn to play guitar if you can just jam out with Guitar Hero instead?

The Invisible cares deeply about his craft. He has likely studied for years, gained credentials, and worked toward a level of expertise that an enthusiast couldn't approach. This is not to say that we all must strive to become experts or not bother doing something at all. But when you can do something a little bit well, and the results are pleasing enough, many decide to stop there. Nearly everyone I know under forty (including myself) it now seems is some combination of amateur photographer, DJ, filmmaker, writer, and craft maker of some sort. Much of what's produced is good, but few devote the necessary time to make something truly great. This is in contrast to the tremendous amount of work and training that's required, when, for example, as an editor or writer you debate over a single word for hours or days until the tone feels just right, or as a guitar player you finally nail that really tricky piece of music you'd been practicing for weeks on end. Invisibles like Giulia Wilkins Ary embody this devotion to get something near perfect. If we pushed ourselves, like they do, to want more than the easy joy of "pretty good," we could achieve the occasional ecstasy of "great."

I'm gonna live forever
I'm gonna learn how to fly
I feel it coming together
People will see me and cry
Fame!
I'm gonna make it to heaven
Light up the sky like a flame
Fame!
I'm gonna live forever
Baby, remember my name.

Let's take a momentary detour from our Invisibles to get a broader perspective on how they fit within the culture today, why their approach to work runs counter to the prevailing current, and what is so important to learn from their example. Why is our culture so hooked on praise and recognition? And how did we get here?

FAME, SUCCESS, AND THE MYTH OF SELF-PROMOTION

Why Attention Doesn't Satisfy Us and Won't Help Your Business Prospects

In April 2009, when Twitter was still in its relative infancy, Michele Catalano was already a veteran user, having joined two years earlier, not long after the service's launch. Up to that point she had been using Twitter mainly as a platform for "jokes and observations about sports," she wrote in an article on Boingboing .net, the widely read culture and technology site. But something unexpected happened: she started gaining followers by the thousands, hitting 28,000 in one week. First, she thought someone was playing a joke on her and the followers were all "bots" (fake accounts). It turned out, inexplicably, she was featured on Twitter's Suggested User List, "sandwiched between celebrities and sports stars," which led to the spike. Within a few months she had *one million* followers.

Having this extraordinary platform, however, wasn't the boon many might assume it to be. In fact, Catalano felt anxious. With so many followers she worried about the gravity of every tweet yet felt pressure to tweet often. "I'd never before in my life been popular. I was that kid . . . at the far end of the lunch table picking at her sandwich while she sat alone. Here I was with a million people listening to me, waiting to see what I would say next," she wrote. "What should have been a 'Wow, this is exciting!' moment for me became a moment of sudden terror instead. I felt like I suddenly moved into a glass house and all my neighbors were armed with rocks." With her tweets being read by so many she not only had to defend the content of her tweets to naysayers, but her overall follower count as well. Overwhelmed, she began to tweet less and less.

Still, she hoped to parlay this unexpected fame into advancing her writing career—with such a massive audience, surely once she tweeted about being a writer, literary agents would fight over one another to represent her. She'd gain choice freelance writing assignments. Perhaps she'd sell that novel she had been working on. But none of that happened. "Having a million followers did not afford me new opportunities. It did not make my life richer or make my teeth brighter. It did quite the opposite. It made me more self-conscious than I already was. It made me feel riddled with self-doubt." She had lost her "voice," she wrote.

After much soul searching, Catalano ultimately decided to resume tweeting but with a return to the attitude she had before she gained all those followers, engaging with friends and telling jokes. Now, when people ask her "Who are you?" to warrant such a following, she responds, "I'm just a regular person."

I'M GONNA LIVE FOREVER . . . BABY, REMEMBER MY NAME

One of the earliest known writings on the exaltation of fame is *The Iliad*. In Homer's ancient Greek epic poem, dating to around the eighth century BC, the heroes are motivated by status and honor in the eyes of other men. Here, the concept of *kleos*, translated as immortal fame or glory, reigns. When heroes behave poorly they don't feel guilt via an inner morality, rather they feel shame for looking bad publicly. Bob Thompson, director of the Bleier Center for Television & Popular Culture at Syracuse University, and who has written widely about fame, told me there is "graffiti of gladiators' names carved into Roman ruins." And there is even some evidence that they "were paid to come to parties the way Paris Hilton types are today."

While fame has been a goal of many throughout history, what has changed are the cultural infrastructures that tell you who is able to achieve it, and who can even aspire to it. "If you are a peasant around a medieval castle you have the same desire for power, wealth, and privilege as an *American Idol* contestant," Thompson said, "but the difference is on some fundamental level the peasant knows he will never achieve it." As Alice Marwick, an assistant professor of communication and media studies at Fordham University, told me, "In pre–mass media people were limited to word of mouth." Now, though, she noted that social media provides a means for the medieval peasant of today—albeit one with an Internet connection— to gain an audience or even celebrity.

It makes sense that people desire fame, Thompson noted, because our culture tells us that it brings us many things we've been programmed to desire—attention, money, power. The problem is that the ability to garner fame, or often times even just recognition, is largely an illusion. For every 10 million videos on YouTube, one goes viral. Thompson likened the unrealistic expectation that you'll be the one behind that video to buying a lottery ticket and believing you're going to win. The novelist Sam Lipsyte spoke of the cruelty of this illusion in an interview with *New York* magazine, where he said, "To me, the whole idea of the loser is a joke, because it's a kind of really oppressive society that's calling you a loser. It's a society that's about celebrity and money and status and all of these things that are not very available to most people. Most people are automatically rendered losers."

Why do so many people buy into this illusion? Thompson chalks it up to an "American sense of optimistic denial," and that we're not a rational people. But what if there is something larger at play?

What if our cultural norms today almost demand this attitude? And what are the consequences of this new norm?

In *Quiet*, her exhaustively researched and thoroughly persuasive book about the importance of introverts in society, Susan Cain suggests that around the early twentieth century there was a change in American culture. She cites the historian Warren Susman's theory that we shifted from a Culture of Character to a Culture of Personality. In the Culture of Character, "what counted was not so much the impression one made in public as how one behaved in private," essentially the opposite value system of Homer's kleos. But when we moved toward a Culture of Personality, "Americans started to focus on how others perceived them. Susman wrote, 'The social role demanded of all in the new Culture of Personality was that of a performer. Every American was to become a performing self.'" In a sense, now, we've regressed back to striving for kleos. Only instead of names etched on stone columns, with apologies to Paul Simon, today the words of the prophets are written on the Facebook walls. Cain goes on to explain that as America became industrialized and urbanized, people found themselves working and living among strangers, an environment that encouraged us to try to "become salesmen who could sell not only their company's latest gizmo but also themselves." This notion is supported by recent research by the UCLA psychologist Patricia Greenfield, who, using a digitized catalog of more than 1.5 million books spanning the past two hundred years, found an increase in prevalence of individualist terms such as *unique*, *individual*, and *self*, mirroring the ascent of urbanization.

I would argue, following Susman's Culture of Character and Culture of Personality, that we are entering a third phase: the Culture of Profile. The digital landscape so many of us operate in is as different from the cities of the early twentieth century as they were from the rural environment their inhabitants came from. When so much time is spent online, though we are physically present in a variety of places, our minds, essentially ourselves, are in that online world. And being engaged in that environment comes with its own biases, including an amplification of the Culture of Personality that

Susman wrote about. In the online environment, especially on social media platforms, as we present ourselves as a series of "likes," links, and lists of favorite stuff, our essence has been reduced yet again—from a personality to a profile.

Stepping back for a moment from today to the middle of the last century, as the Culture of Personality was gaining ground, a reserve, some would say repression, still held sway in much of the society. With the idea of the Company Man dominating that era, a quiet uniformity was in many ways the ostensible norm. As the century tilted toward its latter half, however, individualism, and Susman's Culture of Personality, finally came to dominate, the starboard oars on our racing shell careening us to the side. A vivid lens through which to view this shift borne out is professional sports.

In 1960, the Chicago White Sox did something revolutionary: they put their players' names on the backs of their uniforms. Up to that time no team in any major sport in college or the pros, which had had organized leagues dating back to the 1800s, had ever done so. The next fall the American Football League followed the Sox. And within a decade—with the exception of three teams—all of Major League Baseball abandoned the No Name on Back uniforms (or NNOBs as they're known in the argot). This shift wasn't arbitrary. "The common denominator was television," Paul Lukas told me. Lukas, the man behind "Uni Watch," an intensely followed column for ESPN that "deconstructs the finer points of sports uniforms in obsessive and excruciating detail," is our nation's preeminent expert on sports uniforms. "Once sports became more televised," he explained, "then fans could read the names on the back. And this was a way to market players as personalities." (It also created a huge revenue stream of selling jerseys of favorite players, he noted.)

Initially, there was some pushback. As John Thorne, Major League Baseball's Official Historian, told me, "There were players who thought this was gauche when it started." A *New York Times* article from 1962, when much of the league had still yet to change from NNOB uniforms, quoted a pregame smack-talking exchange, where a New York Met ribbed, "I see where the Cardinals have their names on the back of their uniforms. I don't like that." Even up to the late 1970s, when the National Hockey League belatedly began mandating NOB (Name on Back) jerseys, Harold Ballard, then owner of the Toronto Maple Leafs, was so against the change that he made GNOBs (Ghost Name on Back) uniforms in protest. They featured nearly invisible blue letters on a blue background. But ultimately the old collectivist mores gave way. Ballard got away with this for just two games. Our march toward individualism and desire to be noticed would not be stopped. As Lukas noted, when a minor leaguer gets called up to the big leagues, the "tangible badge of having 'made it' is seeing your name on the back of the jersey." It's hard to imagine, today, football players doing touchdown dances and other self-celebratory theatrics if their names weren't on their backs. If you want to witness our country's descent from collectivist attitudes to heralding the individual above all else, look no further than sports uniforms.

As a thought experiment it's worth considering that disproportionate success has fallen on the few teams in collegiate and professional sports that do feature NNOBs. The pre-scandal-era Penn State football team famously went without names on their uniforms, and Notre Dame's football team, which has used NNOBs off and on over the years, are both storied programs. The Yankees, the winningest team in baseball, have NNOBs. The Red Sox, whose home uniforms are NNOBs, after a notorious drought, have won the World Series twice in the past ten-plus years. And most interestingly, the San Francisco Giants, who adopted NNOBs for their home uniforms in 2000, have won the Series twice since the sartorial change. Peter Magowan, who was the managing general partner of the Giants when they made the change, told me they wanted to promote the team's history and tradition with a nod to their classic uniforms, and part of that was "to promote the Giants as a team, as opposed to individual players." To his surprise the players were enthusiastic about the change. Perhaps the NNOBs' "expression of team unity and collectivist spirit," as Magowan views it, offers some—albeit highly anecdotal—evidence of what can be gained when individuals aren't as concerned with calling attention to themselves.

THE AGE OF THE OVERSHARE

The NNOB teams, though, of course, are outliers. Beyond the observational theory above, the rise of individualism, desire for recognition, and even narcissism can be traced together in several telling studies and polls. In an analysis of word usage in over 700,000 American books, dovetailing with UCLA psychologist Patricia Greenfield's study cited earlier, researchers found "the use of first person singular pronouns (I, me) increased 42%," from 1960 to 2008. In a nationwide meta-analysis of college students' scores on the NPI (Narcissistic Personality Inventory) from the 1980s through 2009, and in a review of a longitudinal study at one university, Jean Twenge, a psychologist at San Diego State University, and her co-author Joshua Foster, a psychologist at the University of South Alabama, found "both studies demonstrate significant increases in narcissism over time." A Pew survey published in 2007 found that just over half of 18-to-25-year-olds said being famous was their generation's most important life goal. (This was second only to "getting rich.")

We're in an environment where we are reliant on recognition for our self-esteem. There is even some suggestion that there is an addiction to praise. In an oft-cited 2010 study on self-esteem, its authors found that college students would rather receive praise than have sex. A *New York Times* article on the study noted, "participants generally 'liked' various activities . . . more than they 'wanted' them." And "the difference between *enjoying* and *wanting* the activity was lowest for activities that boosted self-esteem [italics mine]. The distinction is important, Dr. Bushman [one of the study's authors] said, because research on addiction suggests that one indication of habituation is that people tend to want or need something more than they actually like or enjoy it."

These poll and study results are no wonder, as this ethos is so embedded in the culture today that it's become part of the pedagogy. From a young age, in fact, we now are being trained that to seek recognition is a princely value. In *Quiet*, Susan Cain writes about a cooperative learning model that has been gaining prominence, where in order to succeed you have to be someone who "calls attention to yourself," a Manhattan fifth-grade teacher was quoted as saying. While there is much value in a cooperative approach, such as learning effective speaking skills, an overemphasis on it is problematic. As Cain goes into great detail illustrating, many people—in school and in business—achieve their most effective results by working in a solo setting; in other words, most definitely not by calling attention to themselves.

We can look to one area more than any other, though, to explain the rise of desire for recognition. As television's influence demonstrated—in professional sports (as cited above), and countless other programming, most notably the domination of reality TV, where, for all the variety of ostensible setups, the common denominator among nearly every show, when you kick the dirt away to reveal the root, is that unfamous people participate in order to become famous—our communications technologies play a large role in fostering a look-at-me performative culture. Specifically, the increasing ubiquity and use of social media and other Internet-based communications are enabling and amplifying an already intrinsic desire to be noticed. For our online and offline worlds are in many circumstances not separate but extensions of each other.

In the Internet Age we are now all being watched and watching one another. "Before, we had the classic panopticon, in which many are observed by the few," wrote Rob Horning in a 6,500-word treatise on fame, technology, and surveillance in the modern era in *The New Inquiry*, a journal of cultural criticism. This scenario recalls Orwell's Big Brother and infamous state security services like East Germany's Stasi. "If you invert this," Horning continued, "you have sousveillance, the few observed by the many," the model of traditional fame, where "the masses gossip about a handful of stars." Today, however, "the ubiquity of social media . . . brings about lateral surveillance or 'participatory surveillance,' the many observing the many." Operating in this environment, where you observe others and know they are observing you, on a mass scale, deeply alters our sense of public and private, normalizing the expectation of recognition for everything you do.

Where has this led us? A 2009 national poll of college students showed that 57 percent agreed that people in their generation use social networking sites for self-promotion, narcissism, and attention seeking. In a German study on the hyper-self-promotional environment of Facebook, presented at a conference in March 2013, the researchers found feelings of envy "rampant" among Facebook users, where many react to this emotion by then posting "even more self-promotional content" to try to match the content among their "friends." The authors of the study describe this phenomenon as the *self-promotion—envy spiral.* In August 2012, TheAwl.com, a website that often features in-depth cultural critiques, published "The Condition: Chronic Self-Disclosure," a piece which observed that "at its most sinister, [the condition] amounts to surveillance, or at least the sense of being watched by no one in particular for reasons both mysterious and transparently dull."

Coupled with this lateral or "participatory" surveillance is the time-extension bias of online communication. In physical space, and to a lesser extent talking on phone, there is no time to edit what we are saying in a conversation. Yet much of how we interact online is not in "real time." This both enables and burdens us with the ability to edit what we say and how we present ourselves. More time is spent on crafting the image of oneself and less time on spontaneous interaction. While pausing to think and craft a narrative produces possibly our most complex thoughts—like books—it also, when directed toward presenting oneself, forces an exaggerated self-awareness.

As Facebook, the world's largest social media platform, attempts to make its service "synonymous with the Internet" by becoming the sole portal through which people operate online through apps like Facebook Zero and Facebook Home, lateral surveillance will dominate even more so than it does now. While websites have been placing tracking cookies in our computers for years, and the Edward Snowden scandal has shown that our government has been following our generic Internet use, there still is a relative anonymity with searching and surfing the Web through browsers. But something profound will be at play when all Internet use becomes a performance, as it effectively will be if every action online goes through a social media platform.

Robert Thompson, the Syracuse professor, always asks his new classes what they most desire, and the answer, echoing the Pew survey, invariably is fame and fortune, with fame usually coming first. In fact, the desire for recognition has so permeated our culture— because fame essentially is just hyper-recognition—that, Thompson noted, it has become an achievement unto itself that people aim for. "A lot of people would be thrilled if they got one million hits on YouTube, even if they had no pride in the video itself," he told me. This hunger for attention is amplified—turned all the way to 11, if you will—because we spend so much time online. While every culture in history has had people desirous of status, there were different paths to measuring it—education, awards, athletic prowess, wealth. But today, online, the size of one's audience is the primary metric for status, noted Alice Marwick, the Fordham professor. Social currency isn't new, she said, it's that it's expressed differently online. Fame itself is now both the means and the end.

DON'T BELIEVE THE HYPE

Way back in 1996, when Facebook founder Mark Zuckerberg was just an unknown twelve-year-old, David Foster Wallace, the novelist, essayist, and critic, published his landmark novel, *Infinite Jest*. He had had some critical renown with earlier works, and was among a crew of young writers, including Jonathan Franzen, who were expected to be the next literary lions of American fiction. But nothing had prepared him, or the intelligentsia, for the book's reception. *IJ* was a thousand-plus-page difficult, postmodern work, featuring a nonlinear narrative and hundreds of endnotes. Despite also being funny and wise and having profound and fresh things to say about our culture, a book of this complexity had no business blowing up the way it did. But it did. Lugging around this doorstop with its *Simpsons*-like clouds on its pale blue cover was, for a time, a marker of "cool" for a certain youngish, writerly clique in our culture. (If you wanted to pick up smart chicks in a college town you could do worse than have *IJ* nonchalantly sitting on your table next to your Danish at a coffee shop.) Wallace had been anointed the "it" writer of the era, immediately entering the pantheon of twentieth-century greats, joining Roth, DeLillo, Mailer, Updike, and the rest. Yet Wallace was keenly aware that part of the reason his novel was so buzzed about was because it was being buzzed about. He was thirty-four as he struggled to enjoy the ride without letting the wave take him under.

The posthumous book *Although of Course You End Up Becoming Yourself* is a 350-page transcript of a multiday road trip interview the writer David Lipsky conducted with Wallace for a *Rolling Stone* article on him as the hysteria around *IJ* was launching him into the literary stratosphere. Out of all of my research, including extensive exchanges with scholars, I found this book to contain some of the most prescient and deeply thoughtful things to be said about the seductions and dangers of recognition. Bear in mind, this is Wallace speaking off the cuff and not part of some carefully crafted essay. "One reason *Rolling Stone* is interested has very little to do with me or the book," he told Lipsky. "It's this kind of miasma of hype around the book, that feeds on itself. . . 60 percent [of the interviewers say] 'I've only read five pages. But what I'm really interested in, is, what do you make of all this attention?' The phenomenon is not lost on me." The first lesson here is how Wallace was able to keep perspective on why he was receiving so much recognition.

But the real meat is when Wallace talks about the catastrophe to one's ego of relying on accolades and recognition for self-esteem. He needed to fight the allure of soaking in the praise because ultimately the rewards are so ephemeral and unfulfilling on a deeper level. "It's flattering to have *Rolling Stone* send you here," he told Lipsky.

> But it doesn't mean to me what it would have meant to me ten years ago. And I realize that that's precious. Because if it means that much to me, then I'm real fragile and real breakable. 'Cause what if you *don't* come? Or what if you don't like me? Or what if the next thing gets a bad review? Then I'm like . . . something made of glass, that has to be treated just a certain way or he breaks. Right?

Wallace went on to compare how he was trying to manage the situation at the time versus how he would have had it happened to him ten years earlier. "It would have been absolutely great [initially].

I would have tried incredibly hard to impress you, in about a thousand different ways . . . You would have left, I would have waited on tenterhooks for the article, the article would have come out. And if it wasn't savage, I would have had exactly an hour of a kind of *greasy thrill* about it. And then there would have been a feeling of utter emptiness. Which is the feeling of, 'Now I'm back to being made of glass, what's the next thing I'm going to find that's gonna handle me just right?'" The emptiness of the greasy thrill calls to mind the gross momentary pleasure of devouring a bag of fries only to be nutritionally bankrupt an hour later.

But Wallace freely admitted this was still a battle. "It's not like I'm not like that at all, anymore . . . I've finally discovered I really love to write this stuff. I really love to work hard. And I'm so terrified that this—that *this* [the interview, the overall hype] is going to somehow twist me. Or turn me into somebody whose hunger for approval keeps it from being fun, you know?" He struggled with maintaining a balance. He wanted to allow himself on some level to accept and enjoy some of the praise, but yet to do so without it affecting his ego. And he said doing this was "extraordinarily . . . hard work inside your head."

Beyond the risks to his sanity over the whole hullabaloo, Wallace also spoke of the dangers posed to the creative process, of simply being able to work, that being overly concerned about recognition can bring.

The I'll-show-people, or, People-are-really-gonna-like-this— thinking that way has hurt me so bad. When I'm thinking that way, I'm not writing . . . in order for me to even start—not to get in the groove, but to get started—I've gotta find some way to turn the volume of that way down . . . And I'm willing to do enormous emotional and psychological gymnastics to avoid thinking that way . . . I know that the biggest part of me is looking forward to all this being over, so I can get back to work. And that that's the most important thing. And that that's good because I can live that way. If I depend on this [the hype, the praise], then I'm gonna be miserable except for once every five years.

Wallace's instincts are borne out by scholarly research. Jennifer Crocker is a psychologist at the University of Michigan who studies self-esteem and contingencies of self-worth. In one of her many studies that support Wallace's mind-set, she found that "college students who based their self-worth on external sources—including appearance, approval from others, and even their academic performance—reported more stress, anger, academic problems, relationship conflicts, and had higher levels of drug and alcohol use." Interestingly, the students who based "their self-worth on academic performance did not receive higher grades despite being highly motivated and studying more hours each week than students who did not rate academic performance as important to their self-esteem." Conversely, "Students who based their self-esteem on internal sources—such as being a virtuous person or adhering to moral standards—were found to receive higher grades and less likely to use alcohol and drugs or to develop eating disorders."

"We really think that if people could adopt goals not focused on their own self-esteem but on something larger than their self—such as what they can create or contribute to others—then they would be less susceptible to some of the negative effects of pursuing self-esteem," Crocker said in an article on her work in a journal of the American Psychological Association. Crocker's work explicitly supports the power of Invisibles' internal motivations and collectivist attitude. Though David Foster Wallace, by the nature of his work as a writer, was hardly invisible, his *approach* to work, and how to find fulfillment, in many respects, mirrors that of Invisibles.

THE BRANDED SELF

It's the early 2000s and Neal Pollack bursts onto the literary scene. His first book, *The Neal Pollack Anthology of American Literature*, a satire of pompous literary types, is the first publication by the hugely influential indie publisher McSweeney's, run by the hugely influential writer Dave Eggers. The book gets so much attention, including landing a prominent review in *The New York Times*, that HarperCollins republishes it. His head swelling, Pollack impulsively moves to the east coast to be closer to the New York publishing world. A few years later, in 2003, his star continuing to rise, Pollack garners a six-figure advance for *Never Mind the Pollacks*, a satire on rock 'n' roll and music critics.

Only there was a bit of a disconnect from the attention he was receiving and his actual sales. According to Pollack, his first book sold around 10,000 copies. And his second, despite the advance, around just 4,000. None of that mattered to Pollack at the time because he was gaining so much attention. And the gatekeepers of the industry didn't seem to mind or notice the (relatively) dismal sales, because for his next book, 2007's *Alternadad*, he once again scored a six-figure advance. This is when Pollack's fame really took off. The book, a memoir about his experience as a new father, was seen by the media as being on the vanguard of a new trend of hipster parents. And they pounced. He and the book were written up in *Time* and *The New York Times*, among many other major outlets. Most of the coverage was as much if not more about him and the "trend" than it was about the book. He made it onto the *Daily Show*. *Nightline* ran a segment on his family. He even started a band that went on a nationwide tour as a cross-promotional shtick tied to the book's launch.

Pollack's ego and ambition balloon. Hollywood calls. He's hired to write a screenplay version of *Alternadad*. He lands a sitcom deal. He uproots his family again, and moves to LA to capitalize on it all. At the same time he attempts to "start an Internet parenting community," he told *The A.V. Club* in a March 2013 interview, from which the quotes in this summary are culled. "I was trying to turn *Alternadad* into some massive multimedia empire. And," he said, "it failed!" Despite the enormous hype around the book and Pollack himself, the book bombed. Pollack said that title, too, sold around just 10,000 copies.

It was 2008 and he was five figures in debt. The movie never got made, the sitcom thing fell through. But Pollack was still "trying to flog *Alternadad*" to studio executives, over and over. "It was kind of humiliating," he said. "Instead of doing what I did well, which was write, I was trying to cash in big time and become some mogul." Pollack was "sad and broke." "I wasn't doing what I dreamed of doing, which was be a writer. Instead I was just a salesman."

Pollack's story reads as a kind of anti-Wallace cautionary tale. Instead of focusing on his work, he focused on the hype. And while he was able to generate a couple significant book advances, spread out over so many years and after two major moves, his finances were in shambles. And he was deeply unhappy. "I spent a lot of years trying to turn myself into a brand because they told us self-branding is a way to success," he said. "But it's not true."

There was a telling comment below Pollack's interview. "I remember tracking Neal during my early days as a professional writer—'02–'05, thereabouts—reading his smaller pieces, like the Slate stuff about his book tour and his 'band' . . . I admired how he tried like hell to create some buzz around his books. Now, a decade later, as I get tired of trying to make myself into a 'brand,' I see that all that effort Neal gave didn't really translate to sales, satisfaction or even lasting monetary rewards. Kinda makes me think the whole 'branding' craze we've gone through over the last decade is BS." The comment was by a freelance writer named Joel Keller. Intrigued, I reached out to him.

Keller's work has appeared in *Fast Company*, *The New York Times*, *The Atlantic*, *The A.V. Club*, and elsewhere. Now forty-one, his goal is to simply make a living as a writer—whether that's as a freelancer, writing books, or working on staff at a publication. "What struck me about the Pollack story is that I remember during the peak of his fame [with all of his cross-promotional tie-ins], I thought, 'That's what you need to do in order to make it,'" Keller told me. This was before the era of social media, he noted, and said that today, with Twitter, Facebook, et cetera, the pressure to promote is an escalation of what Pollack did a decade before. "*They* keep telling you you need a certain Klout* score or this many followers on Twitter or Facebook or Tumblr or wherever," he said ruefully.

But who is this "they?" And why do so many people feel compelled to follow the conventional wisdom? Keller attributes the problem largely to the media. "It's like the way my profession makes

---

* Klout is a company that tracks peoples' social media presence then gives them a score of 1–100 ranking their supposed influence.

[the critically acclaimed but not widely viewed HBO series] *Girls* seem like the most popular show on TV because of all its coverage. It's the same with personal branding," he says. "Because media people write about personal branding so much it seems like it's more necessary than it is to get ahead. And it's not exclusive to media jobs. It's for a guy, for example, who wants to get a job as a banker and makes a viral video as his résumé and gets the job."

Keller's observations are not without merit. A *Wired* article from 2012 on Klout began with what some would view as a modern-day horror story. Sam Fiorella was recruited for a "VP position at a large Toronto marketing agency." He had fifteen years of experience and had consulted for major brands like AOL, Kraft, and Ford. But he was turned down for the job because his Klout score was too low. The interviewer actually pulled up Fiorella's score on his computer and turned the screen to him so he could see his undoing.

In a piece for *Forbes*, Glenn Llopis, a speaker and consultant who focuses on "leadership" and "career advancement," wrote, "Developing your personal brand is essential for the advancement of your career and development as a leader . . . I always advise those who want to have a social media presence to think carefully about their intentions and objectives before opening an account. Why? Because the moment you start—you must not allow yourself to stop . . . Personal branding, much like social media, is about making a full-time commitment to the journey of defining yourself as a leader." I was going to italicize part of Llopis's quote to emphasize how doctrinaire it is, but I realized I would have ended up italicizing the whole thing.

Gary Vaynerchuk, a social media branding consultant, whose book *Crush It!* was an instant bestseller, is just one of the many gurus telling us how to build personal brands using social media. Vaynerchuck, like most of them, encourages the merging of the personal and the professional, and being active online to grow your "brand." The reality, as Keller sees it though, is that "there are very few people who come from no previous platform and follow this model and then become successful." The success, if they experience it at all, is usually either short-lived or simply a perception of success based on the amount of noise surrounding the person. In Neal Pollack's example, both were true.

In late 2006, Julia Allison, at the time a dating columnist for a free, local paper, *am New York*, began appearing on the media gossip site Gawker.com. Continuing for several years, the coverage of her exploits around town was relentless, and often cruel. But for Allison, whose sole mission seemed to be to gain attention, well, as they say, any publicity is good publicity. She received so much attention all over the Web, in fact, that she was the subject of a cover story in *Wired* in 2008 that explored how she so successfully promoted herself. The copy read: "She can't act. She can't sing. She's not rich. But thanks to her genius for self-promotion, she's become an Internet celebrity." Like Pollack, she parlayed her fame into a brief fling with Hollywood, appearing on a reality TV show (what else would you expect?) about dating advice. But she essentially has dropped off the radar. After her *Wired* cover story she wrote to the magazine's editor that her "real goal was never fame at all." That her real ambition was to make it as a writer, citing Nora Ephron as a role model. For someone who received thousands upon thousands of words written about her on blogs, who had a cover story on her in a prestigious magazine, and who has had countless culture pundit gigs on TV, alas, she wasn't able to leverage all the notice into a solid, or even semi-solid writing career. As Joel Keller told me, "You gain a lot of followers by doing work. Having a lot of followers doesn't get you work." A telling postscript on Allison: It was only after several years of a precipitous drop in her coverage in the gossip blogosphere that she finally landed the until-then-elusive Book Deal in late 2013.

And that's the irony of all of this noise about the need for self-promotion, especially so online. In some ways it seems just a vast myth that the culture at large has bought into. Jonah Berger, a marketing expert who teaches at Wharton, and is the author of *Contagious: Why Things Catch On*, alluded to this. In an interview with *Fast Company*, Berger was quoted pushing back against his publisher, who wanted him to use social media to promote himself and his book, and said, "These things [Twitter and social media] are great because you can see them, but it doesn't necessarily mean they are effective, or are more effective than other things that are harder to see." And this is coming from a guy who apparently is called

"The Twitter Whisperer." There's even some evidence the myth extends to businesses. A 2013 corporate study by Coca-Cola "found that online buzz had no quantifiable impact on short-term sales."

Something interesting happened to Neal Pollack in LA just after he bottomed out. He moved, yet again, but this time to the more manageable town of Austin. And he began to focus on his writing. He self-published a novel that sold around 500 copies. But then the mystery/thriller imprint of Amazon's publishing arm picked it up. Ironically, it, too, sold around 10,000 copies, the same as his earlier big-time releases. Except 10,000 copies ends up bringing in decent money, if you can take advantage of the near-zero lead time of online publishing and write a new book every five months. Another Amazon novel followed. Pollack recognizes that not all authors can write, nor can all books be done, in this condensed time frame, but his new work can. He found his niche. "If I can churn out book after book that sells ten thousand copies, I'm thrilled because I'm doing what I want to do," he said. He's also begun supplementing his thriller income with freelance writing gigs. It was only when Pollack focused on his work that he found not only some financial stability, but also fulfillment. At the end, when the *A.V. Club* interviewer pointed out that [despite his lower status today] Pollack is making a living as a writer, and that that was "a victory in itself," he replied, "I'm grateful."

THE MACHINE

Keller's "they," who push the idea of the need to brand oneself, indeed includes the media and limitless numbers of marketing consultants. But what if the notion of the branded self is embedded in the fabric of social media itself, in the very structure of the social Web?

"Facebook wants us to see our profiles as brand identities," wrote Chris Baraniuk, a London-based writer who has written extensively about the social impacts of technology for *The Atlantic* and *Wired*, among other publications, and whose work is heavily followed by academics who study media and technology. I talked with Baraniuk to get him to elaborate. "Every Facebook user is subject to the sense that their identity on the site is, first and foremost, a quantifiable entity," he said. "An online identity in many cases is evaluated, even if not exclusively, in terms of the number of contacts, the number of posts, the number of comments, likes, messages, et cetera." He continued, "Facebook equates brand identity success with social identity success by encouraging us to have populated, highly active profiles. (The reasons for this from Facebook's side, of course, are commercial)."

Ultimately, Baraniuk argued, "it doesn't really matter whether or not you like to think of yourself as a brand, or information about your life as a commodity. That's what you are within a network like Facebook. Something happens to your personality and your social life as soon as it enters the doors of Facebook, which transforms those things into units on an endless product line." Rob Horning, *the New Inquiry* writer, views self-promotion in this context not as a choice but as compulsory. In the same essay about surveillance referenced earlier, he wrote about how "microfame" is related to "coping with mandatory requirements to construct identity online." "In using social media, we become fatally aware of how we can sell ourselves and thus intensify self-marketing practices," he continued. "We put ourselves forward as a brand in order to register in these commercially oriented, quantification-driven systems. As use of these sites become more pervasive and normative, we start to seem to have no choice but to self-brand because it is the only way to take the measure of ourselves." Microfame, Horning suggests, "means feeling unduly neglected, not feeling slightly famous." When success is viewed as a quantifiable metric—be it fame or wealth—one never is fully satisfied.

Alice Marwick, a Fordham University media studies professor, is also the author of *Status Update: Celebrity Attention and Social Media*. The book explores how people market themselves online, essentially as objects to be sold. When you participate in a lot of online groups, Marwick told me, "attention and visibility are a status metric. Every single website that has a social component has some way to differentiate its users based on this concept. Amazon has the 'Expert Reviewer' tag. Etsy has 'Top Sellers.' Et cetera." She added, "I don't think this is something that people necessarily want to do," but they feel obligated.

As if this commodification of the self weren't troubling enough, there is now a double bind in how to navigate the terrain. "Interestingly, unlike brands, social identities are not evaluated as more successful because they have more followers," Baraniuk told me. "Often, there is a certain threshold of followers beyond which a person, within specific social groups, will be perceived as 'narcissistic' or over-networked!" Baraniuk said. "If someone starts to look like they treat their identity like a brand, in other words, their Facebook profile tumbles into the uncanny valley."* So, we must simultaneously work relentlessly to mold our branded self online, yet do it in such a way that it doesn't appear we are overtly branding ourselves. It's a dissonant charade.

At times we've all done some variation of this dance offline when we've tried to achieve something without appearing overeager—there's a reason the expression "he looks like he's trying too hard" is such an embarrassing pejorative. Yet conducting an online extension of oneself requires a continued and heightened management of this dance, due to the frameworks that our profiles exist in (as Baraniuk argued) and due to their constancy (even if we're not online our profiles are almost always still visible). In blunt terms, it takes a ton of time, and it's a hell of a lot of work—both intellectually and emotionally—for many of us to maintain our online avatars.

Joel Keller's relationship with Twitter speaks to this. He joined in 2008. He used to tweet "a lot" he said, and over the years he's amassed 1,200 or so followers. But now, he says, "I don't tweet that actively because the format feels like it takes too much time and mental bandwidth to follow threads and interact with people. Every so often I start again, but I stop because it's too exhausting." I asked Keller if he ever considered devoting, say, three months or so to see

---

* By 'uncanny valley,' Baraniuk is referring to the notion that when representations of human beings—as robots or in computer animation, for example—are extremely realistic, but just a little bit off from actual people, the slight imperfections in the replicas can provoke unease or disgust. (This effect is also cited when someone gets too much Botox or cosmetic surgery.)

if he could build a larger following, to see where that would take him. He replied, "In that three months I could write part of a novel, or I could land a bunch of freelance gigs that pay. It's taken me a while but I've realized there are more productive ways to spend my time."

Not surprisingly there is a growing backlash against all the self-promotion, evidenced not just by people personally avoiding it as Keller has done, but by many people actively starting to speak out against the whole notion. Just a brief search yields innumerable blog posts and screeds by people fed up, even offended by the trend. A presentation at the 2011 South By Southwest, the annual music, film, and interactive conference, was titled "Why Personal Branding Is Bullshit." "You're Personal Branding Yourself a Narcissistic A-Hole" is one of the more colorful blog posts. TechCrunch, the widely read technology news site, ran a piece in 2012 titled "Here's to the Death of Personal Branding on the Internet." From the article: "Personal branding has become a topic for every other South By Southwest session and for a zillion e-books that sell for $4.99 a piece. It's fake, it's not productive, and it's actually holding all of us back from being actual humans . . . What's happening right now is that people who have found a way to get a bunch of Twitter followers, make a fancy website, and write a book are preying upon people who are self conscious and shy."

So, aside from the time invested/wasted in promoting yourself online, and thinking about how to promote yourself, that could likely be better spent actually working on whatever it is you do, creating stuff, rather than marketing yourself as someone who creates stuff, there's now the real risk of alienating the people you are trying to impress. Because it's become so pervasive, there's a growing sense that when someone is branding or promoting themselves too much or in too overt a way, that they are dishonest. Because after all, branding, if not inherently dishonest, certainly is about only promoting the positive. (Recall the self-promotion envy spiral. How many of your "friends" on Facebook regularly post unflattering news about themselves?) One personal branding writer defended the term, saying "personal brand" is just another way of saying "reputation." But it doesn't matter what you call it. Even if the brand you create is accurate, and not purposefully intended as a promotional lie, the problem still is the fact that you are spending too much time worrying about how you appear to others.

The days of reclusive authors like Salinger and Pynchon appear to be long behind us. If for no other reason, no major publisher today would allow their authors to just disappear (unless it was some sort of calculated marketing stunt). In fact, it's a mark of elite stature to not need to partake in self-promotion. Years ago, when David Foster Wallace was still alive, I used to periodically type his name into my Firefox address bar, quixotically hoping to see that he had finally started a personal Web page. To this day Jonathan Franzen still doesn't have a website (other than the one linked to his publisher's site); amazingly, he has a Facebook page but it's "managed" by his publisher (you can tell he wants no part in it—even his photo shows him looking away). Danah Boyd, a fellow at Harvard's Berkman Center for Internet and Society, has closely studied Internet usage, and in particular social media use, among young people. She said there's "near saturation" of around 95 percent of youth having online access. In fact, of the very few types who opt out, she told me, it's "a conscious choice by a certain class of privileged youth who feel as though they don't need to stay connected and don't want to because others will come to them."

For the rest of us who aren't superstars, we generally need to opt in. I'm not suggesting that some types of professionals don't need to self-promote. Many of us do. Only that there's probably a better chance that success will find you if you keep plugging away with your work, doing things because they're rewarding to you, rather than burning a ton of energy trying to garner attention for yourself, both toward some concept of a personal brand and to boost your ego. Roy Baumeister, a psychologist at Florida State University who has studied self-esteem for decades, was quoted in a *Psychology Today* article as having said: "My recommendation is this: Forget about self-esteem and concentrate more on self-control and self-discipline. Recent work suggests this would be good for the individual and good for society." This is, at its core, the message of the Invisibles. To let go of the ego and worries of recognition, and instead focus on the work.

6.

THE SINGULAR VISION AND THE ART OF COLLABORATION

Composing Light While Remaining in Another's Shadow

Quick—name five movie directors. Okay.

Now name one cinematographer.

Stumped? You're not alone. While actors and big-time directors are household names, movies are, of course, collaborative endeavors, relying on a whole ecosystem of Invisible workers (that
eternal scroll of names at the end of every film isn't for nothing).
And out of that scroll, after the director, no one is more responsible for the overall look and feel of a film than the cinematographer
(also called a director of photography or DP). "In essence, cinematographers are responsible for lighting the movie," Robert Elswit
told me. But much like saying a quarterback's job is "to throw a
football," this definition is—to put it mildly—misleading in its simplicity.

On a raw November evening I'm standing on the corner of
Stuyvesant Street and East 10th in New York City's East Village
under the warm orange glow of a classic sodium vapor streetlight.

Actually, it's a "space light" on a scaffold twenty feet up, but down here on set it *feels* like a streetlamp. This is the magic of moviemaking, in particular lighting—artificiality employed to create the illusion of the real. Robert Elswit is a name you probably don't know, but if you were riveted by Tom Cruise scaling the wall of the Burj Khalifa skyscraper in *Mission: Impossible—Ghost Protocol*, if you felt George Clooney's movie-star aura in *Michael Clayton* or *Syriana*, if you were transported to a 1970s porn flick by the crude colors in *Boogie Nights*, you've seen his work. In fact, if you've seen just about any Paul Thomas Anderson movie, including *There Will Be Blood*, for which Elswit won an Academy Award, his genius and craft has entertained, perhaps even moved you. He is the rare breed of artist who has achieved both critical and commercial success. And yet awareness of his gift is always in the shadow of the directors he works under.

We're on set for the pilot for *Criminal Justice*, an HBO miniseries produced by the late James Gandolfini. It's an unusual circumstance for Elswit. It's not a feature film, normally his only format, and it's his first major project to be shot digitally. But both of these factors are ultimately of little relevance to the job at hand. Though the budget is smaller than the major releases he shoots, like *The Bourne Legacy*, HBO is known for its production values. And, surprisingly, Elswit told me, whether shooting digitally or on film, the essence of his role is the same: figure out the best way to shoot the movie (or in this case, TV show).

Elswit, in a gray baseball-style cap, readers, black sweater, jeans, and sneakers, is studying dailies on his iPad with the key grip (the head of the camera equipment) and the head gaffer (electrician). There's a problem with the space light. You can see its reflection in the windshield of a car that's in the scene. The position of the light is adjusted until Elswit is satisfied that all that is seen on screen is its diffuse glow. Around me, and a block over on Second Avenue on an adjacent set to be used later tonight, is an army of worker bees, each with their specialty, many under Elswit's charge. In a skilled balance of authority yet practiced courtesy, the first assistant director (AD) is barking orders, though very politely, at the crew. He is the megaphone for Elswit and Steve Zaillian, the director of the pilot, who won, among other awards, an Oscar for writing the screenplay for *Schindler's List*.

The First AD storms up to me. "Who are you? What are these notes you're taking?" Elswit introduces me, I sense about one moment before thugs would have arrived to throw me into the crowd of bystanders watching the set from across the street. Elswit takes his readers off to look through a camera's viewfinder. He calls out, "I'd love to have all the sound equipment, the crew, everything, people away—not you [to me]—everything away except my junk!" It's a strange sensation to be here, on the inside of a scene I've witnessed a million times living in New York. I'm right *here*, next to the cameras. Even most of the crew have been ordered back. But I'm with Robert Elswit. For the rest of the night no one will question me again. I try not to abuse my position and take a step back from the camera onto the curb.

I chat up a young man, Sean Mount, who is the "scenic" for the shoot. His job is to paint sets. He's here tonight just in case, for example, a part of the taxi they're filming is too bright and Elswit asks him to dull the finish. There are lots of tricks of the trade for accomplishing little fixes like this—sometimes he'll rub antiperspirant onto the offending surface. Other times he'll smear soap onto headlights to tone them down. But he's done nothing so far tonight, and didn't do anything yesterday on set either. It's no wonder films cost so much to make. As a union member, he gets paid no matter what. But film sets are dynamic environments and all the bees are needed nearby—just in case. Mount becomes my guide and confidante for much of the night. He's knowledgeable and gregarious, and I feel more comfortable giving Elswit a respectable distance. I find myself secretly rooting for Mount to get called into action tonight. The cliché about crew and actors sitting around on film sets doing nothing most of the time is true. One of the few who doesn't stop all night, though, is Robert Elswit. Over the hours upon hours the shoot lasts overnight, I don't see him take one break. (With a toddler at home who's recently been waking up at 5:30 every morning, I, on the other hand, slink away repeatedly to the food truck around the corner, recharging with Swiss Miss hot chocolates and other nutritionally suspect goodies.)

The thing is, Elswit's time on set is only the most obvious of his work. "I still find the creative aspect of cinematography an enormous challenge and really fascinating," he told me when we met for an extended interview a few weeks earlier. "And I think about it all the time. I'm thinking about it now. For the next many days, I have to figure out how I'm going to light—how I'm going to create the world that this movie, or this HBO pilot takes place in. It's all in New York; it's all night. It has to feel unlit. It's available light. It's dark, dingy interiors; it's cars. How do I help tell this story? I mean, this is what I think about all the time."

Elswit's command of the set happens only because he spends so much time preparing beforehand. Like elite athletes, or Giulia Wilkins Ary interpreting in the booth, what appears effortless or simply a natural gift is actually the result of meticulous groundwork. "Movies cost so much money every day. So it's often essential that you plan things as specifically as you possibly can," he said. For big-budget films like *Mission Impossible* and *Bourne* the prep was ten weeks. For a complex action scene like Tom Cruise scaling the façade of the Burj, they "make very, very specific storyboards that move, called animatics" to map out where the cameras are going to be. "A lot of it was shot from a helicopter, but a lot of it was shot on the real building from camera positions where we took windows out—you know, you're actually angling the cameras out and shooting Tom while he was actually hanging from one wire fourteen hundred feet in the air. We also had a three-story set that was built nearby, where we shot some of the tighter angles." On sequences like this he'll also work with a visual effects supervisor. The creative aspect of figuring out the shots is "hopefully a collaboration with the director and production designer, with the director leading the way. But how to technically shoot it falls on me," Elswit said.

He'll also review the scouted locations, make decisions about things like whether to shoot a scene with a handheld versus a dolly, and have lengthy meetings with the director and production designer about colors and light. Often he'll study other films with the director during prep as reference points for a certain look. "Paul [Thomas Anderson] and I looked at [the 1940s John Huston classic] *The Treasure of the Sierra Madre* when we were thinking about doing *There Will Be Blood*. For *Punch Drunk Love* we looked at the wonderful Godard film *A Woman Is a Woman*. Paul drew an enormous amount of inspiration from that movie—not the least of which was Adam Sandler's electric-blue suit." You don't just walk onto the set and figure things out there.

Part of the prep work entails discussions about color. Deciding the "temperature" of the color is always done in collaboration with the director, of course, but also, critically, the production designer and costume designers. While Sandler was in that blue suit, Emily Watson, his co-star, was always in autumnal colors, not overly saturated. "Paul wanted Adam's suit to pop on the white-gray scenes, to take banal locations and beautify them," Elswit explained.

Color, if used well, can subtly tell part of the story. After seeing an exhibit of Caravaggio at the Met, the director Sidney Lumet said he wanted everything in his film *The Verdict* to feel like that artist's world—autumnal. However, certain components—a furniture piece, something in the background—would be a deep, wine red, highlighting elements of the story, unifying it, even if the viewer wasn't actively aware of this. (Even in the trailer I immediately noticed a burgundy couch in one scene, and a ketchup bottle on a table in another, popping from the otherwise dark picture.) As Elswit explained it, "Lindsay Crouse [the actress] comes to court and wins the case by telling the truth. Everything in the courtroom is dark, brown woods, et cetera. But here she is in this Caravaggio red dress!" He went on, "Real-world colors are distracting. You have to control them to make them meaningful."

Color is discussed in three ways. The *hue* (the actual color), the *value* (how light or dark is that color), and the *saturation* (how rich the color is). When you hear "temperature" in regards to color there's a literal basis for the term. A nineteenth-century scientist, Lord Kelvin, figured out that when you burned a carbon rod at different temperatures the color of its glow changed. He used this system of different temperatures to represent different colors. For example,

5,600 degrees is pointing a light meter at the sun. A 60-watt bulb is 2,200. Elswit also explained in great detail about different film stocks designed for different temperatures, and how they function. It was one of many riffs on technical subjects where he spoke as nonchalantly and fluently as he did about Hollywood mores or the details of a film shoot. Like David Apel, the perfumer who could go toe-to-toe with a PhD chemist, Elswit's breezy mastery of the science of his craft undergirds his artistry.

Finally, on the importance of prep, I was reminded of the carpentry adage measure twice, cut once. I ask Elswit if he ever gets blamed for something going wrong. "I don't let it go that far," he said. "I can see it coming. I see how all the sets are designed, I get floor plans, I get elevations, I get drawings. If something's wrong, I address it then." Since time literally equals money on set, "where cinematographers get into trouble is when they take too long. That's really it." And yet, Elswit said, on set nearly all the time things don't turn out as planned. "What I learned from Paul—which is the greatest thing, really—is not to try to control everything, and to let things happen." Elswit's work process could be summed up as this: Plan meticulously, then expect at least some of those plans to go awry and be ready to adapt.

For over forty-five minutes Elswit has been conversing with various crew members on set before they've even done one shot tonight. I ask Sean, the "scenic," if there's always this much discussion before every shot. He says no, but "that's why this is going to look so good." Beyond obvious great acting performances, it's hard to put your finger on why certain films look transcendent, and others just ok. But it's these forty-five-minute discussions over generally unseen (at least not consciously) details that separates good from great; in this regard—the devotion to details, to excellence, that is absent in much of the culture—Elswit is a quintessential Invisible. There are multiple Oscar winners on the crew. These discussions aren't happening because they don't know what they're doing.

Car work requires its own particular prep work. In planning for tonight's shoot, Elswit set up a "pre-call" with the grip and electricians who have to "mechanically attach shit to the car," like the camera on the hood of this taxi looking through the windshield, before the actors arrive. Despite the prep, something still isn't looking right with the taxi that is the focus of this scene. A truck drives by spritzing the street to make it look as if it had rained. I ask Elswit why, because I could see on the monitors that the cameras were going to be filming only inside the car, not the pavement. "It probably won't be picked up on screen," he says, "but *maybe* it'll be way in the distance, in the background." As critical as it is, this attention to detail seems a bit excessive. He then tells me that the wet ground will definitely be seen in the next shot, and I feel a little relieved.

7:40 p.m. Rehearsals with the actors commence. In addition to the camera on the hood looking through the windshield of the cab, another is attached to the front passenger door window. There's lot of talk between Elswit and Zaillian, the director, about how the passengers should get in the car and where they sit to get just the right amount of their faces visible on screen. The driver, who is the protagonist of the pilot (and series if it gets green-lit) is trying to get the "on duty" light to shut off and in the process does the proverbial accidental turning on of the wipers. These people climb in the cab because his light is on but he doesn't want to pick up any fares. He just can't get the damn light off. An undercover police car pulls up next to the cab but the driver misses his mark so they cut. Someone on set calls out for "alcohol, glue, and razorblades."

8:00 p.m. Elswit views footage from an earlier shoot on his iPad, discussing it with various people. The lead actor, Riz Ahmed, a Brit of Pakistani heritage, walks up and Elswit shows him a scene of him and a slight, dark-haired young beauty (the actress Sofia Black-D'Elia, who had been on the hit shows *Gossip Girl* and *Skins*). In the scene, Ahmed and Black-D'Elia are talking at night with the George Washington Bridge lit up, twinkling enchantingly in the background. Elswit introduces me to Ahmed: "This is David. He's writing a book about British actors coming to the U.S." Later, to the director: "This is David. He's writing a book about failed film sets."

Elswit, renowned within the industry and among cinephiles as a top-tier director of photography, has built a reputation as a master of film (literally *film*, as in celluloid). Partly this has to do with his permanent association with Paul Thomas Anderson, very much an auteur, who is known for his own devotion to celluloid. (Anderson has worked with Elswit on every one of his films except *The Master*, where he was forced to use someone else because Elswit was recovering from a neck injury during the shoot. The pair resumed work together in 2013, filming *Inherent Vice*.) So it's particularly surprising how matter-of-fact he is about working digitally on this shoot. Elswit told me that recording digitally doesn't offer the same exposure range as film, and that the images tend to be flatter, with less contrast. But, he said, "digital capture right now works really well in low light." Though it was just a daily on an iPad this seemed borne out. I felt a twinge of nostalgia and delight at its beauty, a grand New York City bridge in the background of a young couple, reminiscent of the iconic shot in Woody Allen's *Manhattan*. Elswit's adaptability to digital despite being so revered for his work with film seems emblematic of his flexibility. After so many years in practice, he has a "way of doing things" yet he's continually altering it as the scene, director, or project demands.

Starting to shiver, I disappear for a few minutes for a rendezvous with my Swiss Miss. When I return I see that Sean is no longer on the sidewalk but is on set, dabbing something on the windshield over the spot where the arm of the rearview mirror connects. I felt the pride and thrill of a parent seeing his child unexpectedly called off the bench to star in the game. He made it in! But surpassing my excitement over seeing Sean in action is when I learn what he was doing. Because this one little thing that he was called on set for encapsulates why Robert Elswit is such a virtuoso of his craft: Two taxis are being used for the pilot, but both are supposed to be the same cab. The other taxi, which is on the second set a couple streets over, and will be used later tonight, had been filmed yesterday. Elswit had noticed that the black spot about the size of a nickel, where the rearview attaches to the windshield, was "one step darker" on the cab in the footage from yesterday, than the spot on this cab here. So Sean was called to make this one darker so they match. I marvel, almost incredulous at Elswit's attention to detail. The minutia! Back on the curb, I turn to Sean, a veteran of many TV and film sets, including *Nurse Jackie* and *The Following*, and he shakes his head, "It's pretty amazing he picked up on that." Would viewers have noticed the discrepancy? One can't know. Perhaps not consciously. But clearly this devotion to perfection has served Elswit well over his career.

"I don't think anybody's short of ego doing what I do. I mean, you have to be [confident]," he told me. And yet as focused as he is on getting the results he desires, Elswit speaks with the same relaxed authority that comes only when you're completely secure in what you do and your position, whether he's in an interview or managing a crew. On set his forty-five-minute discussions, despite the time pressure, all remain conversational in tone. "There are sometimes sixty or seventy people who are hired directly or indirectly by me who have to want to come to work every day. The gaffers, the grips, the camera crew," he said. "If I spend my time making them feel like shit, if they aren't happy to see me, if they don't want to come to work, if they don't enjoy what they're doing, then my work suffers. I think the biggest thing I had to learn early on was just how important it was that I'm actually part of management in a strange way. I worked for DPs when I was younger who were assholes. I just desperately don't want to be that guy."

This respectful, collaborative approach is nowhere more important than in his relationship with key personnel, like the production designer and, most of all, the director. Shooting movies is "so complicated and requires so much energy," Elswit told me, that he and the director have to agree on how things will be done. "And quite honestly," he said, "if I don't agree, tough luck. I still do it the way the director asks to do it." Because "you know what? It's not my movie," he told me. "A gaffer I've worked with a lot—he was an Alcoholics Anonymous guy—once said 'You know what you are? You're an enabler!' And I went, 'Yeah, that's true!' But directors of feature films are under enormous pressure. Someone's handed them twenty, thirty, eighty, a hundred-fifty million dollars. If you're not there to help them, then what are you doing?" And this support begins way before they're on set. A big function of the time spent on prep is to give him "an insight into supporting a director's ideas, because that's what it's all about."

It's amazing that for all of Elswit's accolades, skills, and experience, he still fully embraces his role as a supporter of the director's vision. It's clear that part of this has to do with his reverence for great directors' gifts. "A lot of people can do what I do," he lied, though I think in his humility he might actually believe this. "But Paul is able to find a poetic connection with the material that didn't exist. It's not something that's on the page." (The rare times when he's "gotten in trouble with some directors" have been when he found he didn't honor his subordinate role. "I had a very difficult time with Ben Affleck, who is the nicest guy in the world. We didn't really see eye to eye creatively at all. And I think I really overstepped the bounds there," he confessed.)

"I love the idea of trying to—within the limitations of my job—figure out the best version of whatever it is that we are doing *together*, with all these people," he told me. "Grips, gaffers, electricians, the camera assistants, the camera operators are really highly skilled," he said. "A lot of these technical jobs which go by in a crawl of a hundred miles per hour at the end of a movie are really skilled positions." Perhaps most important of the crew to Elswit is the production designer, who, because of their senior role in affecting the look of the film, he mentioned more often than anyone else in our many hours of interviews. Speaking of Anderson, but he really could have been speaking about himself, Elswit said, "he understands that the skill level of those people directly impacts the quality of the movie. If you find people who are good at those jobs, you want to hold on to them." By contrast, "studio executives, for the most part, and certainly some producers, they're all interchangeable widgets."

Elswit's respect for the crew under him, his acceptance, embrace even, of his subordinate role to the director, and his relentless work ethic on set, all point to a larger truth about why he's been so successful. Adam Grant, a highly influential Wharton professor and author of *Give and Take*, a bestseller about the importance of collaboration and generosity for achieving effective results in business, offers a lens through which to view how Robert Elswit's approach and demeanor are so closely tied to his success.

When I reached out to him, Grant was remarkably enthusiastic about Invisibles as a group and concept, and we had extensive conversations about how they fit within the framework of his scholarly research. "In my experience," he told me, "Invisibles focus more on giving than taking," and this often results in them ultimately being the most successful people within an organization or their field. Part of being a "giver" is understanding the importance of collaboration. (In the course of my own research, as the recipient of the generosity of so many prominent academics like Grant, the merit of *Give and Take*'s premise became self-evident.)

In his book, Grant explains how Frank Lloyd Wright, an iconoclast, creative genius, worked prolifically "throughout the first quarter of the twentieth century." Wright tended to work alone, and was, to put it mildly, a hard-ass. (When his son John, whom he hired to work on several projects as an assistant, asked to be paid, Wright "sent him a bill itemizing the total amount of money that John had cost over the course of his life, from birth to present.") This attitude served him but only for so long. For nearly a decade, from 1925 to 1933, Wright's career crashed. By 1932 he had the distinction of being a world-famous architect who was essentially unemployed. Wright's career, in fact, resurrected only when he began to collaborate with skilled apprentices.* Grant goes on to say that collaboration isn't only critical for creative fields. He cites a study of cardiac surgeons that showed they didn't generate better surgical outcomes from practice alone, but from repeatedly working with the same teams of nurses, anesthesiologists, and others on the OR crews. It was, specifically, the relationships they developed with the surgical teams that lowered the risk of patient mortality.

This phenomenon has also been demonstrated in the financial sector. Researchers at Harvard found that when star analysts moved alone "to a different firm, their performance dropped," and it was only the analysts who brought members of their team with them who maintained their success after switching firms. It's not a surprise, then, that Robert Elswit tends to use the same crews in New York and Los Angeles for nearly every film, regardless of the

---

* Wright's lack of interest and ability to collaborate, you may recall from chapter 3, was also evident in his hubristic, and ultimately invalidated, dismissal of engineers.

director. "If it's a *Bourne* movie it's just more people. If it's a Paul Thomas Anderson movie it's fewer," he told me. In researching Elswit, I found, even beyond his Academy Award win and nominations, the renown he has received among cinephiles and within the industry as a brilliant and visionary cinematographer is uncontestable. I would have thought, quite honestly, he'd have more of a Hollywood big-shot attitude. He's paid handsomely for his work and he's in charge of large teams of people in complex and dynamic work environments. But it's his role as the subordinate to the director, and as a collaborator with the crew, with which he most identifies. It's this perspective that drives his success.

Trailing Elswit, I was reminded of Dennis Poon. He also works in another's shadow, in his circumstance, the architect. And he, too, is in charge of large teams of people on highly complex, expensive projects. And yet Poon repeatedly emphasized to me his role not as a leader but more as a collaborator. "We are just structural engineers. We try to coordinate with each trade—the wind tunnel consultants, the mechanical, electrical, plumbing, et cetera—as a team," he said. After much back-and-forth I got Poon to admit that he oversees the structural design of the building, *which incorporates all of these elements*, and he acknowledged that because his firm has extensive supertall experience they can spot a lot of things that perhaps some of the other consultants may not see as readily. But he visibly tensed when framing himself in a unilateral leadership role. This is a man who is a vice chairman of a global firm and who has engineered many of the tallest buildings in the world. It's also worth noting that he reflexively uses the word *we* rather than *I* when talking about his work. Jim Harding and David Apel share this semantic tendency as well. (Apel's case is particularly telling of Invisibles' collaborative mind-set because his success is so dependent on his personal creativity.)

When Robert Elswit and his wife, Helen, were getting their house built in LA, the plans for the kitchen called for a large U-shaped island. Robert was away on a shoot while the work was being done, so Helen oversaw the construction. When he returned home from the shoot, Helen told me, he instantly said, "Something's wrong." "But the U looks perfect!" she said to him. What the architect had missed was that in Robert's specifications the U was supposed to be asymmetrical. "Robert wanted one side nine inches shorter because with it cut back it would give a better flow and sight line leading to a large picture window. So they redid it. And he was right." When I later recounted the story to Elswit he said, "If you go to any DP's house, you'll look at the kind of lighting built into their house, how it's sited, where the sun comes up and goes down. All of that stuff plays into every DP's thinking all the time so naturally when you come home you think about it there, too."

When Robert and Helen were first together he took roll after roll of photos of her. Helen thought, "Wow, this guy really likes me! He's infatuated!" She later realized he was taking pictures only when the light was hitting her face a certain way, or the sky in the background had a certain hue he wanted to capture. To this day, Helen told me, "he always has a Leica around his neck." Robert Elswit loves motion pictures and he loves working with light. And loving what you do, of course, cannot be underestimated for its effect on your success.

When I asked Elswit, as I did with every Invisible, about his feelings regarding his lack of recognition among the public, despite his outsized role in creating films millions enjoy, instead of answering directly, by way of explanation he told me about *why* he got into film. He grew up in LA and watched hundreds of black-and-white films on TV as a kid. He was amazed that despite seemingly taking place all over the world, all were actually made "within like five miles" of his house. But he was most attracted to "the way they looked. I was truly in awe. And the way they looked was the most interesting thing to me because they made me feel a certain way, and I connected at that level." Elswit was obsessed. When he was ten he had memorized the names of all the top cinematographers at the time. When he was thirteen he even arranged to have lunch at the Friars Club with a great old cinematographer. To Elswit, this was all I needed to know to understand why he doesn't care if he's unknown to the public, always in the shadow of the director.

And yet he didn't start on some sort of fast track to becoming a

DP. He started by trying to get into lighting and production design in theater, but since he lacked the skills—"I wasn't a good stage carpenter!"—he got up his courage and applied to film school. "It seemed like an impossible road," he told me. But he didn't worry about it. "After film school I was so intent on just finding a job, working as an assistant, figuring stuff out," it didn't matter that his path was unclear. In the late '70s he worked for a number of years doing special effects photography, including a stint at George Lucas's famed Industrial Light and Magic visual effects company, working on films like *E.T.* and *Return of the Jedi.* In the '80s he segued to doing cinematography for TV movies and shows, slowly advancing to feature films. It wasn't until 1994, when he shot *The River Wild*, a big-budget action-adventure film starring Meryl Streep and Kevin Bacon, that he hit the big leagues. Two years later he would shoot *Hard Eight*, beginning his storied relationship with Anderson, with his skills and the quality of the films he's worked on growing from there.

He's now at the stage that he can turn down projects that don't interest him or feel like a good match. "I turned down every Nora Ephron film because," he said, "I'm a comedy killer. No one will laugh if I shoot that movie." But what does it mean to not know how, or want, to shoot a comedy well? "If you're doing a romantic comedy with Meryl Streep and you don't make her look fantastic, you get fired," he told me. "There are more special effects, probably, in *Mamma Mia!* than in *The Incredible Hulk*. Every single close-up of these women was retouched in post. It's done all the time now."

Elswit said that many high-caliber female stars even demand specific lighting techniques. Sometimes this is to the detriment of portraying reality. In *The Prince of Tides*, he said, "Streisand is standing in front of a window, a *window* looking outside during the day," yet because she was lit front-on (apparently at her demand), "she's actually throwing a shadow onto the window. Which is," he notes, of course, practically "impossible."

He went on to explain the difference between the film traditions in the United States and Britain, where the actors aren't as concerned with looking perfect. For the right projects, though, Elswit is inspired to try to walk the line. "I knew *Michael Clayton* couldn't feel artificial, but at the same time, it's a movie-star movie. And you had to introduce George Clooney—he has to feel a certain way." When shooting Angelina Jolie he had to start with what she looked like in every scene. "Whereas in a lot of movies, you start with the room, the space" that the characters are in, he said. One of the reasons I approached Elswit, versus other DPs, was because I have felt such a deep connection to much of his work. There's a realism in many of his films that feels absent from most big-budget Hollywood productions. I wasn't able to articulate what it was about the look of *Boogie Nights* or *Syriana* or *There Will Be Blood* that so moved me, and what it is about the look of so many romantic comedies or "tent pole" films that, while sometimes entertaining, don't affect me in the same emotional way. But now I understand—it's the lighting. This is Robert Elswit's magic.

The thing that I am the luckiest with is I'll get a script like *Michael Clayton*, and *Michael Clayton* is not a film about a guy who tries to solve the murder of his best friend and sort of fails and then figures out some way of blackmailing the woman who has murdered all these people. *Michael Clayton* is about a guy who finds himself at the age of forty-eight completely bereft of any personal sense of dignity, who has slowly lost every part of him that he used to think was important. He has no self-respect left. He is a shill; he is a prostitute; he is a living version of everything that when he was twenty-two years old probably disgusted him. And it happened so slowly he never figured it out. And he's given the opportunity at some point to find himself again. That's what *Michael Clayton* is about.

The above text is not from George Clooney expounding on his motivation. It's Elswit simply talking about the film. While we've established his deference to his directors, and his respect for his collaborators, his ultimate duty is servicing the story. Elswit is gregarious and generous with his time. During all of our extensive interactions, meeting in person for lengthy interviews, meeting on set, and multiple phone conversations, the thing that struck me was that he was as animated, if not more so, talking about the stories that drive the films he's worked on or admires as he was discussing the specifics of his craft. It's this macro view of his role that ultimately informs his work. (What's amazing is that, unlike, say, many CEOs, whose role is to provide a 30,000-foot view of a company's strategies, and unlike technicians who spend every day buried in the details of their work, Elswit merges both roles.)

"If you have a multi-character film," and you've done the right prep, "you've made real choices about what's different between the five stories you're telling," he said. "For instance, in *Syriana*: Jeffrey Wright's role, Matt Damon's role, George Clooney's role. Each of these characters are lit the same. Or slightly differently. Or do we light the locations differently? It's always story-driven and story-specific. Or character-driven and character-specific."

"What cinematographers know is that lighting, because of the way people see, the way people view pictures—going all the way back to art-history land, when they're looking at figurative art—is the most direct way of communicating with someone's feelings," Elswit told me. "Other than music, in movies, it's the most direct way to speak to someone's feelings. And a lot of directors don't think that way or they don't care. But cinematographers do." He went on, "It's really about how you're lighting human beings and how you're lighting the rooms they live in or the spaces they're in. You're trying to make an emotional link in some way between what's going on in the story and what it looks like. It's about feelings, and it's about emotion."

In the 1930s, film stocks of the time had technical limitations that required a lot of light. And the brighter it has to be on set, oftentimes the less realistically you can light a space. "Creating a soft ambient light, like what we're being lit with now," Elswit told me (it's a bright October afternoon, and we're in a hotel bar with large windows in Manhattan), "was difficult or impossible in the thirties, forties, fifties, until film stocks got faster." The advance of film technology helps explain, at least in part, why starting with the late 1960s, and especially the 1970s, "there was a wonderful shift toward naturalism or realism," as he explained it. This look that I fell in love with, not surprisingly, was a huge influence on Elswit. The DPs followed a "more naturalistic style of light that was less self-conscious in a way, less theatrical" than the artificiality of what had been done on Hollywood sets, "but very, very dramatic. And there's a big difference between dramatic and theatrical."

Elswit's love of that era speaks to his overall technical approach and why it's not just a stylistic choice but almost a philosophical one. "It's all content-driven. It's all about the script, and what the characters are doing or thinking or feeling within the scenes." He added, "So if you're doing something that calls attention to itself in a way that doesn't make sense, you're probably doing something wrong." Elswit's approach to making films is a metaphor for the Invisibles' approach to work.

9:30 p.m. Elswit is now smoking a pipe while he shoots. The night has gotten colder. The assistant director calls out in his megaphone to the crew, "This is the East Village! You have to be really nice to these people," motioning to the crowd across the street. "They've been through a hurricane!" (This was shortly after Sandy had devastated New York.) The undercover cop car pulls up next to the taxi and stops. The cop and the cabbie talk, the cop pulls away, but only just out of frame, needing to stay within the cordoned-off area of the set. It needs to appear on screen as if the cop has driven away, but with him idling just out of frame, his flashing light—the kind you rarely see in real life but somehow are used by practically every undercover police car in movies—is still visible on screen, ruining the illusion that he's actually driven away. They set up for the next take. After he pulls away this time he shuts off the flashing light and all is good. Except—now the reflection of his brake lights is visible. They decide that on the next take he needs to cut the engine as soon as he pulls away.

On and on this went until the wee hours of the morning. There's a beauty in witnessing an expert perform and succeed at his challenge. It's like the sublime pleasure of watching your favorite team win a close game. You don't want them to lose, and you don't want them to win by a blowout. You *want* the stress and the reward—they feed each other.

As the assorted grips and camera operators reset positions, the police car slowly rolls back out of frame to get ready for the next take. Sean and I look on from the curb, warming our hands around paper cups of yet more hot chocolate and coffee. Elswit confers with Zaillian for a few seconds then steps back, holding his pipe, lost in thought for a moment.

MASTERY OF CRAFT IN SERVICE TO A "FRONT MAN"

How to Disappear Completely

Plank is a man whose identity is so aligned with his work that his name is slang for guitar. Formally known as Pete Clements, his relationship to the instrument, and the copious gear that goes along with it, however, is not as a musician. For the past twenty years Plank has been the guitar tech for Radiohead, one of the most critically acclaimed and successful bands of a generation. As their fans at sold-out concerts around the world bask in the wall of sound from high-decibel electric guitars all they think about is the music, and all they see are brilliant performers on stage. But without Plank, the arena would be silent.

Radiohead are known for their sonic wizardry, their three guitar players using countless effects pedals and other gear all complexly linked together to create the beautiful noise. But if just one piece of equipment falters, the whole chain can be broken. If Plank performs his job perfectly (and if luck's on his side), he remains in the shadows—and that's exactly as he wants it. Because Plank, like most Invisibles, is only thought of if something goes wrong.

His instinct to shirk attention is so strong that meeting with him here in Cologne, Germany, for a sold-out show on the band's worldwide 2012 tour, almost didn't happen. Though he's all but unknown to the band's millions of fans, Pete (as I tended to call him) does occasionally get interview requests from guitar magazines and the like looking for insights into Radiohead's elusive sound. When you're so intimately tied to an entity with this immense and devoted of a following (the band has sold over 30 million albums and routinely packs arenas around the world), the particularly devoted seek back doors for access to information about the stars and their creative process. As a rule, he's always turned them down. There are a variety of reasons for this, mostly relating to the band's privacy, but more than anything he's simply shy. Much of the time we were together he displayed an almost palpable discomfort with the attention. It's telling that what ultimately sold him on the profile was the notion of being seen as part of a collective of Invisible workers; it was the only way to tolerate the recognition.

The Lanxess Arena seats around 20,000 people. It's an odd and strangely thrilling experience to be inside a venue like this while it's empty. There's an energy in quiet grand spaces, especially so when their sole purpose is to be loud and filled. I've been going to concerts since I was a teenager, with a good number at arenas like this, and I felt an illicit high as I circumvented the main doors, instead strutting through a specified unmarked entrance, and made my way past layer upon layer of security with my coveted VIP All Access Pass. It's 9:15 a.m. as I head backstage. Plank's workday, which will extend through early tomorrow morning, has already begun.

Plank is officially the backline crew chief. The "backline" is the term for all of the band's musical gear—the drum set, guitars, amplifiers, effects pedals, et cetera. Each member of the band has their own designated tech. Ed O'Brien and Jonny Greenwood, the band's two main guitar players, are looked after by Adam and Duncan. Adam also manages the gear for Colin Greenwood, the band's bass player, because bass players' rigs tend to be low-key affairs. Philip Selway, the drummer, has his equipment managed by Simon. In addition to overseeing the backline crew, Plank also is the personal tech to Thom Yorke, the band's enigmatic lead singer and guitar player. On a tour of this magnitude, involving massive lighting rigs and sound equipment, the backline is actually one of the smaller components of all the gear that gets transported around the world in ten tractor trailers. But it's the most precious. If the touring crew can be thought of as the armed forces, the backline are the Navy SEALs.

While the lighting rig is being assembled where the stage will be, ultimately being raised to the ceiling, the actual stage is in the middle of the floor. This way the backline crew can set up their gear on the stage and the lighting crew can build their rig at the same time. It's one of many tactics the crew employs to maximize efficiency. Later in the day, when the lighting is mostly set, there will be a big pushback as the stage is rolled into place.

Tonight, I'm hoping to be with Plank, just off to the side of the stage, watching him in action during the show, but he didn't guarantee it. The band doesn't know that I'm here with him and he doesn't know what their reaction is going to be when they find out. For now, the only certainty is that I can follow him around during the day while he sets up. The preparation leading up to showtime is the bulk of his work, so it's hardly a poor consolation, but the show itself, the briefest part of the whole process, is, of course, also the most intense. It's "two hours of being ON," as he told me. Plank gives me a ticket for the general-admission section on the floor right in front of the stage, unsure of how things are going to play out. Beyond the band's reaction, he's hesitant himself to have someone in his space, hovering next to him during the peak of his job, as he works in real time making sure everything runs smoothly for his boss in front of 20,000 fans.

With all the electronics, the movement of heavy equipment, and some scary circus-like scaling of dangling ladders for rigging the lighting and PA speakers near the ceiling, there is a testosterone-fueled vibe to the operation. Indeed, every person working here is a man. And they *all* are in some shade of black. Plank, fit and trim with thinning salt-and-pepper hair cropped tight with sideburns, has on a North Face fleece with a "Radiohead" logo tastefully embroidered on the back left shoulder, dark gray cargo pants, sporty hiking boots, and professorial rimless reading glasses. Though there's much clanking and grinding of various boxes and parts colliding and unloading, overall it's surprisingly quiet; everyone knows what to do and is each going about their business like so many ants carrying food and leaves.

There are sixty backline cases alone. A color-coded system of triangles adorns the cases, indicating how they should be loaded into the truck, and also where they should be placed and unloaded in the venue relative to the stage. Right/Center/Left = Red/Green/Blue. Without this system, the load-in would be a chaotic mess of inefficiency. In addition to the forty-odd crew who travel with the band, every show involves local crews as well—which are a mix of grunt workers and some skilled technicians. Plank calls out to some local crew working with his team where the boxes should go. They, of course, don't know his system. "Being polite to local crew is very important," he tells me. "If you're an asshole they can be very unhelpful."

It's a bitter October day in Cologne. I walked to the arena from my hotel under gray skies, enduring strong gusts of frigid wind, and pinging light rain. While inside the empty arena is an improvement over the Germanic drizzle, it's unmistakably cold in here. I wonder if it's so cold inside because the arena management is only concerned about making it comfortable for paying fans, not workers, or if it's purposeful because they know the callisthenic workout required of the crew in setting up for any event.

Even with the efficiencies, getting all of this equipment into place takes a long, long time. It's noon when the backline setup itself actually begins. Despite my fingertips having taken on a bluish hue, Plank's North Face comes off after one minute into unloading the gear, revealing a T-shirt (black, of course) and forearms adorned with faded tattoos. Like a boxer removing his robe on the way into the ring, when the cases start to open, jacket off, it's Go Time. Because of his tenure with the band and the nature of his work, Plank is, if not technically the most senior out of the several-dozen-strong traveling crew, then unofficially so. He has perhaps the most critical, and certainly the most intimate responsibility on the tour. After all, if a light goes out, the show continues. But if a guitar's signal doesn't come out of an amp, the show stops.

Unique among the crew, Plank works for Radiohead throughout the year as a salaried employee. When not on tour, he's with them in the studio, maintaining their instruments and amps, assists them in their various solo projects, and oversees some of the administrative tasks for storing and managing the touring equipment in off times. (After the tour ends in Australia all of the gear will go back to the UK on a slow boat. The band has a mirror set of gear that sits in storage in the States that he looks after because it's cheaper to have two sets than to repeatedly transport one across the Atlantic.)

Despite his privileged relationship with the band, he's helpful and kind to whomever he's in contact with. This attitude is a noticeable contrast to many of the managers, handlers, and assistants for the numerous executives or "talent" I've dealt with over the years, either as a co-worker at a company or as a journalist or fact-checker trying to access someone from the outside. Throughout the day Plank claims, with a trace of guilt, that in his managerial role now he doesn't do as much of the physical labor of the setup as he used to. Nevertheless, I continually find him wheeling cases with the local grunts, and pitching in with a hoisting of some ungodly heavy box or beam wherever he sees it's needed. He can't seem to help himself from, literally, getting his hands dirty. Despite his responsibilities as a technician for the band's front man, he also must manage his senior role in the touring apparatus. He's repeatedly answering questions from crew members on where things should go or weighing in on how to resolve one issue or another. Either job, technician or manager, is a lot to handle on its own, yet he glides back and forth from one role to the other. You get the sense he views them as one and the same. He has a personal stake, an emotional interest, in making this thing, this unwieldy enterprise of a world-famous rock band on tour, work.

The local crews, whom he'll never see again, won't be hanging out with Thom Yorke telling him how great Plank is. And imagining Plank reading this, I can feel his discomfort at being praised. His motivation is simply, with great reserve, to get the job done. Yet somehow the band must notice. You don't employ someone for two decades and entrust him with your most valuable assets unless you know he's exceptional at his job. "My research shows that we give much more respect to those who thought their generosity would be anonymous or unrecognized," says Robb Willer, the Stanford sociologist, who has conducted research on the effect on people's status who do unrewarded work. "This sort of anonymous kindness is tremendously impressive and meritorious in our eyes because we can be sure that it was likely driven by sincere desires to benefit others," he said. Willer described to me his research which shows that "we respect people who we believe labor, not for acclaim, but instead to benefit others," and this respect positively affects their work status and career advancement.

A study by the Stanford professor Frank Flynn, recounted in Adam Grant's *Give and Take*, echoes Willer's findings. He studied engineers at a large telecommunications firm and identified which ones were, in Grant's groupings, "givers," "takers," or "matchers" (people who balance their generosity with receiving favors from others). They found, not surprisingly, that the takers had the lowest status and the givers had the highest. But the givers "paid a productivity price." Of the three groups, givers tended to end up on the bottom: They were the least productive and with the worst-quality work. Grant also found this to be the case for salespeople. If you're always helping others, your own work suffers. Yet, surprisingly, the people at the very top of the success and productivity spectrum weren't the takers or the matchers. They, too, were givers. What separated these givers at the very top was that they gave *more*. Interestingly, "the givers only took a productivity dive when they gave infrequently," Grant wrote. Plank has made it to the absolute top of his profession and to a senior role in this large organization because he goes all in with his work and with helping others.

This "giver" attitude not only has correlations with business leadership but is also tied to high levels of personal fulfillment as well. A theory of motivation called Self Determination Theory, initially developed by the psychologists Edward L. Deci and Richard M. Ryan at the University of Rochester, is now studied and advanced by a large contingent of researchers. I e-mailed with Dr. Ryan about the premise of *Invisibles* and he told me: "It does fit with SDT's assumptions about basic psychological need satisfactions—indeed that doing for others is especially need satisfying, and that helping motivated by extrinsic outcomes—rewards, recognition, et cetera—is less fulfilling."

From the very beginning Pete Clements has been drawn to being a behind-the-scenes helper, an anonymous worker part of the apparatus, rather than seeking glory as a front man. In 1979 he was playing guitar in a punk band in Oxford, England. The band broke up but some of the members started a new band and rather than aim to continue performing, Clements bought a van "very deliberately" with the intention of driving the band around to gigs. Around the same time he got involved with sidecar motorbike racing and ended up being the mechanic for a racing crew. He described the role this way: "Put everything in the truck, go to the track, get everything out. Make it all work. The bike has to be kept tip-top." Just substitute guitar for bike and it's essentially the same role he has now. He told me he loved the notion of "go somewhere, get everything out, make it work properly, absolutely right, then on to the next place." It was just like being on tour. It seems Plank is meant to be on the road, despite its known hardships. Some Invisibles fall into their careers, and over time find the rewards of their role and their work. Yet Pete Clements seems to always have known the joys of working with his hands and the rewards of being part of a team. Plank is vivid proof that being shy doesn't equate with not being successful nor even the need to work alone. He is a master collaborator, but just chooses to stay away from the spotlight.

In the early '80s, Plank started a workshop in Oxford making and repairing guitars for local musicians.* He continued this work for about a decade until one day, in December 1992, Ed O'Brien showed up with a couple guitars he needed fixed. It was the first

---

* Though Plank doesn't make guitars at present, Ed and Thom, along with Billy Duffy of the Cult and Joe Strummer of the Clash, among others, bought/play guitars he's made.

time Plank had heard of him or Radiohead. "I fixed his guitars and we sat chatting for a while and ended up talking about his band," he told me. Radiohead was still in its early stages and didn't have a guitar tech and needed one. Riding around in the van to gigs was the band, Plank, Tim Greaves, who was the band's tour manager until about five years ago, and Jim Warren, who is still the band's main sound guy today. Plank was working with the Kinks around the same time, but when that obligation ended he basically started full time with Radiohead. When the band went to record *The Bends*, the follow up to their smash debut *Pablo Honey*, he was asked to join them in the studio. (For bands at this level of success, and for techs at Plank's level of expertise, it's not unusual for the tech to be tied with the band not only for tours but for recording as well. This is the case for Dallas Schoo, the long-term tech for U2's guitar player, The Edge.) In the early years Plank handled all three guitar players and the bass, but over time, as the band's success grew, more members were added to the backline crew. Recalling the early era, Plank marveled at how he was able to manage so much by himself.

Eventually, the Radiohead responsibilities became so consuming that Plank gave up doing workshop stuff back in Oxford for a long time. In the last few years, however, he's managed to resume some of that work because he enjoys it so much. He's also begun a small business making flight cases for instruments. His interest in building and tinkering with things is insatiable. It's curious how he's able to marry that tendency for such solitary work with his responsibilities of management and collaboration on tour. But then it doesn't seem so strange when you realize that both provide him with internal, unseen rewards.

12:30. A female(!) piano tuner starts plinking some keys. The notes drifting into the cavernous arena are a soothing contrast to the clanking, grinding, and slamming of massive metal flight cases being wheeled around; pipes being locked together; the engine of a forklift; and whine of the electric drill and wrench of the tour carpenter that now fill the air. I find out later that there are actually four women on the tour—a production assistant, massage therapist, the band's chef, and a computers person. (The piano tuner is local.)

12:40. The main sound board moves roughly into place in the back center of the floor area. Behind me I hear toms being lightly hit, skins adjusted.

A massive horizontal truss with lights ascends thirty-plus feet straight up into place at the end of the floor above where the stage will ultimately be. It's a direct echo of the time-lapse footage that imprinted my teenage brain with the lighting rig being assembled in the opening of Def Leppard's video for their 1988 classic "Pour Some Sugar on Me." (As I view the video sitting at a desk in my shared writers' office space, the hot '80s metal chicks shakin' it in front of the camera, I want to explain to the woman walking by my desk, "No, really, I'm doing research for my book!") But while time-lapse is a great effect to watch, we simply lack the imaginative tools to truly flesh out all that condensed time. Until today, as I walk through this empty arena, experiencing the hours of setup, I simply couldn't appreciate the time and coordinated effort it takes to put these massive lighting rigs together, not to mention the backline, soundboard, and everything else.

Plank opens one of the large flight cases, a giant metal trunk with hard foam insulation inside, revealing ten guitars, each in its own regular carrying case, arranged in symbiotic head-to-toe layers and side by side. Like the color-coded symbols on the outside of the cases, the packing inside adheres to a system. On the inner lid of each case is a schematic that Plank has drawn for quick reference. Each of these guitars has been packed in a precise order and position. Like nearly every other Invisible, Plank's ritualized routine of packing and unpacking the gear exhibits a hyper-meticulous nature.

12:50. Someone tells Simon, the drum tech, to stop playing so the piano tuner can hear what she's doing. The gender difference lends a chivalrous obligation to the request, which is honored, of course. But due to the uniform professionalism of everyone on the tour crew I suspect it would have been honored right away even if the piano tuner was a six-foot-two guy named Brutus. The smell of oil and exhaust from the forklift pollute the air as it scoots by me, the two prongs sticking out the front like anxious fangs. I decide to step back from the area and move into the first tier of seats. As I walk across the floor PA speakers are being connected by thick metal chains to cross bars being hoisted above me. In an increasingly fast *swoo-swoo-swoo-swoo* just to my right a large rope is dropped from the ceiling to the floor, piling upon itself. From thirty feet up this would cause some serious damage if it hit your head. Perhaps it's because of The Accident that befell the tour earlier this year but I'm becoming keenly aware of danger, and I wonder if the overt businesslike atmosphere of the crew is also a result of it.

The previous spring, as part of this year-long tour, hours before a sold-out crowd of 40,000 was set to enter a park in Toronto, the roof of a temporary outdoor stage collapsed, killing the band's drum technician and injuring three others. Plank was on the stage at the time. He was very reluctant to discuss the incident but said he "heard a cracking sound, then ran." The band canceled a number of shows following the disaster. Now, four months later, the tragedy still hangs in the air. (The Ontario Ministry of Labor ultimately issued thirteen charges against the concert promoter Live Nation Canada, a staging company, and an engineer. The charges claim that they failed to ensure that the temporary stage was designed and constructed "to support or resist all loads and forces to which it is likely to be subjected without exceeding the allowable unit stress" for the building materials. I've found many connections between the disparate Invisibles in the book, but this is the only dispiriting one: Thornton Tomasetti, Dennis Poon's firm, was hired to do the forensic engineering on the collapse.)

Akai Head Rush, EHX Iron Lung Vocoder, Telenordia Kompressor, Telenordia Treble Booster, Crowther Hotcake, Line 6 DL4, EHX Holy Grail, EHX Small Stone Nano, Boss TU-2, Tech 21 XXL, Turbo Rat, Voodoo Lab Pedal Power 2 Plus, Radial Engineering direct boxes, and a Boss AB-2 switch for acoustic lines.

What does it take to create "cutting-edge advances in sound," what the *New Yorker* music critic Alex Ross fawningly called the "layer upon layer of weird beauty" and the "byzantine musical designs" of Radiohead's three guitar players? It takes formidable song-writing talent and performative skills. It also takes some serious equipment. The list that begins this section is not fanciful vocabulary from a science fiction book. They are some of the effects pedals that Thom Yorke uses during every show, which Plank is fastidiously laying out in a specific order on the stage floor where Yorke will be standing tonight. Seeing the first of the backline gear finally getting set up bumps my anticipation for the show up about ten levels. The behemoth lighting rigs are neat, but *this* is what makes the magic.

If you're unfamiliar with setups for rock guitar players, you should know it's extremely rare for them to simply plug straight into an amplifier. One of the things that makes rock guitar so versatile is the range of sounds it can make utilizing various effects pedals and units, which electronically modify the guitar's tone and signal. Those seraphic arpeggios that cascade onto themselves which The Edge plays at the beginning of U2's "Where the Streets Have No Name" couldn't happen without a delay unit. Same thing for the intro Slash plays on Guns N' Roses' "Welcome to the Jungle." That spaceship sweep on the legendary riff to Van Halen's "Ain't Talkin' 'Bout Love" is from a flanger. Even a seemingly straight-up distorted rock guitar is more often than not the result of a distortion pedal (that would be the Turbo Rat from the list, if you're wondering). The signal processing occurs inside the pedals themselves, as is the case in Yorke's setup, or inside "rackmount gear," effects machines housed away from the guitar player, with a designated pedal attached, like a wired remote control, to change settings on the machine. For extremely complex setups involving vast amounts of rackmount gear and foot pedals, special customized foot switchboards are used to enable the guitar player to turn on and off pre-programmed combinations of effects with the click of one button.

Different effects not only are used on different songs but often are changed throughout the course of any given song. This is the reason they are effects *pedals*—so the guitar player can switch the effects on and off with his foot, leaving his hands free to keep playing uninterrupted. In Nirvana's "Smells Like Teen Spirit," to shift the tone from the tight staccato chords that open the song into the explosive wall of distortion that hits when the band kicks in, Kurt Cobain stomped on a Boss DS-1. When the song moves to the verse section he turns off the DS-1 and steps on a "chorus" pedal, creating that warbly effect of the two notes you hear ringing. Now, picture a guitar player rocking out on stage—effects pedals are often called "stomp boxes" for a reason. They take a lot of abuse.

Plank links all of the pedals together in daisy chains with quarter-inch cables. He has to make sure they are connected in a particular order, that they're all functioning properly, and that they each have the proper settings on their knobs. With Yorke's dozen-plus pedals, *each of which* has two, three, or four knobs, you can imagine the amount of settings there are in total. Needless to say, Plank keeps detailed records of each pedal's settings. Rudimentarily yet critically, he also must make sure they have fresh batteries. If a pedal breaks or is malfunctioning a tech will either have to get a replacement, or in the case of a master technician like Plank, attempt to fix it, operating on the wiring and circuits inside. In addition to the pedals, Plank also maintains Yorke's amplifiers. A main amp is used—on this tour a customized Vox AC30—with a backup AC30 sitting behind it on stage. Each amp has its own array of knobs—treble, bass, presence, pre-amp, volume, et cetera—to be set. To keep track and for efficiency, all the amps have hash marks on them noting where each knob should be turned. "Consistency" is the key, Plank told me. (To give an idea of how precious this specialized gear is to the musicians, The Edge's tech, Dallas Schoo, has flown with his customized AC30 sitting next to him in its own first-class seat.)

Last, of course, are the instruments themselves. For this tour Yorke is using twelve different guitars. Plank takes them out of their cases and lines them up in two racks of six. Two Gibson SGs, two Epiphone Casinos, a Guild M85, a Martin 000-18, among others. Plank's favorite is a 1962 black Fender Jazzmaster. Some of the guitars are in pristine condition, others are deeply weathered from years of use—paint rubbed away on the front by the right forearm from a hundred thousand strums, nicks on the center of the back from countless belt-buckles, finish darkened along the neck and fretboard from the left hand's sweat and oil from one million notes played. Guitar players are known for using favorite axes for decades or even their whole careers, their idiosyncratic blemishes and contours personalizing them like the most perfect pair of old jeans.

All the guitars must be restrung regularly and, as showtime draws nearer, retuned constantly. Most have their own volume and tone knobs that need to be set, and switches for different pickups that need to be set up, down, or in between. (Pickups are the little rectangles on the face of the guitar under the strings that are essentially microphones that "pick up" the sound of the vibrating strings.) The pickup closer to the neck of the guitar gives an entirely different tone than the one closer to the bridge, so making sure the right pickups are selected is critical. And each guitar will often use different settings for different songs. Plank also needs to know which songs require a capo—a bar that gets locked on the neck to raise the pitch—and what fret it needs to be placed on. He has six capos, each with different preset openings calibrated for the thickness of the neck on the guitar it will be used on. Some songs require nonstandard tunings, so Plank needs to know that as well to have the guitar tuned accordingly, then tune it back to standard after the song if it's to be used again later.

How the hell does Plank keep track of all this? He's got a system.

At least a few hours before each show the backline crew are given that night's set list. Unlike some acts who perform the same show over and over, Radiohead plays any combination of songs from their roughly hundred-song catalog on any given night. Plank knows the settings for pretty much every song in his head but he keeps a master file on hand for reference. Once he gets the set list he writes down a code next to each track so, amid the intensity of the concert, without thinking, he can immediately see which guitar to use for the next track, how it should be set, and what, if any, changes he needs to make to effects pedals.

Later in the afternoon, during a brief spell of downtime before the show, over hot chocolate at a quiet café a short walk from the arena, Plank took out the set list from a show a couple nights before in Paris to show me how it's done. Without my experience playing guitar professionally for a number of years (and being a general nerd about this stuff as a teenager) I would have had a much tougher time

following along with his explanations. I'll decipher just a couple tracks to give you an idea:

"Airbag" code: *JAZ* = Fender Jazzmaster guitar; *b/a* = b string tuned down to an A; *XXL* = Tech 21 XXL distortion pedal; *b* = bridge pickup.

"Bloom" code: *W JAZ* = White Fender Jazzmaster guitar; *n* = neck pickup; *T7* = treble knob turned to 7; *OFF↑* = turn off the (super noisy) XXL pedal used on the previous song immediately.

13:20. Plank and the other techs are in discussions about moving the line check—a test to make sure sound from every amp and microphone is coming out of the main PA properly—back from 2:00 p.m. to 3:00 p.m. Though there's always a schedule for setup, with so many moving parts things often get delayed. But there won't be a sound check by the band tonight (he's not sure why), so a later line check won't cause any problems. Plank's twenty-eight-year-old son calls. His face lights up as he sees the number on his screen. ". . . You don't ever have to be sorry for ringing me! You know that . . ."

Plank was on tour a lot when his son was younger. It was difficult for the family at times. "When your kids are small, it's very, very hard. When my kids were really tiny I was doing heavy metal tours—Yngwie Malmsteen, stuff like that—and [on those tours] generally nobody was married with kids and so they went out and partied all the time," he says. "And if you're a guy who's got small kids it doesn't really fit together. I spent plenty of time walking around. I'm very happy on my own." Plank's wife, a painter, used to not meet him on the road often, but is doing so a little more now. When there's a day off on one side of a gig they might connect. "I miss her, too," he says. "We've been together a long time, since we were kids."

"At the start of a tour you're busy and you're figuring everything out. It takes up every waking moment sorting everything out. But about ten days or so into it, it usually hits me," he says. "I tend to get a bit down for a couple of days. If you can see the end when you start it, if you're away for two or three weeks, it's not too bad." Plank told me later via e-mail: "The duration and number of dates in a tour can vary wildly from a week to a couple of years. It's mainly dictated by money and geography. Often tours are routed in the most practical way as far as cost/distance are concerned. The bigger tours are able to factor in breaks and it's nice to get home for a few days here and there. I tend to get fed up if each leg is 4 weeks or more but, generally, you get an itinerary and it tells you where and when, rather than the other way round."

But the road offers a type of fraternity not easily found elsewhere. "Quite often with touring you might get to know groups of twos and threes or fives of different people that tend to spend their days off together," he told me. "I love the environment. The camaraderie, the workshop banter, you know. Just being with one or two or more people and you can have a laugh, and still get on with what you're doing and do it perfectly well. And the people you meet doing this kind of thing tend to be strong-minded, and you can end up having great conversations about anything—gear, but also science things, nature stuff, bikes, cars, flying. Pretty much my happiest touring days are the ones with the very long drives, when it's a whole day or two traveling on the bus in Canada or in America going across somewhere like New Mexico or Arizona, talking endlessly about the most random subjects, eating giant boxes of cereal and stopping at the occasional truck stop where a number of random and funny purchases are often made, most being unusable or uneatable. Those are fun and much needed days without the stresses and pressure of gig day."

There are five buses on this tour. The backline bus of Plank, Adam, Duncan, and Simon also carries the tour accountant and two merchandising guys. "Our bus is generally quiet and happy, particularly as most of us are friends outside touring," he told me. Sometimes they go motorbiking or climbing or some other outdoors activity together. What's unusual for Plank is that after the tours end most everyone else goes off and does other stuff but he continues to work for the band. "It takes up nearly all my time. Between the studio and managing the vast amount of gear. Things always need fixing or maintenance," he said. "Or I'm organizing and buying more stuff." This special relationship, to a degree, does set him apart from the rest of the crew. They used to share hotel rooms for a long time but now Plank gets his own. Sometimes they don't get a hotel room at all, though. They sleep on the bus if they are traveling at night from one city to the next, like they did from Amsterdam to Cologne. When there are three shows in a row in three different cities, a lack of sleep always must be contended with.

With the guitars in their racks and the effects pedals lined up, Plank begins taking each guitar down, one by one, and poking at a small black box Velcroed and wrapped to the back of each of the twelve guitar straps. Thom Yorke is the only member of the band to use a wireless system for his guitars. It offers freedom from long, dangling cords, which, when you're moving around on a huge stage, are prone to tangling, but creates another concern for Plank. One of the more critical moments during the live show is when he swaps guitars with Yorke in between each song. For a split second the wireless radios on both guitars are turned on. If he doesn't immediately shut off the radio on the guitar he just was handed, within about one second there's a high risk for a squall of feedback. This would be disastrous during a show. But Plank has come up with a crafty solution to increase the speed of the changeover.

The black boxes he is poking are the transmitters for the wireless system. They're all running on the same UHF frequency to a receiver, which he keeps behind the amps (a cable is then run from the receiver to the effects pedals, then from the pedals to the amp). The main on/off switch for each transmitter is located behind a small latch. To bypass having to open the latch and flip the switch, Plank has drilled a 2.5 mm hole in the front of each transmitter, leaving the on/off circuitry exposed, effectively hotwiring the boxes. Using the blank end of 2 mm drill bit, bound with bright tape so he can see it in the dark, he merely has to poke the hole to turn the box on or off, shaving precious seconds off the procedure.

Implementing ideas like this is one of the reasons Plank has been entrusted with being the lead tech for Radiohead for two decades. To get to the top of your field, you need to do more than simply perform your job well. To be exceptional, you need to perform your job *differently* from what is prescribed. The beauty of this is that this type of creativity is what Plank loves. Being innovative, tinkering with the norm, is where he gets his fulfillment. This isn't surprising, because being a successful Invisible, both professionally and personally, means being motivated by personal rewards, enjoying the process of finding unique solutions to challenges.

"Oh yeah, I love doing that," Plank told me when I later brought up his wireless modification. "That's what I'm most interested in, really. And if I'm honest, whether it's a guitar or something else, it's doing those kind of things and it's making things work, seeing what happens if you do this or you do that, it's all about that really. I love the creative process of having the idea and making something work, just seeing something and trying to make it better or to modify it to your own purpose, to make it do something it wasn't even supposed to do in the first place."

Plank has always taken "everything" apart. "My mum bought me a watch when I was about eight, and I remember taking that all to pieces and bits," he told me. "I laid them all out in order." His creativity also ties in to his desire to help. Plank simply wants things to work. He wants the larger endeavor to be successful, and to achieve that you must take care of all the little things. "I get bored easily," he told me. And his answer to boredom is productivity.

Interestingly, his pride isn't even in the results as much as seizing a challenge. I asked him about the tradition of rock musicians trashing their equipment, and how someone who so fastidiously maintains all the gear reacts when it's destroyed. Radiohead doesn't really damage their equipment anymore, but years ago "Thom used to kick off all the strings or do stuff like that," Plank said. "But I never felt precious about it. It never was 'oh, I spent all day fixing that and you wrecked it.' You know, if you want to smash a guitar it's up to you." He tells a great anecdote about working for (the '80s band) Katrina and the Waves. One night Katrina "smashed her guitar to pieces, the whole body, neck, everything, like 'I never want to see it again.' The gig we had the next day was at some amusement park in Scandinavia, and there was a workshop there. I went in and spent all day—screwed it and glued it, pinned it, got all of it back together. That night she came on, did a couple songs, then I walked out with this guitar and it was like, 'I fucking fixed it, ha!' The look on her face!"

As an expert musician and songwriter intimately familiar with his equipment, Yorke certainly has an understanding of the skill required for much of Plank's work, but it's doubtful he ponders the nuances or is aware of all Plank's special tricks; he just knows that things are working properly. Like fact-checkers and anesthesiologists, for the most part, the better Plank performs his job the more invisible he becomes. Plank's mission is for Thom Yorke to never have to think about his gear functioning during a performance; if he does, something has gone wrong. I ask him, Does the band ever say to you "Great job, man! Thanks for fixing . . . ?" "Nah, no it's not . . ." He trails off. They just expect him and the gear to be perfect. It's like you never say 'thanks for not killing me' to an anesthesiologist, you just expect him to not kill you in surgery. "Yeah, that's what we're doing there, that's what we get paid for, to do as best we can." (Notice, again, like his fellow Invisibles, the use of *we* instead of *I*; and the humility in the face of a mission toward perfection.) Perhaps, when, unlike most people, you work toward invisibility, the only way to approach the job is with humility, because you'll never be done, and like Dr. Meltzer, the anesthesiologist, noted, you'll never get the fruit basket.

And of course it's larger than the work itself, it's about the interaction, managing relationships with members of the team, but especially so the front man. "It's interesting, the relationship between the technician—in my position—and the artist," Plank tells me. "You're not just dealing with a thing working or not, there's the whole person and the personality. Just reading people, which can be difficult too," is critical as well. "And not being flustered, so that they're confident in you. Even if something is fucked up you have to think of your appearance, to appear confident, calm."

16:00. I'm with Plank, ensconced between racks of guitars on the side of the stage. Ed O'Brien, one of the band's guitarists, walks by us to speak with his tech, Adam. He glances my way but otherwise gives no indication that he's noticed me. I want to hide. Radiohead, serious, intellectual, and brilliant, with a front man who reportedly can be a bit prickly,* are a relatively closed circuit. Their concerns with press aren't how to get more of it, but how to manage their sanity and privacy in the face of worldwide stardom. Plank walks over to O'Brien. What if he says no to Plank and they throw me out? Will Yorke also have a say in this? From a few feet away all I can make out are hushed tones, murmurs. Plank motions toward me while they talk. I give a half-smile, not sure what else to do.

For many of the Invisibles profiled in the book some extreme and sustained tenacity was required in order to gain access to their worlds. But none was more difficult than a major rock band's guitar tech. Bands at this level operate in a bubble of obdurately maintained isolation. I had made a hit list—the bands had to be very well known (the more so, the better), they had to be known for their musicianship (the more so, the better), and they had to be on tour during

---

* Yorke, after all, does start a song "Yesterday I woke up sucking a lemon," and it doesn't sound like he's joking.

the writing of the book. Ironically, after repeated dead-ends and Kaf-kaesque runarounds by countless handlers, publicists, and managers, the one band where I finally broke through had been my first choice all along. It was like getting rejected by Michigan, Cornell, and Oberlin and accepted to Harvard. I've made it so far just to be here in Cologne, but now, in the forbidden zone of the backline, I may have pushed too far. I am in the innermost sanctum of off-limits territories. There are whole blogs devoted strictly to Radiohead's gear. For guitar nerds, even reformed ones like myself, it's like being a thirteen-year-old boy and finding yourself in the girls' locker room.

Straining to discern the conversation, I hear O'Brien clearly say, in a relaxed British lilt, while just barely turning my way for a mo-ment, "All right."

"Ed gave me a 'Who the fuck is that' look when he saw you stand-ing with the guitars," Plank tells me. But after he then explained the premise of the book, that was enough to satisfy him. Plank told me he had been taking some ribbing from some of the other crew mem-bers after they found out he was going to be written about, but inter-estingly, O'Brien doesn't even seem to crack a smile over the weirdness of a guitar tech as the subject of a profile. To a certain degree the band's isolation—physically, emotionally—isn't only from the media and their fans, but also from the crew. Even Plank, having spent so much time with them over the years, who's there in the studio, their most intimate of atmospheres, who has been made many times privy to their private lives, is, ultimately, still part of the staff.

Earlier, I had asked Plank, why, with twelve different guitars, aren't certain ones simply designated for the alternate tunings so he doesn't have to do drastic retunings in the middle of the high-pressure, time-starved environment of a show. This is pretty irratio-nal for a man who has highly rational systems for everything. His response is measured, guarded, vague. And I realize it's the wrong question to ask. Yorke's job isn't to make things easy or logical for Plank. His job is to create, to perform, to be an artist. And Plank's job is to help him in that role any way he can. If Yorke wants to use the same guitar with three wildly different tunings, so be it. He and these men—and by now, the band and much of the longtime crew are no longer inchoate boys, but, indeed, grown men—have had a close relationship for decades, and part of Plank's role is knowing how to navigate the murky territory of friend and employee.

Backstage pass has long been one of those terms that connoted the ultimate in access to power, excitement, celebrity. An entrée, albeit a temporary one, into the privileged world. But tonight I have something better. I am actually *on*stage for the show. Plank and Adam and all of Ed, Colin, and Thom's gear are on a riser stage right, just two steps down from the main stage. (Duncan and Jonny's gear are the same on stage left.) We're kept in the shadows, but we are right here, looking out to the crowd. As far as I'm aware, Yorke was never told of my presence at the show, but with O'Brien's approval Plank is, for the most part, comfortable now with me joining him.

20:45. In between the opening act and Radiohead, Plank is onstage and off, strumming guitars, turning effects pedals on and off. I'm standing as far back as possible in this tight area between all the guitars and Plank's mini-workshop. He's quickly but calmly tuning and retuning every guitar. He adjusts the gooseneck pinpoint light he's fashioned above an old Boss tuner, then hastily solders some wires in a device I can't quite see. I won't be asking what it is. There will be no more talking. Plank's readers are on as he watches the LEDs light up on the tuner. He tests the wireless radios and double checks their Velcro straps. With this last task, I think of Hollywood depictions of SEALs, doing a final check of their gear before rappelling out of a Black Hawk.

21:01. Plank inserts his custom in-ear monitors.

21:02. The house lights go out. Twenty thousand German Radiohead fans erupt.

21:03. Enveloped in a roar of adulation, the band files on stage in the dark.

21:04. Plank walks onstage and hands Yorke his guitar.

Being here on the actual stage with earplugs in, it's not that it's too loud for my ears, but like a sonic weapon the mega-low hertz are rattling my brain inside my skull. I think of how terrifying this event would be for someone from the pre-electric era. This noise, so loud and powerful that it's not just heard, but felt deep within your bones, is a bit of an oddity as a purposeful, seemingly pleasurable experience. There is so much vibration that Plank told me it makes tuning the acoustic guitars near impossible. He doesn't have to hear the strings; he's wired the acoustics with pickups and plugs them directly into the tuner, which gives light indicators for sharp and flat, but the body and strings vibrate so much during a show that it's hard to get the tuner to give a clean readout.

Plank's demeanor isn't so much one of anxiety but of focused concern. He and Adam are both chewing gum with a bit of a manic subconscious rhythm. A few songs into the show I catch Plank resting for the first time since before they hit the stage, watching the band, taking in the music. But after a moment he turns and picks up the on-deck guitar and starts fine-tuning it, again. Guitars are fickle instruments as far as staying in tune is concerned. The wood and the strings (which is a misnomer because they're actually wires) are constantly stretching and shrinking, adjusting to changes in temperature and tension. As you tune one string its changing tautness or slackness then affects the overall tension and the other strings start to shift. By the time you get to the bottom E the top E can be out of tune again. But at this stage of repeated tunings, it'd be a surprise if the pitches needed to change more than a cent, if at all. The ritual of it seems to have as much value in keeping Plank busy as it does in actual utility.

I watch Plank perform the same task during each song—consult the set list for a second then grab the on-deck guitar, tune it and check all the other settings, then wait watching the stage, holding it by its neck, ready to exchange it with Yorke as soon as the song ends. His on/off wireless transmitter move is like that of a skilled surgeon, fast but deliberate, and easy to miss if you're not specifically looking out for it.

During the encore I finally take Plank up on his offer to go into the crowd with my floor ticket. I hop down gingerly off the stage and wade through a thicket of python wires, and cross from the super-extreme-coveted backstage area into the merely highly coveted front general admission section of the floor in front of the stage. For the first time I feel like I am off duty, just watching, enjoying the show as a fan. I didn't realize it at the time, but standing with Plank I was internalizing his stress, his dutifulness, his attentiveness to the details. As cool as it is to be a part of a highly regarded entertainment spectacle, it's a job. And while you are working, it is of course not your role, nor is it even possible, to be a fan.

Yorke is playing an acoustic during "Paranoid Android," a crowd favorite that features an extreme array of textures from syncopated beats, soft acoustic guitars and explosive electric guitar riffs, and switches in between these disparate sections both unexpectedly yet fluidly, like a cheetah shifting direction while sprinting at full speed. The guitar has two "channels" or outputs and runs through an A/B switch that Yorke clicks to shift from channel 1—a direct signal path for a straight "clean" sound during the softer parts, to channel 2—running through a distortion pedal during the heavier sections. At one of the song's section changes Yorke stomps the A/B switch to shift from the distorted to the clean sound, only the guitar stays distorted through the clean section. I've been playing guitar for most of my life, and professionally through my twenties. I know rock music, and I know pedals and concerts. And yet, here's the thing: I didn't realize this mishap occurred until after the show when Plank does a postmortem with me.

"Yep, the A/B switch stuck," he sighed. "It happens. The switches inside wear out, and often falter if they get dirty. I'll take it apart tomorrow, and see if a little cleaning will fix it. If not I may have to do some rewiring or buy a new one." I could tell the notion of buying a new one disappointed him. Not being able to fix the pedal would be a sort of defeat.

After he tells me about the incident I can picture the moment this happened, but it's not clear to me if it's a false memory from the power of suggestion or real. To my perception of the crowd's ecstatic energy during this song, it was likely the peak of the show. The point is, for all of the band's delicate nuances, during a blazing number like "Android," leaving the distortion on either wasn't noticed by anyone, or if it was, was surely assumed to be a purpose-ful choice. And yet of course Plank, and surely Yorke as well, no-ticed.

Within minutes after the show ends 99 percent of the fans have already filed out of the arena. Reversing the setup earlier in the day, the stage gets pushed back into the center of the floor, where thou-sands of fans had been just minutes ago. Plank and the backline crew immediately start dismantling their gear and loading it back into the flight cases. Grunt workers on the local crew are loitering nearby waiting for instructions. By around midnight the flight cases are mostly packed and Plank is directing grunts on where to bring them out to the trucks.

They begin loading the backline cases into an eighteen-wheeler in a freezing open garage area. Plank's schematics for how to load the truck are taped to the front side. At his invitation I am now standing inside the truck. "Dave, stand next to the red boxes!" he yells. "DON'T MOVE and you're safe!" I am inside a live 3D Tetris as each new flight case rumbles up the ramp into the truck, thundering past me. The local crew doesn't know the rules. They don't do this every day, and they don't have the memory of a terrible accident on another continent months before. They keep wheeling the massive cases, the small ones of which are the size and weight of a large trunk, into the truck with a bit too much careless zeal. Things feel a little out of control. *Pddddtttth. Bam! Pddddtttth. Bam!* Up the ramp then into the bay, the cases are slamming into place all around me. My second-worst fear of standing amid all this madness has been realized: I've been boxed in. In Tetris I am in that space that you curse, that one open square preventing you from clearing a row. But here in the truck, this is my salvation. Things seem to be hap-pening very quickly, loudly, and something about heavy cases being too-quickly moved about by bleary-eyed unskilled workers, who presumably are eager to finish the job and get out of the cold, is making me fast feel that taking Plank up on his offer to join the Tetris was a very, very poor decision. The cases continue to thud around me. Plank spots me in my boxed-in space and swiftly guides several cases out of the way himself without saying a word so I can escape. I jump out of the truck before my worst fear can be realized—getting crushed to dust.

Plank's organizational schematics and lists aren't just for packing efficiency. In his supervisory role he's also in charge of the carnet, the list of gear to be signed off on at customs. "Making this list is quite a job. Customs can scroll a finger down the list and randomly pick something and say 'show me that.' Or open a box and then say, "show me *this* on this list." But for someone charged with overseeing, he still can't stop himself from getting in there and helping with the heavy labor. While some of the other crew are directing grunts where boxes should go, Plank is *in* the truck pushing the cases with them. And it's not a micromanaging thing; he clearly just wants to pitch in. He's wired from the two-plus hours of the show and said, "After, loading the truck, even though I'm not generally doing the major physical lifting anymore, being in that physical environment helps me unwind, come down." It's amazing to me how oblivious he seems to the amount of work he's doing. It's freezing—I'm in a long-sleeve thermal T-shirt, a zip-up black hoodie, and a thin army jacket over top, but Plank has now stripped down to a T-shirt again and is sweating. The guy loves to work.

I had asked Plank earlier if he ever thinks about how others on the crew view him or treat him, considering that everyone knows his privileged position with the band as their oldest-serving, and perhaps most-trusted confidant. He replied, "I hadn't thought about that, really." And I get the sense he's not playing some false humility angle. Not only does he work toward invisibility with the fans, but wants to melt into the community of the crew as well. In the early years when there was a skeletal touring staff he had to perform far more jobs than he does now, and he wouldn't have been promoted to his current role amid the larger crew if he hadn't demonstrated the ability to do that well. So it's not a matter of growing into his present position, but rather a matter of his present position having grown to suit his already demonstrated level of responsibility. He doesn't care as much as he does because he's a senior crew member now. He's a senior member now because he had always cared so much.

Stephen Sauer, the Cornell business professor quoted earlier, has a specialty in Leadership and Influence in Management Teams. When I discussed the Three Traits with him he explained that not seeking outward recognition for one's work, Trait 1, matches well with a highly influential "leadership concept called 'Level 5 leadership,'" developed by Jim Collins, a former Stanford business school professor, and author of a number of business bestsellers, including *Built to Last* and *Good to Great*. These Level 5 people, who have attained in Collins's view the highest level of executive capability, have a "paradoxical mix of personal humility and professional will." As Collins notes in his literature, what he has observed in Level 5 Leaders is a "burning, passionate, obsessive ambition for the cause, company, *the work*, not themselves." Sauer added that there is much empirical research into a concept called "transformational leadership" by a host of scholars that further supports Collins's concepts.

Many years back, around 1994, when Radiohead did their first "Apollo-sized tour," as Plank called it, he was asked to become the production manager, technically a big step up. While performing that role he continued to take care of the guitars, but after many nights he realized he was "going to burn out" with the dual jobs. "I had to make a choice," he said. But the choice was easy: "Guitars are what I know best and enjoy doing." Plank indeed has the characteristics of Level 5 leadership yet, perhaps to the chagrin of some business school professors, he chose to step down from a more senior position so he could spend all his time doing the job he loves most. We're taught that being in the limelight is the greatest glory, but Plank knows that simply isn't true for himself. Being subordinate doesn't reduce your importance to the overall enterprise, or even your stature within it. Plank knows that recognition and singularly focusing on "advancement" don't bring lasting fulfillment. Dignity and reward come from a devotion to expertise and your commitment to the work itself.

Prior to my trip I had assumed being on stage with Plank during the show would be the highlight of the day. I've been a Radiohead fan for my whole adult life. Moments on their albums *OK Computer* and

The Bends still ignite something inside of me the way they did nearly twenty years ago. These guys are musical heroes to me. And having a brush with the band, being so close to the power of their celebrity, and looking out from the stage, was indeed terrific. Yet, to my surprise, what engaged me the most, and where I had the most fun, was spending the afternoon with Plank watching him perform his work.

THE BALANCE OF PRIDE AND HUMILITY

A Bear Comes to Pittsburgh

The Tongass National Forest stretches along hundreds of miles of coastline and encompasses thousands of islands, mist-shrouded fjords, and alpine meadows in southeastern Alaska. It is the largest intact temperate rainforest in the world and receives up to an astonishing 20 feet of annual rainfall in areas. On the land, massive hemlocks and cedars thrive, as do myriad other flora. One particularly majestic species of tree in the Tongass, however, Sitka spruce, that reaches heights of over two hundred feet and can live to more than seven hundred years old, possess some very unique properties. The foggy, cold, and rainy climate of the Tongass enables the trees to grow slowly, which is advantageous for unusually clear wood and tight grain. The spruce also has very long and uniform fibers, and a remarkably high strength-to-weight ratio. These properties are prized by, among others, a relatively small but highly influential industry for one main reason: sound resonance. Companies like Gibson, Taylor, and Martin have long relied on the wood for their guitars, but perhaps no company is as tied to this wood as the venerable 160-year-old piano maker Steinway.

The Steinway D, the apex of the firm's line, is used by well over 90 percent of the major concert halls in the world. Aside from a 345-pound cast-iron plate, strings, and small parts, 85 percent of the piano is wood. Its sides are made of hard rock maple, which is painstakingly bent into its telltale curvy shape. But the heart of the instrument, weighing just 27 pounds, and what enables it to be heard above a full orchestra, is the soundboard, made exclusively of Sitka spruce. Only 130-odd Steinway Ds are made each year, and their recommended lifespan for top concert halls is just ten to twelve years. The D at Heinz Hall, the home of the Pittsburgh Symphony Orchestra, is nearing thirteen.

It's a Wednesday afternoon in February and Peter Stumpf, the piano technician for the PSO, is backstage at Heinz Hall working on "the instrument," as he calls it, preparing it for Friday night's concert. Perhaps even more so than Plank, his fellow technician behind musical front men, Stumpf and his work aren't thought of by the audience. When people hear a live symphony and they praise the sound, they think of the musicians, and perhaps the acoustics of the hall. They may even think of the instruments themselves. And yet without the technician who spent days expertly tuning and tweaking the piano for that specific performance and space, the sound would not have been so sublime.

In this book I've included two Invisibles who work for musical front men because while ostensibly they perform similar tasks, in reality the details and circumstances of their jobs differ enormously. They are as far apart as fact-checkers and anesthesiologists—which is to say, wildly. Unlike Plank, whose work entails maintaining numerous guitars plus all of their related electronic gear, in preparing for a concert, Stumpf is responsible for just one instrument. And while Plank's job continues during the performance itself, culminating in high-tension real-time work, much like Giulia Wilkins Ary performing simultaneous interpretation, Stumpf has plenty of time to prepare but his work must be complete before the lights go down. If something is wrong at showtime it's too late to fix. And yet for all the differences between their work, and the obvious divergence in atmospheres of a touring rock band and a staid classical orchestra, Plank and Stumpf both are technicians, tinkerers, men who still use their hands for something other than typing. But, more fundamentally, like all Invisibles, they share the same core traits.

Stumpf's work relies on a creative application of deep theoretical knowledge in the way David Apel uses his foundation in chemistry and olfactory science as a launch point for the artistry of developing his fragrances. Remarkably, at the elite level, tuning and caring for an exquisitely nuanced instrument like the Steinway Concert Grand Model D only in the most gross sense has to do with getting it "in tune." In fact, for a virtuoso like Stumpf, there isn't even a fixed notion of being in tune. Concert grands are massive instruments, just under nine feet in length and weighing nearly a thousand pounds: Everything about them says *permanence*. Yet to Stumpf, they are as adaptable and customizable as a car off the lot is to a hot-rodder or code is to a hacker. Through his creative vision they are asking to be tailored to his needs.

As I meet Stumpf—who is in jeans, a white long-sleeve T-shirt with a blue striped button-down overtop with the sleeves rolled up, with a white goatee, and glasses, and whose face and head recalls the actor Ed Harris, though with a touch more hair—that is exactly what he is doing. With a tool he made himself, a thin copper rod with a brass insert and a sewing needle sticking out the end, evoking an instrument of Victorian dental torture, his arm is inside the open piano and he is pricking one of the felt hammers. This is known as voicing and it alters the tone of the piano. On guitars and other stringed instruments, the older the strings, the mellower the sound that gets produced. On a piano, however, while the strings do wear, often the older it is, the brighter it gets. Over time, from repeated contact, the felt of the hammers where they strike the strings becomes compressed and hardened, resulting in a brighter tone. If the felt is too hard, the tone can become overly bright and take on a harsh quality. "Think of fluffing up a pillow before you go to bed, to make it nice and soft, that's what I'm doing here," Stumpf tells me as he pokes away. "This gets rid of the brightness. But you really need to be careful with this or you'll turn the felt into a dishrag."

Since most of the piano's eighty-eight keys and corresponding hammers strike three strings each, depending on how each note sounds, Stumpf may voice one, two, or all three spots on each hammer until the tone is where he wants it. It's a painstaking process, and like much of his adjustments, requires a combination of skilled hands and ears.

If a string breaks, especially if it's right before a concert, his preference is to try to tie it and keep it, even though knots are only 90 percent successful, he says. If you replace the string, the tone on the new one will differ greatly from the rest of the strings and a lot of voicing on the hammer will be required to get the tone to match. Either option is unpleasant if an audience is already filing into their seats. "You have to be fearless," Stumpf says. "Whether it's true or not, I believe I'm as good at what I do as the orchestra members are at what they do. This is my craft. I have to be confident. But with this bag," he pats a small leather satchel filled with assorted tools resting on the piano, "I feel like Superman." Despite the claim, Stumpf's tone isn't boastful. He simply possesses the earned confidence and aplomb necessary to perform his job at this level.

The Pittsburgh Symphony Orchestra's reputation for excellence transcends the city's relatively modest population (its greater metropolitan area is ranked twenty-second in the United States) and limited influence on the nation's socioeconomic stage. As you enter the airport, the first big sign you see reads, HOME OF HEINZ KETCHUP, indicating who butters the bread—excuse me, dresses the burger— here. With The Heinz Endowments and others donating in the seven figures, the PSO enjoys an outsized ability to foster a renowned orchestra. In an article on the PSO's residency at Musikverein Hall in Vienna, home to what is considered one of the top two or three orchestras in the world, a Viennese classical music critic said, "Only the best orchestras will receive this invitation. Therefore, the [PSO] can be considered as one of the best orchestras in the world." With this reputation comes superstar visiting soloists, including many pianists, and an expectation that the instrument's quality will be on par with their renown.

Though I've been at the hall for only a short while, there's an

evident buzz about the upcoming concert series. Despite its distinction, like orchestras around the country the PSO has struggled to
stay on the cultural radar. But this series is sold out. As staff walk
by I hear bits and pieces of expectant conversations, and when I
meet one of the Hall's executives she's almost effervescent. Stumpf's
private clients are begging him for tickets. Part of the reason for the
sellout is the popular program chosen—bombastic Rachmaninoff
and Mussorgsky numbers—but the main driver is the visiting pianist,
a thirty-eight-year-old Russian phenom, Denis Matsuev. Known as
the Siberian Bear, Matsuev is a six-foot-four beast of a man and "an
absolute powerhouse of a pianist." "He makes the piano move in
ways you wouldn't normally see," Stumpf says. "I've never witnessed
someone do such things with just their fingers. He played here a year
ago and the joke was he was trying to break the proscenium. He's
that strong." But like the best NFL linemen, the wow factor of Matsuev's brawn overshadows his finesse. He has won countless awards,
including the International Tchaikovsky Competition when he was
just twenty-three, and performs with the world's top orchestras. As a
writer at the *Los Angeles Times* wrote, he has "the fastest paws in the
Arctic and maybe anywhere else." Still, because of the Bear's power,
and the thunderous music chosen for his concerto, Stumpf is undertaking extraordinary measures to prepare the piano. The task will
require all of his faculties and experience. "Someone asked me why I
was working so much this week," Stumpf tells me, "and I said, 'I've
got to get it ready for the Bear!'"

Growing up, I remember once in a while, probably whenever my
parents randomly thought of it, a man came to the house to tune our
baby grand. But tuning—adjusting the string tensions to alter their
pitch—is only one aspect of maintenance. Pianos, especially those
played by top artists, require physical alterations to their parts as
well, like the voicing Stumpf did earlier, and regulation, adjusting
the mechanical aspects of the instrument. According to Stumpf,
there are some thirty to thirty-five different things that can be adjusted on every single key. Deciding what to do, how to do it, and
executing the work is a mix of science, art, and craft. While he

won't nearly be addressing all thirty-five, on an instrument this far along in its lifespan for premier work, Stumpf needs to be aggressive to keep it in top condition.

"Dave, I need you to step back for a moment," Stumpf says. He removes the blocks at either end of the keyboard, sets them aside, and quickly yet gingerly pulls out the action—the full keyboard and all the attached levers and hammers—from the frame of the piano, laying it on a workbench. Seeing the delicate mechanical innards pulled out from their protective case arouses a queasiness in me akin to witnessing surgery. Indeed, Stumpf makes a medical analogy: "You must never, and I mean *never* drop an action. It's like an OB-GYN dropping a baby. You get zero chances in your career." (Later I watched a few videos of technicians taking actions out and it seemed a laborious, slightly clunky, and nerve-racking process for them. I then watched a video I had taken of Stumpf performing the same task and, confirming my recollection, his motion by contrast was fluid, his demeanor focused but relaxed. His expertise, like other Invisibles, again echoes the illusion of ease a gifted athlete creates while executing incredibly challenging moves.)

Stumpf strokes a coarse strip of sandpaper vertically up the sides of the hammers as they lie exposed, slowly working his way down the length of the action. The ideal shape of a hammer is ovoid. Yet over time through use the tops of the hammers flatten and develop grooves where they contact the strings. Though Stumpf's technique removes a bit of the felt each time, reducing the life of the hammers, it's essential for reshaping them for optimal performance. "If too wide an area of the hammer strikes the string, it changes the sound, especially so in the pianissimo [soft] mode," he explains. "If you play softly you ideally just have a kiss of the string, you want one point on the string excited. If the hammer is too wide it produces an interference or distortion, makes it less musical. On the other hand, if the hammer is too sharp it doesn't give you enough contact. To get it just right you want it almost like an egg shape."

While certain tasks, like the shaping of the hammers, have a somewhat universal standard that's aimed for, much of Stumpf's other preparations enter an artistic realm, where he customizes his work to the performer and music. "Virtually everything I do is a deviation from the standard spec," he tells me. "For example, where the hammer sits at rest, Steinway likes it a little higher than how I have it. The reason I have it a little lower, giving extra 'blow distance,' for this concerto is it gives the artist more control over their power," he says. If you envision yourself punching someone, you're going to have more power and control if you can cock your fist back a little bit than if you are holding it just an inch from their face. Stumpf is following the same principle by moving the resting spot of the hammers farther from the strings. Rachmaninoff's Piano Concerto No. 2 is a propulsive piece of music, so in providing an artist of Matsuev's power and finesse extra room to work his gifts on this piece, Stumpf's work, in effect, becomes part of the performer's magic.

But he must be careful not to go too far. "It will now take another microsecond for the hammer to reach the strings," he says. "This is why the artist needs to adapt himself. He needs to play slightly ahead because there is a little lag time from when his fingertip hits the key and when the sound is produced, a few milliseconds. Even at Steinway spec there's a lag, but I've made more." Most artists, as they warm up, says Stumpf, "will adapt to the instrument. They'll notice this subtle difference, tactilely."

Some neat basic physics plays a big role in how a piano functions. If you press a key very, very softly, the hammer won't reach the strings at all, even with the key pressed all the way down. This is due to what's called "let off," which Stumpf is now testing key by key, the distance where the hammer disengages the jack and its movement is solely carried by inertia. You need a certain base level of velocity for them to go the full distance. "You can go too far with this if the let off is too close to the string. The last thing you want is for it to still be lifting when it hits the string, because then the hammer will simultaneously strike and dampen the piano," he says.

Each nuanced adjustment carries its own detailed methodology for the optimal setting and where Stumpf thinks is best for the upcoming concert. And each adjustment is part of a cascade of intervention, one change creating a domino effect—the let off affects the drop, the shaving of the felt to improve the surface also lowers the hammer levels, on and on. "I am a rule breaker," he says. "I do a lot of tailoring but you have to know where you're going to get away with going through the speed trap."

After the work on the hammers, Stumpf starts pounding the keys in an unnatural, unmusical way, like my two-year-old son does with great joy on his toy piano. The aggression is surprising, off-putting, and almost scary. "You hear I'm really beating it in." He smashes the key again very hard. "When your tuner comes to your home he is not pounding it like I am now. If I don't BEAT"—he pounds a note on the word *beat* like an audible italic—"it into tune, the Bear will beat it out of tune." Stumpf directs my attention to one of the zillion metal tuning pins inside the piano. "When I turn this pin the wire gets tighter. It's essentially just the first segment of wire—from the tuning pin to what's called the agraffe, which is the first of several termination points—that gets tight first. And you need to overcome that pressure right there and the best way to do it is with that shock."

Once, a note did get beaten out of tune during a performance. "It was during Brahms's First concerto, in D minor, Opus 15. The note was C sharp 5 up against the strut break," he says, like a soldier recalling the details of a war story. "I happened to be sitting in the fourth row and I would have paid a hundred dollars for fifteen seconds just to be able to go up on stage and pull that in. It wasn't terribly out but I heard it."

Though Stumpf's work requires composure, and the orchestral environment certainly is one of reserve, I've come to realize that like Giulia Wilkins Ary, Stumpf is a bit of an adrenaline junkie himself. There's a thrill I can see in his eyes when he talks about pushing the limits of what he's "supposed" to do in order to get the absolute most of the instrument. Everything he's doing today is with the imagined performance in his mind of the Bear pounding Rachmaninoff out to the last row of the balcony. And like Wilkins Ary, there is this synergistic relationship between extreme focus and endorphins, Csíkszentmihályi's flow. As Stumpf later told me when we discussed the phenomenon: "It happens most often when doing the most tedious jobs—concert voicing, regulation, et cetera—that require all my faculties. It is as if time loses its mastery over me and becomes irrelevant. I've gone ten hours without eating, I don't hear my phone. I'm chasing down excellence. No one will ever be able to tell how long I worked, but that doesn't matter. The process of striving toward perfection is the reward."

Because of his verve for this type of minute work, Stumpf's attention to detail seems innate. But like Marc Levitt, the graphic designer who gained his meticulousness through repetition of particular tasks in design school, Peter Stumpf was taught an appreciation early on for the subtleties of his craft. "When I was in school at Shenandoah [a conservatory], my teacher took a human hair and put it under a page in a phone book and said 'Can you feel that?' Of course, I could. Then he folded a few more pages overtop and said, 'Can you feel it?' Then folded a few more over, and even at something like nine pages you could still feel the hair underneath," he told me. "Your fingertip has amazing ability to sense extremely fine, little things. And the difference between a piano the artists love and a piano that's 'meh' is sometimes that minute, subtle difference."

"I started out falling in love with the sound of the piano. I was a very intermediate pianist. But I loved the sound and the instrument and I began to wonder how it worked, how I could get more out of it," Stumpf told me over dinner outside the Hall one night. "And the piano technician would come over to the house and I would always sit with him, and pick his brain and drive him crazy. When I graduated from high school I knew this was what I wanted to do but my guidance counselor talked me out of it. He said a piano is archaic, this isn't a good profession. 'You have a good mind for math, become an accountant or an engineer or something.'" Stumpf was a business major at the University of Pittsburgh for two and a half years before quitting. He then went to work in a print shop for a number of years ("at least I was working with my hands"). It wasn't until Stumpf was thirty that he "got back on track," he said.

He summoned up the courage to go against what was advised and instead follow what he loved and enrolled in a one-year program to become certified as a piano technician. (Stumpf guesses that about a third of piano technicians have official education, certification, and the rest learn by mentoring, with the odd few who read a book or somehow figure it out by themselves.) "After I got certified, I moved back to Pittsburgh. I had skills but zero customers," he said. He was determined to make it work. "I wrote letters to school districts, churches, and said, 'I'm a new tech looking for work, and if I have the opportunity . . .' The first Halloween I gave away Symphony candy bars and put in coupons for like ten dollars off piano tuning and I got a few customers. The Upper Saint Clair [a suburb of Pittsburgh] school district had a regular tech who couldn't make it once and contacted me and became one of my first customers. I didn't mean to usurp anyone, but I just grew and sought opportunities." Slowly, his tenacity paid off. For the first couple of years he continued operating printing equipment to help pay the bills. But he then got busy enough that he exclusively was working on pianos. At that point, "the referrals started to roll," he told me.

Stumpf spent sixteen years as a successful piano technician in the greater Pittsburgh area, working in people's homes, churches, and schools. "I would do the rebuilding process, replacing strings, et cetera. I positioned myself as a full technician, not just a tuner. There are plenty of guys doing that, and I didn't want to compete with them," he said. In 2006, two big breaks came that launched him to "the big leagues"—he got hired by Carnegie Mellon University, where (in addition to being the sole technician for the PSO) he is a staff member taking care of their five Ds. And he got called to audition to work for the PSO. How did he make the leap?

"I was fortunate to have picked up some very skilled and demanding customers early in my career, performers or teachers at universities," he told me. "They would push me to the limit. It was hard for me to deliver on everything they wanted but over time I developed the skills. They really brought out the best in me." I asked Stumpf if his goal was to ultimately move up to a prestige job like working for the PSO. "I *never* expected to get this job. There was another technician who had been here for fifteen years. He was and is an excellent technician, but his [lack of] people skills ultimately led to his dismissal. Scrambling, they brought in someone from the Cleveland Institute of Music while simultaneously interviewing techs in the area. They called some of those very fussy people that I was servicing, asking who they used." Stumpf made it on the short list of people invited to audition for the job.

The PSO has three pianos—the concerto, orchestra, and practice. The concerto, what Stumpf is working on for Matsuev, is the prized instrument and is used only by visiting pianists performing concertos (music where one instrument—in this case, piano—is the featured component). The orchestra piano is played by the staff pianist as part of regular concerts. And the practice is as titled. The technician must maintain all three instruments, though the concerto is, of course, the most critical. At first Stumpf was allowed to work only on the orchestra piano. "At the time the Cleveland fellow was doing the solo work [concerto piano], and it was costing them a fortune to bring him in. I worked on the orchestra piano and I treated it like it was a concerto. I really threw myself at it. Rodrigo Ojeda, the orchestra staff pianist, sat down at the piano after I had worked on it and said it was noticeably improved. Lastly, there was a concerto where the guy from Cleveland, I guess, stumbled. There were some complaints, so they dismissed him and gave me the opportunity."

As his test, Stumpf had to prepare the instrument back to back for two giants of the classical world, Yefim (The Brontosaur)* Bronfman and Emanuel Ax. "The very first time I was tuning for Bronfman, there was a two o'clock rehearsal and at one twenty a string breaks during the tuning." This has happened only once on the concerto in twelve years. "I devoted thirty seconds to screaming silently in my head every profanity I knew, then I got to work." Stumpf has a crash kit backstage at the Hall with a full set of Steinway Model D strings. Since the break was at the tuning pin, he "was able to keep the original string by borrowing an inch from its hitch-pin buddy. It had to work, and it did," he said. "I kid you not, I was pulling it finally up to tune as I saw him walk on stage. He asked 'How's the piano?' And I lied and said, 'Never been better!' The last thing I wanted was to say 'I broke a string, I hope it holds, it should be okay.' You have to project confidence." This managing of the psyche of the front man is one element that Stumpf and Plank do share. Plank told

---

* Yes, I, too, would like to see a battle of the beasts between the Brontosaur and the Bear! Those classical music journalists love their nicknames.

me how he always stays calm and never looks worried in front of Thom Yorke, so as not to rattle him when he's performing in front of thousands. Stumpf said, "I wasn't taught to do that, of course. I just intuited that's what had to happen. If they see me nervous that will of course affect their perception of the instrument."

After Stumpf's nearly twenty-five years of work, his confidence and skill are well rewarded. According to Stumpf, the best and busiest techs in the nation earn in the range of $150,000 a year. While his income is culled from CMU and some private clients (including work on a few orchestra members' home pianos) in addition to the PSO, this generous remuneration, at least as an economic metric of value, supports Stumpf's belief that his expertise in his own craft is on par with that of the musicians of the PSO (whose base pay is just north of $100,000). Beyond the deep fulfillment so many Invisibles derive from their work, this comfortable wage also buttresses the argument of Matthew Crawford's 2010 book *Shop Class as Soulcraft*, which extolled the value of working as a tradesperson, especially so with one's hands. If our culture could get beyond biases toward recognition and desk jobs over technical or craftswork, especially that which isn't typically seen by the public, some otherwise unhappy and underpaid middle managers could be enjoying better lives. (This isn't to say there aren't untold numbers of fulfilled Invisible workers in office environments—such as Peter Canby, the *New Yorker* fact-checker—only that an elite craftsman or tradesperson in a small city can do quite well.)

For all of the importance of the other tasks Stumpf performs, when it comes down to it, they're irrelevant if the piano isn't in tune. This is the most obvious, and therefore critical, adjustment Stumpf will make. Surprisingly, he uses just one tuning fork for one note—the A above middle C set to vibrate at 440 cycles per second, known as "A 440," generally the standard pitch of orchestras around the world. Once that A is set to 440, matching the tuning fork, then everything else gets based off of that key. "It's a lot like being a surveyor," he says. "That A440 is like pounding a stake in the ground and saying 'This is where I'm starting' and then everything is measured out from that."

I've always loved playing twelve-string guitars, but they're a pain in the ass to tune because you not only have to tune the main six strings, but then the other six parallel strings. In this regard a piano is like a twelve-string guitar but almost immeasurably worse because seventy-five of the eighty-eight keys have three strings each. (Another five keys have two strings, and eight keys have just one.) The parallel strings for each key need to match each other in pitch, which is done by eliminating audible beats—that *wah-wah-wah-wah* oscillating sound—between them. (When the strings are nearly in pitch but just slightly off from each other it creates a "chorusing" effect, which is sometimes employed on purpose by guitar players via a chorus pedal*). But getting the three strings for each note perfectly in pitch or unison with one another is just one step of tuning. The really hard part comes when you then have to get each of the notes in tune with one another. "It's like sudoku," Stumpf told me. If you do one note off, all the rest that follow will be off.

In Western music, one octave is broken into twelve pieces (aka notes). The spaces between each note are called intervals. Three spaces is a third, five is a fifth, and so on. In "equal temperament," which, for obvious practical purposes over time became the standard, the intervals remain the same throughout the piano so a fifth in one octave sounds the same as a fifth in another octave.

The thing about hearing a note on a piano is you're not just hearing the note. When you plunk a middle C you recognize the root note of the C, called the fundamental, but there also are harmonics, overtones that vibrate at certain multiples of the fundamental frequency, resounding. If you listen carefully, when a note is played on a piano it oscillates; it's never a flat line of tone. The key to tuning is being able to listen to the beats or oscillations of two different notes and syncing them depending on which harmonics they have in common.

"Sometimes before a rehearsal, I'll be there ten to fifteen minutes before it starts and everyone is warming up, and I like to listen to the oboe and follow what that instrument is playing, and follow that melody no matter where it goes," says Stumpf as he ever so slightly turns

---

* As used by Kurt Cobain in the verses of Nirvana's "Smells Like Teen Spirit," referenced in the previous chapter.

one of the pins. His tuning wrench is another of his custom tools, though he had this one made by a machinist. Often, tuning wrenches have beautiful wood shafts and handles, with a thin steel rod inside the shaft. Stumpf's is all steel, though, and thicker than standard. "This won't bend" he says, trying to do a strongman bend on it. "An NFL lineman can't do it!" A normal wrench can bend when you stress it over time. Also, he demands the control of knowing there is no flex, which is especially critical on the tuning pegs on the high notes because the most minute movement changes the pitch.

He plays two notes together. "If I want to tune this third properly you'll hear the beats of the two notes. These two notes share a common harmonic up here." Demonstrating, he repeatedly hits a high note—the harmonic of the two lower notes—at the rate we heard the beats oscillating while the two lower notes rang out. "Remember, each one has a whole harmonic series and they happen to meet right here—" He hits the high note again. "So instead of listening to the whole rest of the note, I'm only listening to this harmonic, like picking the oboe out of the cacophony."

Things are about to increase multiple levels of crazy, so hold on: You'd think based on equal temperament that all of the notes would be perfectly placed apart up and down the keyboard. But some strange things happen with the math, where to have two notes sound perfectly in pitch the distance between them will actually be a touch more than a precise third or fifth or whatever interval you're playing. This is a natural "stretching" of the octave, caused by inharmonicity, where the harmonics or partials given off by each string don't work perfectly mathematically. For example, one octave above A440 should be 880 but it's not; depending on the piano, it could be 881.223 or something like that. But the tuner listens to the beats, so he doesn't have to know the exact pitch. It's essentially impossible to tune two pianos perfectly with each other because of this inharmonicity and octave stretching.

As if this isn't confusing enough, Stumpf is employing some rogue moves to the tuning, specifically designed for the Bear and for the Rachmaninoff he'll be playing, to make the piano stand out from the orchestra. The decision to even attempt the following moves at all, as well as how to implement them, is highly subjective. This is where Peter Stumpf's artistry truly reveals itself.

Let's start with the slightly easier to understand of the two moves. As you know, an octave is broken into twelve notes. Those twelve notes are divided into 1,200 cents. Now, remember that the orchestra will all be tuned to A440. Without telling anyone, including the pianist, Stumpf is tuning the whole piano one cent sharp (roughly 440.264). According to Stumpf, sounding just slightly sharp can be registered as a pleasingly bright quality to human ears. When something is a little bit flat, however, it's immediately unpleasant to us. "By being sharp," Stumpf explained, "even just the single cent, it will put the piano on a 'musical pedestal' of sorts. Much like how the conductor will be better seen standing elevated, so will the piano by staying on top of the pitch."

The more complex stealthy move that Stumpf is making for the piano to stand out is spreading the temperament octave (beyond its natural stretch explained before).

DISCLAIMER: Before we go any further I must warn you we're delving into some deep waters here. If this hasn't been making sense to you thus far, 1) feel free to skip ahead to the next section and 2) don't feel bad. I spent more time trying to understand the basics of temperaments, harmonics, overtones, intervals, et cetera than I did on any other niche of information for any of the book's profiles. The mathematical concepts here are just heinously complex (there's a lot of talk of Pythagoras in the literature). Going back to junior high algebra, I've found math theory to be incredibly obtuse and frustrating until I get the "eureka" moment when it clicks. My problem with trying to understand the theory behind tuning is the click never came. The deeper I dug in trying to achieve that eureka moment of clarity—and I indeed went deep, reading countless articles, speaking with multiple musical theorists, and going back and forth in extensive e-mails with Stumpf—the more elusive the "click" became. But I don't want to write about anything that I don't understand, even if I know what I am writing is correct. It feels fraudulent. So I became stuck in a downward spiral—the more I learned, the more out of grasp the click, so the more I kept researching. Despite my OCD pulling me into this vortex, I confess, the laws of tuning defeated me here. I gave up without getting the click. The process did teach me something, though: Having a true expertise in piano tuning, being able to veer from the safety of orthodoxy as your inner artist deems fit, as Stumpf does, is an extraordinary skill.

"Expanding the octave will do much to make the piano clearer and colored to a particular style, and will be at its best when playing sans orchestra," Stumpf explained. "Whatever I do to the temperament octave must be replicated over the entire piano, or it will just sound like I didn't do a good job tuning. Done properly, it gives the player more colors to play with." Remember that an octave is 1,200 cents. But Stumpf is stretching the octaves to, say, 1,202 cents, making every interval slightly larger. Think of the octave like a pizza cut into twelve even slices. If the pizza size is increased overall in diameter, each slice would be slightly larger. By expanding the temperament octave, the first octave that gets tuned and is the template for all remaining tuning, Stumpf can "purify" the fifths over the whole piano. "The thirds, however," he explained, "are already among the fastest-beating intervals in the temperament, and this practice will speed them up even more, bringing a heightened energy, clarity, and edge to solo playing."

He goes on: "I use a temperament octave from F3 to F4. So, if I make the F3 to F4 octave two cents wide (the F4 will be tuned two cents sharp of pure), every octave will need to be two cents wide, coast to coast on the keyboard. One must be careful with this. For example, F4 is now two cents wide of F3. F5 will then be two cents wide from F4 and F6 will be another two cents wide. You get the idea. F1 and F7 can easily sound quite out of tune with each other if you go too far." But Stumpf believes this work can help distinguish one performance from another. "And," he says, "much of the time, the artist doesn't know exactly how I got there. It is much like eating at a restaurant. You like the food, but can't exactly place all the nuances of the flavor."

In my quest to understand Stumpf's black art I began crafting diagrams to try to visualize what he was doing. Following is my fourth attempt, which he verified for me does give a rough idea of spreading the temperament in Example 1, and tuning the whole piano two cents sharp in Example 2.

Example 1. Each octave is 1202 cents, and the pitch increases incrementally sharper up the keyboard.

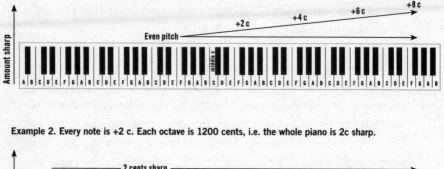

Example 2. Every note is +2 c. Each octave is 1200 cents, i.e. the whole piano is 2c sharp.

Stumpf uses an expanded temperament for composers like Rachmaninoff, Gershwin, Prokofiev, and others where a "higher octane" experience is desired. Further, Stumpf says it works with the ensemble because in bigger works, the pitch of the orchestra rises anyway and this will help the piano to "keep up." (The rise in pitch has to do with the Doppler effect. Higher volumes, especially from brass instruments, will drive the pitch up a small amount, perhaps a few cents.)

Incidentally, you can do the opposite of stretching an octave, for example by compacting it to 1,199 cents. By playing with the pitch as well, you can "mellow out" the tuning, making for a nicer Brahms waltz or Chopin Nocturne, said Stumpf. In conclusion, Stumpf explains: "Expanding the octave is like giving it caffeine. Compacting is giving it a beer. These practices need to be meted out so carefully that even the orchestra members are not on to it." (An irony I enjoy about Stumpf is that his name loosely translates to "dull" in German, and yet through his passion for his work, evident in both his focused demeanor and endless supply of colorful metaphors, he is anything but dull.)

THURSDAY

I enter backstage while rehearsal is in session. I cannot see the orchestra. I am behind a movable wall that is the stage's backdrop. They are playing Mussorgsky and I'm confronted with wonderful bombast: timpani thundering, brass blasting triumphantly, strings swirling. In a world dominated by electric sounds—our phones, the chime of the subway doors opening, the MS Windows three-second start-up song, even nearly all of our live music is electric, amplified—one loses sight (or, ahem, sound) of how special live "real" acoustic sound is. Not being able to see the orchestra right now, I am directed to focus solely on the sound. Who knew—the best seat in the house is one without a view. For a rock music fan who spends nearly all of his time—as most of us do—listening to music that's been pre-recorded, I am taken aback by the majesty of a live symphony.

Experiencing the sonic characters of these instruments not replicated or projected through speakers is unparalleled. The music takes on an almost synesthetic quality, there is a three-dimensionality, a sense of the moving parts, each instrument's sections' sound moving in the air, the complexity and grandeur of the symphony can only be in full relief live like this. I've always thought it's criminal to hear a great rock song at low volume or through tinny, mediocre earbuds. But, actually, the real crime is that classical music has been banished to dentists' waiting rooms, elevators, malls, and old people's radios with one speaker and no dynamic range (like the one that was playing in my hotel dining room at breakfast)—relegated to the role of ambiance in public spaces. This does a profound injustice to the music. It's neutered at low volume, not to mention being reproduced electronically. Forget about The Who blowing out your eardrums. *This music* must be live! And it must be loud! A simple solution to help classical music thrive (as audiences for much of the world's orchestras are a sea of white hair), and capture a new generation of fans, is to bring anyone in the community who's willing to come, not to mention class trips, as many people as can fit, and have them stand right here behind the temporary back wall scenery while the orchestra is rehearsing. They'll never be the same.

When the orchestra takes a break for lunch, Stumpf and I head over to the piano, which has been moved from the back yesterday to the stage, where it will remain through the concert series. Stumpf is going to make some final adjustments before Matsuev arrives to rehearse with the orchestra. Starting around 1 p.m., the first few musicians arrive back from lunch, warming up, tweaking their instruments, like a basketball team doing a pregame shoot around. The previous PSO technician would fight the atmosphere. "The first musician would come out and he would confront the person and say, 'Do you mind, I'm trying to finish this tuning.' And maybe that person would go backstage or to another area to warm up," Stumpf tells me. "But then another person would come, and then another. And it's ten, twenty, sixty people on stage and he couldn't fight it and he would get frustrated and angry. It was like trying to hold the ocean back with a broom." After several long days with the instrument, the bulk of Stumpf's work has to be finished by this time, and he must be able to complete his job without being isolated. "I can't view what I'm doing as more important than anyone else's role. We all have a critical role," he says. "It's a privilege to be out here mingling with them."

Stumpf's continued awe of the orchestra as a whole and his place within it, even after so many years, is unambiguous. He's able to maintain a supreme confidence in his work while remaining humble about his place within the larger endeavor. Being onstage, looking out into the grand hall, the endless rows of velvet seats, the ornate gilded ceilings, I get the first flutters of excitement about the upcoming concert. As Stumpf plays a few notes I remark how great the reverb sounds now that we're onstage in the hall. "I get such a rush being here," he says. I assume he's referring to being onstage like a performer. But I soon realize the rush is from something else. "When I'm onstage, especially alone, the hall is dark except for a ghost light on me," he says. "I love the sound of a piano, and where better to hear it than a concert hall such as this! This is where it's meant to be, like a racecar at the Indy track." Yesterday, as he worked on the piano backstage and discussed the minutiae of his craft, despite it being centered on a musical instrument there was a certain detached scientific feel to it all. We were in a dingy room, among the ropes and pulleys and various gear that comprises a backstage area. Yet now, here on stage, as the piano's sound is given room to breathe, to soar actually, Stumpf's work takes on a new relevance, grandeur even.

"It feeds me in a way that I can't even fully describe in words," he says. "It's so satisfying. Even a simple phrase"—he plays a melancholy passage for a few seconds, the warm, rich tones ringing out—"just listening to that, it stirs something in me. It's a good thing. It's rain on a parched prairie. And I look forward to the next time." I ask Stumpf if he ever dreamed of being a performer. "*This* is now the dream. I suppose there was a time as a teenager or young man when I wanted to perform. But I find this far more satisfying," he says. "I have more control over the sound than Denis Matsuev does. I love the unseen-artist nature of the work."

When I talked with Jean Twenge, the psychologist and co-author of *The Narcissism Epidemic*, about the premise of Invisibles, that people who are ambivalent toward recognition, surprisingly, tend to be more fulfilled than the many in society at large who are increasingly desirous of attention, she replied: "I agree. Those who are motivated by intrinsic joy and connections to others are happier and less prone to mental health issues than those who are driven by money, fame, and image. Narcissists are one example of this. When they are young, they are often happy and satisfied as they seek attention for themselves. As they get older, they grow increasingly unhappy as they don't get the recognition they feel they deserve."

If you have a pride and confidence in what you do, as Stumpf so clearly does, the rewards you reap come from within, which are, perhaps, the only true and lasting rewards. In this regard pride—and I'm not talking about the biblical connotation of pride as sin, but pride as respect for yourself, your work, your effort—is just an extension of the Invisible core trait of drawing fulfillment from the work itself, not outside acknowledgment for it.

Csíkszentmihályi, the psychologist behind "flow," is also known for his writings about "autotelics," people who are internally driven, rather than externally driven where the motivating factors are things like money or recognition. The word is derived from the Greek, where *auto* means "self" and *telos* means "goal." He wrote:

An autotelic person needs few material possessions and little entertainment, comfort, power, or fame because so much of what he or she does is already rewarding . . . They are less dependent on the external rewards that keep others motivated to go on with a life composed of routines. They are more autonomous and independent because they cannot be as easily manipulated with threats or rewards from the outside. At the same time, they are more involved with everything around them because they are fully immersed in the current of life.

The notion of the autotelic is reinforced by Self Determination Theory, the theory of motivation developed by Richard Ryan, referenced earlier in the book. Claude Fernet, a researcher in the Department of Management at the University of Quebec, and a scholar in the SDT field, co-authored a study on "job strain" that found "highly autonomously motivated employees experience less psychological distress in the presence of job demands than their less autonomously motivated counterparts." When I e-mailed with him about Invisibles, Fernet told me: "Individuals who have an autonomous motivation do not specifically (or intentionally) aim to be 'invisible.' The idea is that what drives them to get up in the morning and engage in their activities is the desire (and ability) to get full satisfaction in what they do. If their successes lead them to be recognized (being visible), this will not be perceived as the ultimate reward, but rather as a simple corollary of their quest for growth, personal development, or the expression of a congruence with their core values."

Tim Kasser is a psychology professor at Knox College whose research, much of which is grounded in SDT, investigates how values relate to well-being. One general type of goal within the field that's been identified is called "extrinsic." "These are goals that are focused on external rewards and the praise of other people," Kasser explained to me. In a 1996 analysis, supported by a grant from the National Institute of Mental Health, he demonstrated "that these values correlated negatively with well-being." They also showed, conversely, that intrinsic aspirations—those grounded in motivations to satisfy an inherent curiosity, to learn, or to actualize our potential without any obvious external reward—were associated with "higher well-being and less distress." He noted to me that the "basic finding has been replicated numerous times."

Drilling down, Kasser has done research that specifically looked at the extrinsic goal of "status/popularity," in other words desiring visibility. (One of the markers in the study was participants' reaction to the line "My name will be known by many different people.") Kasser found "its relative importance to be associated with lower self-actualization and vitality, lower diary reports of positive emotion, and more narcissism." Peter Stumpf's desire to work behind the scenes, the fulfillment he derives from the challenge and value of the work itself, even if no one in the audience (or even the musicians) is aware of his work's effect on the performance, is clearly supported by this body of research.

Stumpf's deeply rooted sense of responsibility to the craft is evident by his attention and care given not only to the showpiece concerto piano but even to the lesser instruments, the orchestra piano and others. Ben Folds, the pop-rock pianist, came to play with the PSO and he wasn't allowed to use the concerto piano. But he demanded to have a choice of pianos beyond just the orchestra, so the PSO rented a brand-new concert-ready Steinway. Comparing the two in the afternoon before the performance, Folds still chose the twenty-five-year-old orchestra piano that Stumpf had worked on.

Matsuev arrives. He's in a beige sweater, has a small potbelly, and takes his rimless glasses off as he sits down to the piano. He's a big dude but not the scary beast I expected; more giant teddy than ferocious bear. He noodles around for a minute or two, fluidly, beautifully playing complex phrases with ease and restraint, the way top tennis players in prematch warm-ups hit the ball to each other, at terrifying pace but an effortless 75 percent of force for them. In the midst of his warming up Matsuev pauses a moment mid-phrase and bangs a high note repeatedly. He and Stumpf don't look at each other but it's clear something is off with this note and they both know it.

Stumpf and I depart to his favorite spot in the Hall, in the balcony, to listen to the piano as Matsuev rehearses with the orchestra. Whispering in our seats, I ask Stumpf what was wrong with the note. "There was a ping to it. Too brassy. I'm going to go and play at it a variety of ways and I'll use the poking tool to soften the hammer until it sounds right," he says. About to begin, the Bear strips down to a black T-shirt. And oddly, instead of laying his phone on the bench, Matsuev places it inside the piano.

Much of the piece is lovely, delicate. But it has its explosions. The Bear's head nods violently at times. In a particularly aggressive section his butt lifts off the bench. At the end of the first movement there is a flourish. After the final note his hands fly off the keys as if he just touched them to a scorching cast-iron pan.

Stumpf and I descend the balcony, walk back through the empty ornate lobby, and continue down quiet halls until we reach the stage. Stumpf approaches Matsuev. The exchange is friendly but short. "It's very sensitive. Very American," the Bear says, laughing. Peter translates this comment for me: "Sensitive means he likes the control. It has a sound that's distinct." Despite the elegant passages, the Bear pounding out Rachmaninoff made me worried for the piano. The musicians file out and Stumpf sits down at the bench to get to work on that offensive ping.

A stagehand wanders by after a while and calls out to Stumpf: "Anything left?"

"It'll be worse tomorrow," Stumpf shouts back. "He holds back for rehearsals."

"Get the glue!"

Stumpf shakes his head and gets back to work. The last time Matsuev was in town he played Tchaikovsky's first piano concerto, Stumpf tells me as he voices the offending hammer. "You're probably familiar with the piece." He hums a few notes then does a dramatic *bum bum BUM!* "And he didn't break a single string on this instrument," he says, trying to reassure himself. "But warming up on the older piano upstairs, he broke eight in the week he was here."

Peter Stumpf is the only Invisible I've featured in a major profile in the book whom I also had briefly interviewed for the *Atlantic* article that was this book's precursor. But something he said in that interview was so outlandishly earnest, so hyperbolic, he sounded either crazy or like an egomaniac. Yet there was something in his voice that told me he was serious, and that what he said was true: "When I see Manny Ax [the renowned pianist] playing, it's him and my piano. I get a tremendous satisfaction. If my child was up there performing with him I would feel about the same. I take great pride in my work, I'm not even in the program, ever. Yet when I am in the audience and I hear Emanuel Ax, I genuinely feel like we're doing a duet—it's my piano and the artist . . . and I don't mind him alone getting the praise because they are thrilled with what he's been able to do with my piano." There was such beauty in the notion of Stumpf's connection to his work, that he's so tied to the instrument that *he feels he is performing a duet* with the pianist. I had to meet this man and see him work, to find out if, indeed, he wasn't crazy.

FRIDAY

The lights go down in the sold-out hall. Stumpf is sitting a few seats over from me (because of the attendance, the office was unable to get us two seats together). The conductor, by way of an introduction, tells the crowd of the news that a meteor had struck the Russian countryside earlier in the day, with some wounded. In a potent, distasteful, but humorous comment he goes on to say that a Russian meteor is about to strike Pittsburgh. There is silence before Matsuev begins. I feel a strange nervousness. After having spent so many hours with Stumpf over the past few days, I've internalized some of his connection with the piano. Matsuev places a small cloth inside the piano that he will later use to wipe his hands and brow during breaks in the music.

The second section of the Rachmaninoff piece is an excellent showcase for piano. There are several credenzas (unaccompanied piano parts), and I find myself savoring each of them. During one of them Matsuev is really going at it, his fingers pumping frenetically like pistons in a redlined engine, motoring up and down the keys. Go Stumpf! He accentuates certain single notes, pounding them, letting them ring out all alone. The tone of the instrument, the sound waves of a lone wool hammer striking strings inside a meticulously crafted wooden box, reverberating out in a massive concert hall, floating in the air, caressing the gold leaf on the far reaches of the back walls. *This* is how a piano is meant to be heard. The piece is complex—it's not just moments of fury, much of it is also soft, graceful. But it ends with a bombastic retard, Matsuev pushing the instrument to its limits.

For an encore it is tradition for visiting pianists to perform a short, unannounced, unaccompanied piece at the end of program. The Bear, so noted for his ferocity, does something unexpected—he plays a tender, elegant piece, almost entirely in the upper register, like a lullaby. (I later learn the selection is called "Musical Snuffbox" a nineteenth-century piece meant to resemble the dream-like plinky sound of music boxes, which were once held inside snuffboxes). It's a brilliant, affecting choice, a relief to Rachmaninoff's thunder, an airy strawberry confection after the 16-ounce steak. With the hushed audience and the piano all alone, I think of that high note Matsuev pounded repeatedly during rehearsal, seemingly as both an assessment and a signal to Stumpf that something was wrong. All of that percussive abuse during Rachmaninoff, any of it could have knocked a note out of tune. And now these little notes, so naked, floating alone among the silent crowd. Surely that discordant ping would ruin the piece. It's a terrifying, perhaps even cruel test of Stumpf, of the piano.

But the ping is gone. And every note flows into the next, chiming in perfect tune. The unspoken sign from pianist to technician the day before, the execution by Stumpf with his custom tool, softening the offending hammer's wool. At the last note, the very highest on the keyboard, there is a perceptible collective sound from the crowd, something between a quiet laugh and a sigh. Peter Stumpf and the piano have withstood the Bear. To his relief and triumph, Stumpf has remained invisible.

I look over at him, his face serene, perhaps with just a hint of a smile as the final rings of sound disappear and the crowd, rising to their feet, applaud.

WHEN THE INVISIBLE BECOMES VISIBLE

Crises and Catastrophes

erfection = *Invisibility*. This is the formula so many Invisibles follow. While most of us gain notice for ourselves when we perform our jobs well, as we've seen, for many Invisibles it's the inverse. The better they do their work, the more they disappear. In fact, it's often only when there's a problem that their work is thought of by the public at all. In this chapter we'll take a brief look at a few memorable examples from the recent past that illustrate just how critical invisible work can be—when things go horribly wrong, work that had long been relatively unknown suddenly can become part of the cultural conversation.

November 7, 2000. Florence Zoltowsky, a Jewish, seventy-year-old, Boynton Beach, Florida, grandmother and Holocaust survivor inadvertently casts her presidential ballot for Patrick Buchanan, an alleged anti-Semite, who "wouldn't sit" at her dining room table, she said. "All the analyses point to Buchanan's vote as a clear and massive outlier," "we can state with 99.9 percent confidence that 2,058 of the 3,407 votes cast for Patrick Buchanan are inconsistent with the demographic characteristics of Palm Beach," the probability of Buchanan correctly receiving his 3,407 votes was about "1 in 25,000"—these are just a few of the conclusions from the deluge of statistical analyses conducted after the election which found a significant number of votes incorrectly having been cast for Buchanan in Palm Beach County. The number was so awry that even Jim Mc-Connell, Buchanan's Florida coordinator, said, "Do I believe these people inadvertently cast their votes for Pat Buchanan? Yes, I do." And Buchanan himself admitted on NBC's *Today* show, "It seems to me that these 3,000 votes people are talking about—most of those are probably not my vote." Additionally, a statistically outlying 19,235 ballots in Palm Beach County were discarded for invalidly casting votes for more than one presidential candidate.

What caused this Floridian fiasco? Why did so many people unintentionally vote for Buchanan or invalidly cast more than one vote?

Political operatives, ideologues, and regular citizens can argue in perpetuity about what cost Al Gore the presidential election in 2000. And in a process as dynamic and complex as a U.S. presidential election, it's indisputable that a variety of factors were at play in the outcome. But what's not under dispute, by members of either party, is that the design of the now-infamous "butterfly ballot" resulted in a significant number of incorrectly cast ballots, the balance of which would have tipped the election in Gore's favor.

What went wrong with the ballot in Palm Beach County? The decision to use a punch-card ballot, for one, has been cited. Punch-card ballots require the voter to "punch" a hole next to their choices, but too often the hole isn't fully punched, leaving a reviled hanging "chad" (the piece of paper in the hole, the Munchkin of the doughnut, so to speak, still attached). Bruce Tognazzini, a consultant for tech firms, a former engineer and designer at Sun Microsystems and Apple, and who has written extensively on human-computer-interaction design wrote in *The Butterfly Ballot: Anatomy of a*

Disaster: "As far back as 1988, the National Institute of Standards and Technology (NIST) strongly recommended the elimination of Votomatic-type [punch] cards just because of this problem." Yet the ballots continued to be used.

But beyond the dubious mechanics of the punchcard, it was the graphic design of the ballot—the typeface, the arrangement of the candidates' names, the overall layout comprising two pages—that was responsible for voter confusion and unintended votes. He continued, "the chad problem alone would not have tipped the balance in the 2000 election . . . it took an atrociously bad design to really foul things up."

"Maps of Election Day votes by precinct and absentee votes by ballot style indicate the decisive effect of the butterfly ballot design in increasing Buchanan support within Palm Beach County alone. Areas of relatively high support for Buchanan go up to the boundary of Palm Beach but do not cross it. However, among absentee votes, there are few differences by county, and no sharp changes at county lines," concluded a report by UC Berkeley political scientists. Richard Grefé, the executive director of the AIGA, the graphic design organization, and Jessica Friedman Hewitt, the managing director of its Design for Democracy program, in a piece for *The New York Times*, wrote: "In Palm Beach County in Florida, a confusing 'butterfly ballot' design for punch-card voting equipment made it easy to miscast votes for the Reform Party candidate Pat Buchanan that were intended for Al Gore. The confusion called national attention to the design of ballots."

Until 2000, thoughts about the design of ballots was largely left to election officials; indeed, this was invisible work. After the election, however, when phrases like "hanging chad" burst from the obscure argot of balloting into the national dialogue, all of that changed. "Our work may at times be invisible but it's not insignificant," Marc Levitt, the graphic designer, said about his profession, in reference to the butterfly-ballot debacle. "It was a lightning-rod moment in my profession, when regular people suddenly became aware of how important design can be."

Let's take a look at the design failure:

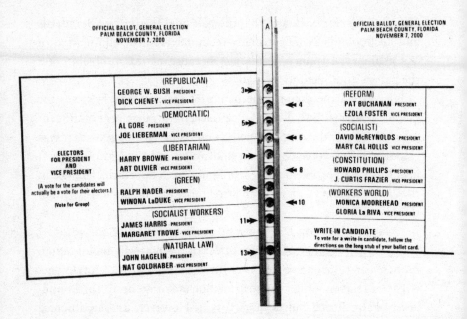

"Not only does it appear that perhaps 4,000 people made the error of punching the second hole on the ballet in the mistaken belief that the second hole represented the second candidate, more than 19,000 people made the error of punching more than one hole, since both were directly alongside their candidate," Tognazzini wrote. The designers "viewed the ballot as a 2X6 staggered matrix with a line of radio buttons in between the two sides. Their cute little arrows appeared to be enough to help people choose the right box from this matrix. The voters saw things very differently."

Calling the creators of the Palm Beach ballot "designers" can only be done from the most general (and generous) perspective. Prior to 2000, ballots mostly were made by election officials with help from the "printers who had inside staff people who laid things out. But it's a different kind of design than what's practiced by those of us in the profession of graphic or, specifically, information design," Marcia Lausen, a principal of Chicago design firm Studio/Lab and a professor at the University of Chicago School of Art and Design told me. After the election, Lausen spearheaded a plan, through the AIGA's Design for Democracy program, to improve ballot design to help make "voting easier and more accurate for all citizens," their literature states.

Lausen, along with AIGA and University of Chicago colleagues, drafted a list of best practices for ballot design to aid election officials around the country. One of the first adopters of their recommendations was Cook County, Illinois, where Lausen was based. The county clerk directly worked with Lausen's team to create a new ballot. It was a byzantine process. Elections in the United States are managed at the county, sometimes even the municipal level, Lausen explained. The election code in Cook County was written in legalese and had all sorts of nonsensical requirements such as demanding the text be done in all caps, and strange measurements of letters—notions that are ludicrous in information design. Before Lausen and her colleagues could implement their new ballot designs they first had to wade through the complex process of influencing local politicians to change the law. But eventually they succeeded. (The very first guideline is: "Use lowercase letters . . . because they are easier to recognize.")

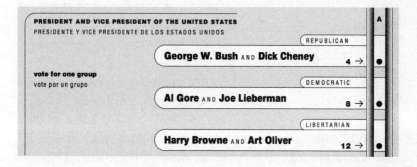

Above is an excerpt of the proposed Cook County ballot by Lausen and colleagues. Notice the use of mixed capital and lowercase letters. There's also a "graphic device" that encapsulates the candidate names and party affiliations, which helps "direct the voter's attention toward each corresponding arrow and punch number," explains *Design for Democracy: Ballot + Election Design*, Lausen and the AIGA's book of guidelines.

"We knew as a profession that when 'ballot design' is on the cover of *The New York Times* that this was an opportunity to make changes," said Lausen of the media coverage after the election. Today, punch-card ballots are virtually obsolete, though many of the recommendations of Design for Democracy are applicable to any type of ballot. Additionally, they've created guidelines for many specific ballot types, including optical scan and touch screen, that have gained prevalence. Unfortunately, many are still poorly designed, but the importance and consequence of quality information design is at least now part of the public conversation and more importantly, that of election officials.

After the election, Theresa LePore, the elections supervisor in Palm Beach County who created the maligned ballot, received hate mail, had a security detail, and even received death threats. Even over a decade later her notoriety still haunts her. In a 2013 interview in *Boca Raton* magazine, she said, "I joke that I have to tip well because everybody knows who I am. It's never gone back to the way it was before that day." Ironically, tragically, LePore created the ballot thinking its design on two pages, allowing for larger type, would help make things clearer for elderly voters. She was well intentioned, yet, as any design professional could have told her, ill-equipped for the task.

Perhaps the most infamous Invisible-becoming-Visible catastrophe was the 9/11 failure of the behind-the-scenes intelligence gatherers from the various alphabet agencies to "connect the dots" of all their data. While field agents like CIA operatives working under code names have long captured our imagination through blockbuster films and airport novels, the role of Invisibles *behind* these Invisibles—the back-office analysts, the data sifters—suddenly gained attention only when there was this terrible breakdown in effectiveness. Today, with the revelations about the government's controversial PRISM surveillance program, the work of these Invisible data analysts is again gaining notice. I cite these Invisibles not as a condonation nor condemnation of the larger policies that their work is conducted under, but to spotlight its impact on the society.

Rather than rehash the debate about 9/11 intelligence failures, below is a brief interview I conducted with one of these "Invisible behind the Invisible" analysts. Her embodiment of the Three Traits is remarkable:

Nina* works as an intelligence analyst in the D.C. field office of one of the federal government's major intelligence agencies. Her critical role is to assess the "big picture stuff, trends, patterns among numerous and varied cases." Her days are spent fastidiously combing through and organizing data. For example, she will cull a year's worth of phone records of a certain suspect or group of suspects in a domestic terrorism case, import the data into a spreadsheet, and slowly start to parse out patterns. The process starts with "the easy stuff, like finding the numbers most called, and gets more involved from there" as she cross-references various suspects, different time frames, locations, et cetera. "I'm a Type-A personality," Nina admits. "I have to be meticulous with my work." When I asked her about the stresses on her due to the importance her work entails, she replied characteristically, "I like the level of responsibility, but I'm just doing my job." And while she said she feels tremendous accomplishment when she finishes an assignment, she lamented that "it's hard because I rarely get feedback on the assessments I write. When I submit an assessment on a big-picture trend to my supervisors, they in turn analyze it, probably in conjunction with other assessments, and communicate their findings to the appropriate undercover agents or whomever else needs to know. But I rarely, if ever, hear back from them about it." Further, she noted, "of course I can't talk about it in any detail in public. Regular people simply don't, rather, *cannot*, know about the work I do every day. Analysts like me just do our work, period. Recognition is not part of the gig." Working day in and day out, secretly, meticulously sorting data that then only goes to people with more seniority, Nina's reward solely lies in the knowledge that she is serving her country. When I asked what drives her, she said simply, "I love the work."

In recent years, especially after the raid on Osama bin Laden's hideout in Pakistan, some of our special forces have garnered the

---

* At her request I have changed her name and cannot reveal which specific agency she is with.

type of romantic fascination from the public that had formerly just been the realm of CIA agents (or their dashing British counterpart, James Bond). But not all of them are happy about their newfound attention from the public. Some Invisibles, in fact, so prize their role of anonymity that they lament when they actually do receive credit for their work. A former Navy SEAL I interviewed, who, considering his views, not surprisingly wished to remain anonymous, complained about the "seemingly incessant fascination with the SEAL Teams" related to the bin Laden raid and other high-profile events. "One thing I can say is that back in the early nineties before the Internet explosion and the political gamesmanship using SEALs as political capital," he continued, "very few knew what we did, how we did it, and where we did it" and, he says, he preferred it that way.

In early 2013 *The New York Times Magazine* ran a fascinating profile of Jason Everman, a Seattle musician who had a brush with rock stardom not once, but twice, as a member of both Soundgarden and Nirvana, only to join the military and enter the elite Army Ranger division. In the piece, Clay Tarver writes: "I wanted to know every detail, but he wouldn't say much. Or couldn't. There's a code among Special Forces: They don't talk about what they do. I actually think this was part of the appeal for Everman. After having such a public rock face, he went for something that wasn't just anonymous; it was classified." When asked about his life now, as a middle-aged student at Columbia University, Everman told him, "It's anonymous. Just the way I like it."

In the lead-up to the Iraq War, the journalist Judith Miller published a series of blockbuster articles in *The New York Times*, many of which asserted, via anonymous sources and defectors, the presence of weapons of mass destruction in the country. As is now known, those assertions were false. Though Miller sometimes used language such as, "There was no means to independently verify Mr. Saeed's allegations," to hedge in case the claims in the articles weren't true, the tenor of the pieces and the fact that they were front-page news in the paper of record overwhelms the caveats. As I was taught as a fact-checker, verifying the attribution of a quote isn't enough. One must also verify the content.

While not quite a WMD, the cloud that engulfed the *Times* in the years that followed the specious articles was poisonous, and brought the practice of fact-checking into the public consciousness (or at least that of media watchers) in a way that accurate reporting never does. Until a problem becomes known, the task of fact-checking remains largely invisible. In 2004, the *Times* issued a mea culpa: "Editors at several levels who should have been challenging reporters and pressing for more skepticism were perhaps too intent on rushing scoops into the paper." Bill Keller, the executive editor of the paper at the time, later said in regards to the debacle, "a lot of people, particularly people on the left, became disenchanted with the *Times* because they saw it as having been cheerleaders for the war." While newspapers do have some fact-checking procedures built in to their editorial process, due to the nature of the news cycle they are a part of, and the great expense, they don't have dedicated fact-checking departments the way top-level American magazines do. As the ballot controversy illustrated, in some circumstances it's the *absence* of the Invisible workers—in the former case, information designers, in this case, fact-checkers—not poor workmanship that brought their field into the spotlight.

A decade after the Miller disaster, subsequent fact-checking scandals, often over content with far less significance, have generated enormous blowback for the writers and the institutions that published their work. Perhaps this increased public awareness of the importance of fact-checking can be seen as a positive offshoot of the WMD misreportage. On one end is the Foxconn scandal. Mike Daisey, a monologist and author, fabricated specifics of worker conditions at an Apple factory in China to a national radio audience (and a record 880,000-plus podcast listeners) during a segment he did for *This American Life*, a popular public radio program. Like the Miller episode did for the *Times*, the Daisey piece rocked many listeners' trust in public radio, and by extension news sources in general. Unfortunately, much of the overall picture that Daisey painted was accurate, but "now, the story isn't [about] Chinese labor abuses anymore. The story is Daisey's own dishonesty, which tinges everything he touched," wrote Max Fisher in *The Atlantic* shortly after the story broke.

On the lighter end of the consequence scale is the Jonah Lehrer scandal, actually scandals, of 2012. The wunderkind best-selling writer first was busted for "self-plagiarizing" in posts on *The New Yorker*'s blog where he recycled material he had written elsewhere. In the scheme of things, a writer reusing some old material is hardly a gross ethical offense. (A dubious career move for sure, but not quite the same as lying.) Yet to many, particularly those in journalism, it indicated a willingness to cut corners that may have led to the extra scrutiny he received later in the year when he was found to have fabricated Bob Dylan quotes in his book *Imagine*. This proved to be his downfall. There was an immediate and fierce eruption of condemnation, much of it from fellow writers. Lehrer was soon out of his job at *The New Yorker*, his books were pulled from stores by his publisher, and *Wired* magazine severed its relationship with him as well after the scandal spurred them to re-fact-check his work there and found numerous inaccuracies in his articles.

Whether it's the reporting of false allegations of a nation's weapons program that helped build support for a war, or merely a pop science writer's almost pathological string of errors, the exigency of fact-checking, normally an invisible craft, is steadily becoming a more regular part of the cultural conversation. To reference some of my own earlier research on the topic, an article I wrote for *The Atlantic* noted as such, where among other examples I cited are "sites like the *Washington Post*'s Fact-Check column and FactCheck.org, which draws hundreds of thousands of unique visitors each month." Nevertheless, as Peter Canby of *The New Yorker* knows, fact-checking, especially when done well, is critical work that is still rarely thought of by the reader.

Ray Hull had been driving with his partner Frankie Ketchens for nearly forty hours straight, round-trip from Nebraska to Texas and back again. He expected to take a rest at the end of the trip before starting work, but when he arrived at the job site a man employed by his contractor was there and he felt pressured to get to work. He began to ascend the cell phone tower he was hired to climb, as he had done on countless other towers over the years, in order to make upgrades to the existing equipment. Then something went horribly wrong. At 240 feet up the tower, "Ketchens made a mistake with the hoist, and a huge piece of steel came crashing down with Hull attached." Incredibly, he lived, due to his safety harness breaking his fall, but he was severely and permanently injured.

As we fiddle with our iPhones most of us likely never think, perhaps not even once, about the physical infrastructure required for them to work. I've thought about the cell network in the abstract of "coverage" across a map, but not the actual towers, let alone the workers who climb them. And yet of course you wouldn't be able to send an e-mail, make a call, or check the weather app on your phone without those climbers building new and updating existing towers. Hull and his tower-climbing peers have remained invisible to the public for decades. But their profession reached a crisis in the early 2000s, when the telecom industry began a frantic push to upgrade and expand the number of towers to meet the exploding demand on their networks. With a death rate ten times greater than that of construction workers, the head of OSHA once called tower climbing "the most dangerous job in America." As mortalities in the field mounted, a flurry of press, including a *Frontline* piece, a DailyKos exposé, and numerous features in influential magazines such as *Mother Jones* and *Outside*, ensued, making these once-invisible workers visible.

We return to our equation: *Perfection = Invisibility.* It's a tough, perhaps impossible standard, and crises show us what happens when Invisibles—either due to their own error or a systemic problem within their field—fall short of embodying the Three Traits.

In the case of the tower climbers, the industry failed them when it stopped using veterans such as Hull (who is a third-generation climber, his father and grandfather having worked on TV and radio towers) as often and, instead, hired inexperienced people for as little as $10 per hour to get this complex, detailed work done faster and cheaper. Many of the deaths were of these newer climbers who lacked the experience and focus of veterans and properly trained climbers. As Ray Hull said, "It takes years and years of training to know the safety of your equipment. There's guys out there now that are foremen within months of working, starting a job. That's ludicrous!" In the rush of expansion, the industry as a whole skipped Trait 2—meticulousness. Unlike veterans, the new climbers often free-climbed (not using safety attachment gear), or were reckless. Beyond the climbers themselves, the subcontractors who hired them weren't meticulous in upkeeping their safety equipment, due to cost pressures.

Until his fall brought him to the public eye, Hull was a classic Invisible. Though he worked to pay his bills, it was his love of the job and pride in his work that brought him satisfaction. "There's probably not a human being alive that loved their job as much as I did," he said. Another former climber, Wally Reardon, shared this attitude: "I loved the adventure. The paycheck was secondary for me." While the Invisibles I've spotlighted in this book are all elite members of their fields and often well remunerated, their approach to work is applicable for all professionals. While a cell phone tower climber doesn't possess the advanced degrees and stature of the featured profiles in the book, the best of them, the veterans, are indeed highly skilled, and as shown above, share traits with all Invisibles. From debacles grand in scale that engaged a nation, to tragedies measured one person at a time that have just edged into public consciousness, invisible work often becomes visible only when something goes wrong. My hope is, after reading this, that it needn't take a disaster to raise awareness. The next time you send a text, pause your thumbs for a second and remember someone had to climb a very tall tower to enable your WTFs and LOLs to reach their destination.

THE VIEW OF INVISIBLES ACROSS CULTURES

International Perspectives

"Since I write personal essays my mom is always telling me, with a desperate hope that for once I'll listen to her, 'Koreans don't air their dirty laundry!'" David Yoo, a freelance writer, and the author of several novels and a collection of essays, told me. Born and raised in Connecticut, Yoo is a first-generation Korean American, and his parents still hold much of their ancestral land's values, much to his consternation. Considering he often mines the territory of late adolescence—budding sexuality, body issues, strained familial relationships, and the like—you have to feel for his mother.

While there is an extraordinary range of personality types and variations on what are considered social traits in every country, a trove of research from the fields of psychology, history, and sociology, among others, does provide evidence of some broad cultural norms in different countries and regions. David Yoo's mom's predilection toward keeping her family's affairs private, for example, is in line with the humility and reserve common to cultures in the so-called Confucian Belt of Korea, China, Vietnam, Japan, and parts of other nations in the region. How do varying cultural norms around the globe affect their inhabitants' views on work and recognition? How do the workers themselves view their place within the culture and the enterprises they work within? In this chapter we're going to take a brief tour of a few select areas around the world to glean answers to these questions. This is not intended as an exhaustive survey, nor the final word on any one region or culture, but as an overview I hope to offer some perspectives on Invisible values and traits across cultures.

Westerners are the protagonists of their autobiographical novels.

*Asians are merely cast members in movies touching on their existences.**

While identifying and comparing societal traits is a highly complex and nebulous affair, within academia there are a few oft-used metrics. One of the best-established means of evaluation is collectivism versus individualism. In collectivist cultures people tend to be loyal to "in-groups" like a family or tribe, and to favor group goals and norms over personal goals. Individualist cultures, on the other hand, tend to have "a loosely-knit social framework in which individuals are expected to take care of themselves and their immediate families only." (Perhaps not surprisingly, the United States is the highest-scoring individualist country on earth.) Through this lens we can form one picture of how Invisible work is viewed within the United States and other individualistic societies compared with how it is valued in strongly collectivist cultures like China and many other Asian countries.

---

* Quote is from Richard Nisbett, a psychologist at the University of Michigan who has studied the differences in Western and East Asian thought processes about the self.

I am a wonderful and very smart person. A funny and hilarious person. A kind and caring person. A good-grade person who is going to go to Cornell. A helpful and cooperative girl.

* * *

I'm a human being. I'm a child. I like to play cards. I'm my mom and dad's child, my grandma and grandpa's grandson. I'm a hardworking good child.

The above self-descriptions are both from six-year-olds. The top one is by a Euro-American, the bottom by a Chinese child. Notice that the first "focuses on the child's own positive depositional traits and qualities, the second attends to the child's social roles and significant relations," writes Qi Wang, a psychologist at Cornell University, in a paper on the development of self-knowledge. Wang, who matriculated both in China and in the States, where she earned her PhD from Harvard, and employs a distinct cross-cultural perspective in her work, told me she views "recognition/fame-seeking" as a modern Western phenomenon "which is related to the conception of the self as a unique and distinct entity defined by one's internal qualities and attributes. It contradicts the Asian ideal of modesty and a relational self."

In a co-authored paper that explored Asian and American concepts of self, Hazel Markus, a Stanford University psychologist who is a leader in the field of social psychology, wrote, "People in different cultures have strikingly different construals of the self, of others, and of the interdependence of the two." In American culture, the paper stated, "individuals seek to maintain their independence from others by . . . expressing their unique inner attributes."

Within the context of this research it's easy to see how the Chinese child quoted above will likely view the value of outside recognition for his work differently than the American girl might. When you see yourself, even from the youngest ages, as part of (or beholden to) a larger system, rather than alone, you may be less likely to strive for or expect praise and recognition as an individual because you view your acts more as part of a collective endeavor.

This collectivist attitude was evident over and over with our Invisibles—Robert Elswit, the Oscar-winning cinematographer who, though in charge of multiple crews on set, stressed the importance of a team atmosphere and viewed his work always in service of the director's vision; Plank, Radiohead's veteran guitar tech, worked tirelessly, doing physical labor he didn't necessarily have to do because his focus was always on making the larger endeavor a success, not just his own work; and as was noted earlier, numerous Invisibles, like Dennis Poon, the lead structural engineer on many of the world's tallest skyscrapers, often used *we* instead of *I* when asked about their work. How have these people become so successful with such nonaggressive and inclusive styles at work? Susan Cain's *Quiet* gives a good indication. She quotes Preston Ni, a Taiwanese-born communications professor who, now in California, teaches courses on extroversion: "In Asian cultures there's often a subtle way to get what you want. It's not always aggressive, but it can be very determined, very skillful. In the end, much is achieved because of it. Aggressive power beats you up; soft power wins you over." Being a successful Invisible is not about being meek and hoping for the best, or even necessarily introverted. To achieve their goals, even as gregarious, sociable people, as some, like Jim Harding, the wayfinding expert, and Elswit struck me, they employ soft power.

WHAT ARE YOU WORTH?

"In the U.S., individuals personally define their self-worth and articulate it through self-presentation and assertiveness. In Asia, direct self-praise is frowned upon and is seen as a sign of immaturity. We are encouraged to reveal our self-worth indirectly, through our group affiliation," Uichol Kim, a professor at the College of Business Administration at Inha University, Korea, who has an expertise in cross-cultural psychology, told me. Even the concept of self-worth itself is mercurial. In a co-authored paper questioning the universal-

ity of a need for positive self-regard, Steven Heine, a social psychologist at the University of British Columbia, wrote, "it is assumed that
people seek positive self-regard." Yet through "anthropological, so-
ciological, and psychological analyses" the authors found that there
is "scant evidence for a need for positive self-regard among Japanese." In America we assume everyone is motivated to "possess,
enhance, and maintain positive self-views," which may connect
with our need for recognition. But in Japan, where even a notion we
accept as intrinsic, desiring a positive view of oneself, is arguably
absent, the need for external praise would be much diminished.

"There is an oft-used saying in Japan—*en no shita no chikara
mochi*—which translates to 'columns that support the stage'; [In-
visibles] are the people who are like the columns that support the
stage, where main actors shine," Shigehiro Oishi, a psychology professor at the University of Virginia who studies culture and well-
being, told me. "Japanese companies try to acknowledge those who
are in a supporting position," he added. At first, the commonly held
Asian trait of not wanting to stand out may strike you as particular
to that region of the world. But, more broadly, perhaps it's our need
to be seen that is the outlier. "The self-centered egotism we reward
in the U.S. is the real anomaly when compared to African, Asian,
and many other societies," Laura Miller, professor of Japanese studies and anthropology at the University of Missouri—St. Louis, told
me. Conversely, "The Three Traits you are focusing on have a prominent place in Japanese cultural ideology." Miller went on to detail
that craftsmanship is an integral part of Japanese culture—from
highly skilled laborers like "the makers of calligraphy brushes . . . to
most of the creative industries like manga and anime. These people
put in long hours and are not famous or financially well-rewarded,"
she said, "but are highly regarded in a Japanese society that has a
history of valuing lifetime dedication to an art, a way of being, or a
martial arts practice."

The Japanese have another time-honored proverb—*deru kugi wa
utareru*—which translates to "the nail that sticks up gets hammered
down." Notably, this sentiment is common among many countries,
and not just collectivist ones. In Australia, a highly individualistic
society, just one notch behind the United States, "the tall poppy gets

cut down" is a popular adage. In Scandinavia, all the countries of which are individualistic cultures, the influential Law of Jante or *Janteloven* has similar connotations. At first the notion that these individualistic societies would highly value not standing out seems strange. One might assume individualism is at the root of personal desire for recognition. And it likely does play a large role. But while individualism versus collectivism is a useful frame, cultures of course are not binary constructs. To parse the nuances further, Geert Hofstede, a Dutch researcher who is considered the pioneer in the field, has often viewed individualism/collectivism as just one of five evaluative categories. Alternatively, numerous researchers cross the individualism/collectivism scale with a horizontal and vertical metric, creating four cultural orientations.

Michelle Nelson, a psychologist at the University of Illinois who specializes in intracultural and international consumer behavior, conducted a study comparing individualism and achievement values in the United States and Denmark. "In a Vertical Individualist culture such as the US—people are rewarded for achievement in a hierarchy, for showing off, for being rich and famous—we have quite a divide between rich and poor. Conversely, in a Horizontal Individualist culture such as Denmark—people are rewarded equally (their socio-economic/tax system is part of this) and do not wish to stand out in the hierarchy," she explained to me. "Modesty is the ingrained social norm . . . in Sweden and Denmark." Further, she suggested that it may be the case that "it is not 'appropriate' to show off or receive recognition in Scandinavian cultures."

With the exception of Argentina, which falls in the middle of the individualism/collectivism rankings, Latin America is largely composed of highly collectivist cultures. Yet status is a prominent feature within these societies. It's not for nothing that "Costco in Mexico sells Burberry bags!" Rossana Johnston, a leadership development coach with an expertise on Latin America, noted to me. Johnston, who travels throughout Latin America consulting for transnational corporations with offices there, told me that from her experience "team building is very difficult in Latin America [though] people may assume the opposite because of its collectivist reputation." Johnston explains the difficulty as part of a culture of vulnerability, where people feel the need to stand out as a "survival mechanism." To that point, much of Latin America scores very high on one of Geert Hofstede's scales, "uncertainty avoidance," where members of the culture "feel threatened by ambiguous or unknown situations." So while many of our neighbors to the south apparently share our propensity for recognition-seeking, the desire may emanate more from a place of protection of one's status, rather than an individualistic impulse as it largely does in the United States.

Like Latin America, Russia ranks as a highly collectivist culture and even higher on the uncertainty avoidance scale. Also, Russians are quite conscious of status, which Hofstede attributes to a great imbalance of power among the populace. Interestingly, though, Russia has a low score on the "masculinity/femininity" scale, another primary Hofstede category. "The fundamental issue here is what motivates people, wanting to be the best (masculine) or liking what you do (feminine)" is how the Hofstede Centre, his affiliated organization, puts it. Here is where things tie in to our questions about invisibility. The Centre states: "Russia's relatively low score of 36 [on the masculinity scale] may surprise with regard to its preference for status symbols, but . . . at second glance one can see that Russians at the workplace as well as when meeting a stranger rather understate their personal achievements, contributions, or capacities. They talk modestly about themselves and scientists, researchers, or doctors are most often expected to live on a very modest standard of living." Hofstede's analysis supported the positions of Tatyana Fertelmeyster, an intercultural and communication consultant for nonprofits and multinational corporations like Ernst & Young and Boeing, who hire her for her expertise on Russian culture, with whom I had spoken prior to reviewing the Hofstede data. "Self-promotion and self-advocacy is normative for the U.S. mainstream," she told me. Whereas "in general, Russians don't self-promote." She noted that in America employees often won't wait for a formal review to talk with their boss to tell him or her what they are doing and what they've accomplished, but in Russia that behavior would be atypical.

"In Russia you have lots of people who are highly skilled but who are quite invisible, known by their colleagues but not by the culture at large," she told me. Some of Russia's complexity, and its apparent respect for invisible work, can be linked with its Communist past, and its lingering effects. The Hero of Socialist Labor was an honorary medal awarded to workers who helped further Soviet agriculture, industry, science, or other fields of endeavor. More than twenty thousand generally unseen, skilled workers received the award during the Soviet era, until it was discontinued in 1991. In 2013 the award was reinstated by Vladimir Putin, though "Socialist" has been removed from the title.

A different type of hero worship, where only the most successful and already visible are lauded, is at play in the United States, suggests Uichol Kim, the psychologist at Inha University in Korea, who also consults with multinational corporations such as BASF on team-building and innovation. He told me that unlike the Asian culture and business environment where teamwork and harmony are key, in the United States "people emphasize leadership and individualized mentoring since the individual is so visible." This is part of a culture of "hero worship," he said, noting that everyone knows who Steve Jobs was, but it's doubtful you could name the CEO of Samsung. Kim's assertion of a culture of hero worship, with little question, explains part of what may drive so many in the United States toward wanting recognition.

"It's likely that people learn to desire that which is valued in their culture and that this preference is internalized," Sharon Shavitt, a psychologist also at the University of Illinois, who researches cross-cultural value judgments, told me. "This would be especially the case in collectivistic societies and contexts where paying attention to norms (what do others want?) is very important," she said. Seemingly, part of people's desire for recognition in our culture is simply a function of this attitude being the norm, not because this innately brings happiness. (The converse, of course, in collectivist cultures is also true, which is why, again, I argue for a balance between these attitudes.) This point runs in tandem with research by Ed Diener, also a psychologist at Illinois, who studies cultural influences on subjective well-being, which shows "people are more satisfied if they have the characteristics valued in their culture," he told me. In other words, generally, people want to fit in, even if, like in America, fitting in means trying to show how much of an individual you are. (A good degree of our advertising is geared toward this seeming paradox, the core message often being: Buy this product that's being sold to millions of others to show how unique you are!) For Invisibles who call America (and other vertically oriented individualistic societies like the U.K.) home, because their traits are not the norm there, this makes their approach to work and high level of fulfillment all the more impressive.

ARCHITECTURE AS INDICATOR

Is the world increasingly headed toward an American-style individualist mind-set, where people crave recognition? There is, of course, no definitive answer to this question. But if we return to Dennis Poon's specialty of skyscrapers for a moment, their production may offer a compelling view on the matter. America, and in particular New York City, was reaching toward its apex of world influence at the same time it was erecting the tallest buildings in the world. The Woolworth, Chrysler, and Empire State buildings were completed in 1913, 1930, and 1931, respectively, the latter two shortly before World War II, which, arguably, thereafter established the United States as a superpower. These buildings' height and grandeur can be seen as classic architectural examples of recognition-seeking on a national level. While the United States is still building supertalls like the new One World Trade Center, now cities like Kuala Lumpur, Dubai, and Shanghai, representing emerging economies, are erecting the tallest buildings on the globe. They are structural shout-outs to the world—Notice us! We're here! Ironically, the financial wisdom of these buildings is often dubious, even though they function as status markers to "advertise and signal economic strength," as Jason Barr, an economics professor at Rutgers University whose work focuses on the economics of skyscrapers, noted in a paper. Barr shared with me some current research still underway comparing skyscraper heights and economics on an international scale. He found that "Asian countries seem to build much taller, on average, than we would expect, given their populations and economies. This is especially true for Arab and Southeast Asian countries." If you want to follow where a culture's attitudes about recognition may be headed, and in Asia's circumstance, where perhaps some traditional values toward downplaying recognition are eroding, these phallic attention-getters may offer a good clue.

A conversation I had with Paul French, a widely published analyst of Chinese culture, who formerly was the chief China market strategist for Mintel, a global market research firm, supports the notion that China is heading in this direction. He told me that "sadly" he thinks the "days of China appreciating craftsmanship, diligence, attention to detail, and skill are long gone." Pre-1949, he said, "China was then a land of guilds and unions and apprenticeships, the essential transmission belts of skill that ensure a new generation of skilled work and an appreciation for it." But now "China is behind the curve in terms of developing a reappreciation for such things." When we talked about Dennis Poon and the Shanghai Tower, French agreed that "it is not the structural engineers but the 'starchitects' that get the media and praise [there] just as elsewhere now." There is a lack of training and apprenticeship today, he said, combined "with three decades of consumerism at its lowest and most naked," reflecting a change in the Chinese culture. He pointed to the excellent *New Yorker* piece by Evan Osnos on the recent high-speed rail tragedy that occurred in China as a result of corruption and poor craftsmanship. In 1995, China represented just 2 percent of the world's luxury good consumers, yet today accounts for 25 percent—it's not outlandish to draw a connection between this consumerist explosion and revised attitudes about recognition. As a citizenry become more involved with appearances and status it stands to reason they may also become more concerned with gaining attention for themselves and their work.

If indeed much of the world is moving toward an American ethos of emphasizing extrinsic values—which focus on things like external rewards and praise by others, values shown to have a negative correlation with well-being—this could be worrisome for broad-scale personal fulfillment. Tim Kasser, the psychologist at Knox College quoted earlier in the book, who studies materialism and values, co-authored a 2007 article that stated "two studies have now provided evidence" suggesting that in societies that mirror "American Corporate Capitalism . . . citizens are more focused on power values, values which share a good deal with Extrinsic values." While China (and others') economic policy is of course different from that of the United States, the similarity I'm highlighting is that as they trend toward consumerist, materialism-based societies, evidence suggests they may also mirror our extrinsic value structure. As Kasser told me, "To the extent that the extrinsic values are adopted and the intrinsic ones are crowded out, that would be the implication."

With all of that said, it's worth emphasizing again that drawing attention to ourselves isn't inherently bad. In fact, as I argue in the book's overview, this trait has been a critical part of America's success. What I suggest, however, is that the tonal balance between this brashness and a more reserved temperament—what I called our American Swing—that served our culture so well is, in recent years, increasingly tipping toward the former trait. Some other societies are arguably skewed unhealthily toward the latter. We can learn from them, though, by pulling the successful elements of their more collectivist and horizontal attitudes while maintaining our unique noise. If we can do that we can get back on course, once again knifing straight ahead through the water. Otherwise we're merely a bunch of oars splashing manically off the side of the boat, not going anywhere.

11.

CONCLUSION

Inspiration for Work and for Life

It's mid-century in New York City. A bright, fawning ingénue charms her way into her theatrical idol's life and inner circle. Before long she's become the idol's understudy in her hit play. But this is just a temporary step for Eve Harrington as she schemes toward her ultimate goal, taking over the lead. "I think *All About Eve* has given many people the wrong impression," Deirdre Madigan, an actor who has performed on and off Broadway for more than twenty-five years, told me, referring to the famed movie. "As understudies we don't want someone's job. Our job is to be prepared to step in and seamlessly become a part of the whole." While, she added, "no actor I know *wants* to be an understudy, I don't act to be the center of attention. I need to tell a story. I want to find a character, and develop it, and make it my own."

Remarkably, in a field so strongly associated with people ravenous for recognition or fame, numerous veterans of the stage I spoke with talked about the satisfaction that can be derived from simply being a part of a production, even in the unseen role of the understudy. While noting that being a "benchwarmer" isn't his first choice, Pete Bradbury, who has appeared extensively on and off Broadway and counts a number of TV shows, including *Boardwalk Empire*, among his credits, told me, "the opportunity to immerse yourself in rich material, no matter the circumstances, is tremendously rewarding. It offers the possibility to improve as an artist/craftsman." Tony Ward, a graduate of Yale School of Drama, who has appeared on and off Broadway, and has had roles on TV shows like *Law & Order* and the NBC series *Smash*, noted that "stage actors are language driven. We thrill to be inside worlds dominated by language and thought," and working "inside a worthy text," even as an understudy, "is satisfying."

Ray Virta, an award-winning actor and director, who has appeared in eleven Broadway productions and teaches at the American Musical and Dramatic Academy in New York, talked with me about the rewards of the unique challenges of understudy work. "Understudying calls for a process unlike anything that is taught in school," he said. "At its most basic, you must imagine yourself the theatrical equivalent of an engineer; your assignment is akin to reverse-engineering an iPod. Pull apart a working model (the original actor's performance), break it down into the components, and manufacture a reasonable facsimile." He also explained, "Since product (an actual performance) is tantalizing yet beyond your hope, you must relish the process. And part of the process is analysis. With great works of art, for example the Tom Stoppard plays I have been privileged to be part of, the challenges demand complete understanding and command. They demand engagement. And even as an understudy, they reward engagement. Think of a Talmudic scholar, sitting alone in a garret, picking apart a text. The challenge is to come to an understanding." Beyond connecting with the text, understudying also provides the opportunity to learn from others. "I've covered Frank Langella [the renowned stage and film actor] twice," Virta said, "and I can assure you that his effortless command and power are not only joyous to watch but worthy of study."

In addition to the artistic rewards there are always practical concerns to consider as well. "Credits are meaningful to out-of-town theatres," Tony Ward told me. "They're keen to put the most capable actors in their shows. If they have a Broadway imprimatur, however it was earned, all the better." In other words, Ward recognizes that even if a gig isn't his first choice, it can lead to other opportunities. In any field, the more you work, even if the role is essentially invisible, the more you open yourself to unforeseen opportunity.

Several of the actors I spoke with talked about the skill of managing their emotions and ego when in the invisible role. Madigan said she turned down a job offer as an understudy for a lead role she initially had auditioned for but didn't get because she feared it would be too hard not to "become bitter." Virta explained, "It takes a certain temperament to be a successful understudy. You have to embrace your role as an insurance policy that is only acknowledged or appreciated by the audience when the unthinkable occurs. It's not for the faint of heart."

Being invisible requires a certain toughness. But the need for that toughness fades when you seek satisfaction in the work itself, and relish your own growth in the process. And like all Invisibles, Ward has an appreciation for the rewards of a collectivist mind-set. "In the case of exceptional productions with a high level of talent from all collaborators," he told me, "some hay can be made about the subjugation of self to a larger good."

I chose to start this chapter with these insights from actors because there isn't a field of work I could imagine more aligned with recognition and attention than theirs. If *these* people can find fulfillment while not being onstage, then we all can find much to embrace about invisibility. It's not that the goal is to be unseen, or specifically to work in an invisible field. It's that visibility or invisibility, ultimately, is not the frame within which to view our work nor the metric for how to value ourselves. Like these veteran actors, unless you are very talented *and* very fortunate, much of your career will likely not be spent in the lead. And we'd all do well to appreciate, savor even, just being a part of the endeavor. Landing the starring role should rightly be a triumph, but it needn't be your only joy. "Right now I am in understudy heaven," Madigan told me. "I have a vital job in a fantastic production of a tremendous play. When I think about it, I am pretty lucky."

We've seen the satisfaction that the Invisible approach to work can bring. Yet the traits these professionals exhibit seem so embedded in their character that one can lose sight of the fact that in many circumstances an Invisible is made, not born. Recall the training that Marc Levitt, the graphic designer, underwent while in design school. He wasn't fastidious by nature, but through repeating exercises that encouraged concentration on minutiae and process, like drawing the same four letters over and over, he developed the trait over time. David Apel spent years in the lab building his scientific knowledge, where he was taught to pay attention to the finest details of the raw materials being analyzed. Later, as a perfumer, he utilized that devotion to detail in his creative work, where he crafts formulas, sometimes composed of hundreds of ingredients, requiring the utmost precision. It's clear that meticulousness, one of the Invisibles' core traits, can be learned.

But what about the traits that can be considered less as a skill and more as values—relishing responsibility, and most important, an ambivalence, even indifference toward recognition? Can they be learned? Even predating our Bronze Age pal Homer and his kleos-seeking soldiers, narrative (fictional or factual) has been employed as a means to instill values and certain mind-sets. Simply through reading the Invisibles' stories, and witnessing their evident successes and fulfillment, we can internalize the power of their values and advance our own embodiment of them. I would call this the osmosis option. But after having spent so much time with and thinking about Invisibles I've come to realize that beyond the Three Traits these disparate professionals share is one other quality in common. And, in some sense, embodying it encapsulates everything else. A gratifying life seems to correlate strongly with following these three words: Be more curious.

Let me explain.

I am not intrinsically a handy person. Growing up, I never bothered to fix things. It was too intimidating. If something broke my instinct was to throw it out. Then, in my twenties, on a whim I bought a thirty-year-old MGB, a British roadster by a brand they don't even sell in the States anymore. They're gorgeous cars and a lot of fun, but stuff in them breaks with distressing regularity. Unless you singlehandedly want to fund an addition on your mechanic's house, you've got to figure out how to do some of the maintenance on your own. While I am far from competent under the hood, the little fixes I learned how to do always provided me with enormous satisfaction (almost comically out of proportion to the complexity of the completed task).

Spending time with Plank, I marveled at his ability and courage to take apart those effects pedals and wireless transmitters, fixing or modifying them for his purposes. It was easy to see the appeal for him. I'll never be a born tinkerer like Plank, but I try to have that take-it-apart attitude in what I do as a writer. I want to know how things work, and I'll keep digging until I figure something out. Every Invisible I interviewed and met with had an enormous reserve of knowledge they had built up about their professions, yet they all still had a palpable desire to keep learning even while at the top of their fields. Spending time with these excellent yet unknown workers, one realizes that, to a good degree, what fuels their embodiment of the Three Traits is curiosity. *They want to learn.* They work more, and they dig deeper even when they don't have to. Because here's the key: When you care about how things work, about the process, and you make the effort to learn the details and implement that knowledge—Giulia Wilkins Ary's joy in studying before the Security Council meetings, Peter Stumpf not just adjusting the piano to spec but personalizing every regulation according to the style of the music and the pianist playing it, Robert Elswit's ever-growing encyclopedic knowledge of his craft—you're less inclined to need the reward of having that work recognized, because the work itself has already rewarded you. In this way, curiosity is directly linked to empowerment (and, as innumerable psychological studies and common sense suggest, empowerment correlates with satisfaction).

Encouragingly, there may be some signs of a burgeoning trend toward curiosity and empowerment. Several new companies, like Code Academy, that teach "regular" people how to write basic computer code are beginning to gain traction. While they're positioned as a means for people to gain employment skills, they also, at a base level, tap into the curiosity-empowerment dynamic. For many of us, so much of our lives are spent online yet we have no idea how that environment is built. Douglas Rushkoff, a media theorist, spoke of this disconnect in his book *Program or Be Programmed*. As he wrote in a related piece for CNN: "It took a few centuries after the invention of text for regular people to learn how to read and write . . . [Today] almost no one still questions the idea that teaching kids to read is a good thing, or that basic literacy makes us more likely to create value for ourselves or our employers." Just as our world once was dominated by print, much of it is now dominated by the online world of apps and networks yet "desperately few of us understand how they work," he argued. I'm not advocating for everyone to become professional programmers. Rather, if we learn a little about how the world—in this instance, the online world—we operate in every day gets created, if we're a little more curious about how it works, we become active rather than passive participants. Or as Rushkoff said, users rather than the used. What Invisibles intuit is that fulfillment is directly descended from engagement.

Mike Rowe, the host of the long-running reality show *Dirty Jobs*, which featured him doing often obscure "blue collar" dirty jobs, started the MikeRoweWorks Foundation which promotes education toward learning skilled trades. While superficially some of these jobs, such as electrician, are quite visible, Rowe argues most of these behind-the-scenes trades—certainly including some of the types of tradesmen on Robert Elswit's film sets and Dennis Poon's buildings—are thought of today as not respectable careers, and for all intents and purposes are indeed invisible for the lack of stature they now hold in our society. The original sin Rowe references is a poster in his high school guidance counselor's office that read "Work Smart, Not Hard," erroneously deriding tradeswork as unrewarding. Rowe's revised motto is "Work Smart *and* Hard." He points to the economic opportunity of the work, citing an astounding 3 million unfilled jobs for skilled labor in the country. But he also stresses the satisfaction of hard work and of understanding how things are made. As he wrote on the foundation's site, "the way a thing gets made is often more interesting than the thing itself." Ultimately, being an Invisible doesn't even depend on whether your work is visible or not, whether you wear a suit or coveralls. It's about a state of mind—do you rely on what others think about you and your work for your self-worth or not? If you don't, you've become liberated from the desire for recognition.

Until more people are liberated, however, the cultural norm of seeking recognition, for personal and business reward, continues to reign. In an article in *Wired* magazine on the growth of microcelebrity, a term connoting when one is "extremely well known" to a relatively small number of people or fans, Theresa Senft, a media studies professor at NYU, whom it's believed coined the term, said, "people are using the same techniques employed on Madison Avenue to manage their personal lives." Not surprisingly, there has been the inevitable wave of articles and consultancies on how to commodify your microcelebrity, with titles like "Maximizing Microcelebrity: Ideas on Turning Popularity into Profits." To give a sense of the metastasizing reach of this ideology, that article title I just quoted is the title of a Facebook post not by a business guru or consulting firm, but, somewhat bizarrely, by an online record-keeping company. It's a worrisome corollary to the oft-cited John D. Rockefeller story about how he knew it was time to get out of the market when his shoeshine boy gave him a stock tip. America—it's time to dial back the volume. As prescient as he was, Warhol's proclamation of a universal fifteen minutes of fame (or its recent variation that everyone will be famous to fifteen people) should not be taken as a raison d'être.

As I've argued, economically we are losing out by no longer valuing critical yet unflashy jobs. And psychologically, the more we view our lives as brands to be commodified, the more disconnected from ourselves and one another we become. It's clear we are increasingly in need of a cultural and personal corrective away from this ethos of attention. The good news is there is a collective of people working silently among us, whose work is not flashy but is critical, and whose lack of need for recognition has led them to business success and personal fulfillment, whom we can follow toward more prosperous, healthier, and grounded lives. They are the Invisibles.

What I love about Invisibles is that their qualities are both relatable and aspirational. Just about all of us, at least in certain aspects of our lives, can identify with feeling invisible, of not gaining recognition for tasks we've toiled on. And yet Invisibles give us much to look up to. That their traits run counter to the prevailing culture makes Invisibles all the more admirable. Any reader of self-help books or just a vaguely culturally aware member of our society knows the pop-psych wisdom that true happiness comes from within. What better embodiment of this philosophy than someone who derives satisfaction from his work, not from an external acknowledgment for it?

The Invisibles' values and ways of being not only advance economic and societal interests, they advance our personal well-being. Learning to embrace responsibility is daunting but ultimately empowering. Striving to work harder and be more meticulous at tasks we value or enjoy offers rewards that cannot be rivaled by accepting just "good enough." Having a silent pride in one's work itself rather than seeking outward recognition is a long-established path to true gratification. It takes courage and effort to pursue the traits of the Invisibles, and I've been humbled by the people I've met who practice and live them in their jobs every day.

When the good folks at Portfolio made an offer to publish this book I was elated. I'd spent the better part of my adult life working in various creative endeavors, and, while I'd had some successes, much of it was a struggle. This was a high point. I'd dreamed of making that victorious call passing the news to my family and friends. Now I was living that moment, and receiving their congratulations felt great. But after a brief spell I strangely didn't feel all that different from how I had felt before. I kept wondering, Why am I still anxious? Why don't I feel happier? Nevertheless, spurred by ambition and fear, I got to work. Though I had a detailed book proposal to work from, I was spending nearly all of my time conceptualizing the shape and scope of the thing. It was hard going. During this phase I'd occasionally bump into an acquaintance or meet someone new and tell them of my good fortune. Then I'd bask in the glow of their wonderment at my awesomeness, feeling pretty high for about five seconds. And then I'd return to wondering, Why aren't I happier?

As time passed, I got deeper into the work on the book. I was beyond conceptualizing, now I was really in *the work*—interviewing people, digging into research, talking with scholars, crystallizing core ideas. I slowly began to feel a little different. I still was my anxious self but at the end of long days a certain satisfaction eased or at least competed with those negative feelings. One afternoon I finally dug into a massive transcript of an interview I had conducted. It was 28,000 words, which is about 90 pages, and I approached it with dread. How would I make sense of it all and weave the threads of a coherent story? I just knew it was going to suck. But something odd happened. After burying myself in it all day, as I walked home in the dark, alone with the soft metronomic tap of my shoes on the sidewalk, the only sound on the otherwise silent, sleeping block, I felt . . . great. Immersed in this person's world, and immersed in my own world of work, time had slipped away from me that afternoon. And, my pace halting mid-stride, I realized an amazing moment of convergence: Hey!, the message of this book I'm writing is the very thing that's making me feel fulfilled. The work itself was making me feel far better than whatever ephemeral ego trip I got from a third-person view of myself as a guy with a book deal. Praise can be hard to come by and fleeting when you do get it but no one can take away pride from, and engagement in, hard work. Like my Invisible subjects, I realized the value of my work, not the volume of my praise, brought me, and still does now, fulfillment. I want recognition, I want success—please, buy five more copies of this book!—but, in the end, what sustains me, what keeps that bogeyman of anxiety at bay, is the work itself.

Let's finish where we began, with some Led Zeppelin. As everyone knows, the archetypal rock quartet has a lead singer and guitar player out front, and a bassist and drummer in the back laying the foundation. Yet too many of us today want to be Robert Plant and Jimmy Page, and not enough are interested in being John Paul Jones (if you're rusty on your classic rock trivia, Jones was Zeppelin's bass player). A band doesn't work without the bass and drums, and a successful society—economically, culturally—needs a foundation as well. A world of front men is just a lot of noise. (And John Paul Jones is pretty awesome.)

AFTERWORD TO THE PAPERBACK EDITION

On June 13, 2014, at 5:30 in the morning, I walked into the deserted lobby of TV station CNBC, in Englewood Cliffs, NJ. A lone security guard waved me through to the studio complex behind him. Just under an hour later I was live on air as a featured guest on *Squawk Box*, the channel's early morning finance and news program, talking about *Invisibles*.

After my segment finished, a stagehand unclipped my lapel microphone and ushered me from the set. "Great job," he said, guiding me gently by the arm. "But, listen, you need to head to the audio suite immediately. The audio engineer needs to speak with you."

"What?" My body tensed. "Is everything OK?"

"You need to go back there and speak with him," he repeated in a measured tone, and pointed the way.

I began to feel sick as I wandered beyond rows of still empty desks in the newsroom toward a distant hallway.

After two solid years of work, it was the day after the book came out and my first TV appearance. Did my mic not work properly? Did they scrub the segment and cut to commercial without me knowing? Expectations were high for the book and this was the first major media coverage. I had been looking forward to a radio interview that afternoon but my spirits were quickly deflating. I knew the show would hardly determine the book's fate, but it was its introduction to a wide audience and I couldn't help but be a little irrational. It was barely dawn as my anxieties about the book's prospects began imploding on my still sleepy brain.

Reaching the end of a long hallway I came upon a windowless room. A man sat with his back to me, alone, facing a bank of computer monitors and blinking audio equipment. "Hello?" I ventured, tentatively.

The man spun around wearing a warm grin. "I just wanted to say thank you. *I'm* an Invisible!" We chatted for no longer than a minute or two, but when I left him my confidence and morale were restored. "No one here, or any of the viewers, thinks about the work I do," he said. "It's only if something goes wrong that I'm thought of at all. But I love what I do, and I don't mind not getting any recognition. I'm happy back here in my sanctum," he motioned to the wall of equipment behind him. "But it was really great to hear you talk about the value of the work professionals like me do."

My encounter with the audio engineer was the first of many such experiences as I made the rounds among radio and TV shows. The hair and makeup women, the cameramen, all the way to the segment producers who booked me, professionals at every rung of the ladder approached me, often sotto voce: "Thank you—that's me." More than one radio show engineer, working the board and my live mic from the other side of the glass, gave me a thumbs-up at some point during my interviews when they realized I was describing their role.

Of course, not everyone behind the scenes is happy there. But the people I encountered, many of whom were working at nationally broadcast shows, some with audiences in the millions—that is, they were at the top of their respective fields—by and large struck me as being satisfied with their jobs. Some may suggest that this is a chicken-or-egg phenomenon, that perhaps they're fulfilled *because* they're successful. But from the extensive time I spent with the featured Invisibles in this book, I know that largely it's the converse. They became successful because they're engaged with their work and spent the bulk of their personal resources on doing excellent work, not on seeking attention for themselves. You can be both very ambitious and not desire your name shouted from the rooftops.

Though the Invisibles' traits do correlate with high levels of achievement, this doesn't have to be, or perhaps shouldn't be, about getting to the top. In fact, we may want to redefine what the top is. Or, as I asked in the beginning of the book: How do you define success?

ACKNOWLEDGMENTS

There was an army of Invisibles behind this book, and leading the professional behind-the-scenes brigade is my agent, Eric Lupfer, at WME. It's impossible for me to overstate Eric's importance in making this book happen. Eric believed in me and this book from its genesis and it was through his intellect, wise consult, and industry savvy that I crafted an effective proposal to sell the book, and more so, improved the book during the writing and publishing process. Eric, I am forever grateful to you for your support. I also want to thank Bill Clegg at WME for his initial interest and work on my behalf. His early excitement was a critical spark for this project.

My gracious editor, Maria Gagliano, is owed a huge debt for her thoughtful suggestions and comments which helped shape and improve this book. In addition to Maria I'd like to thank the entire team at Portfolio, especially Adrian Zackheim for believing in this book, Will Weisser, Rachel Moore, Bria Sandford, Justin Hargett, and Kathy Daneman, and to Brooke Carey who helped get this book off the ground.

J. J. Gould and Eleanor Barkhorn at *The Atlantic* deserve special acknowledgment. J. J. was my first point of contact at *The Atlantic* and I'm grateful to him for connecting me with Eleanor, who then edited several of my pieces, including "What Do Fact-Checkers and Anesthesiologists Have in Common," the article that inspired this book.

I'm grateful to Dave Yoo who has been a reader, editor, and mentor to me for many years as I've slowly progressed as a writer. Dave, you been an invaluable source of advice on both the mechanics and business of writing. The other Dave I'm eager to thank is David Levithan, who helped me navigate the waters of publishing.

A thanks to my friends at the Brooklyn Writers Space, especially Corey Mead and Michael Shein, who were great sounding boards all through the writing process; Lara Shapiro; and Kate Cortesi for her generous feedback along the way.

A special shout out to the Shivs—Aaron, Darren, Marc, Matt, and Jesse—for their friendship. And to Scott Moshen, Lisa Jane Persky, Pamela Ryckman, Jason Corlis, and Brian Gresko.

I am grateful beyond what can be expressed here in this space to the featured Invisibles in this book—Jim Harding, David Apel, Giulia Wilkins Ary, Dennis Poon, Robert Elswit, Pete Clements, and Peter Stumpf. You were incredibly generous to let me into your worlds, and my readers and I are indebted to you. I never could have imagined the extraordinary amount I was going to learn about your work, be inspired by you, and, plainly, how much fun it would be spending time with you. If I had more lives and my druthers I'd write a full book about each of you and your work. It was a privilege to get to know each of you.

Behind each of the featured Invisibles there are of course more Invisibles. I'm thankful to Jorge Cortes at Hartsfield-Jackson; Cindy in the lab at Symrise; Hossam Fahr, Kathryn Young, and Myriam at the UN Interpretation Service; James Kent at Thornton Tomasetti; Grant Illes and Wayne Fitterman at United Talent; Brain Message at ATC Management and Julie Calland; Julie Stumpf for her scheduling help and for showing me the great view from the top of the incline, and The Pittsburgh Symphony Orchestra staff, in particular, Sonja Winkler.

A special thanks go to my sister, Susan, for her unfailing enthusiasm for all of my creative endeavors over the years; and to my parents, Anne and Barry, who gave me the means to live and think freely to pursue a path I find rewarding and meaningful.

Through their generous correspondence or interviews, the following people contributed critical information, quotes, and/or research material for this book:

Simon Zagorski-Thomas and Aaron Liu-Rosenbaum for providing so much detailed, historical, technical information about early rock recording techniques; Jesse Barber; Julia Payne; Deborah Rivera; James Galbraith; Francesca Viano; Jasper van den Broek;

Sonja Lyubomirsky; Leroy Huizenga; Ellen Lupton; Martin Moeller; Barry Lewis; Matthew Shepatin; Daniel Paisner; Stephen Sauer. A special thank you to Cynthia Cathcart at the CondéNast library for helping me track down that old *Vogue* issue. Dirk Bekkering for insights into architecture and Chinese culture. Dan Winey and Monica Schaffer at Gensler, Derek Kelly at RWDI, Cameron Anderson, Daniel Safarik, Robb Willer, Rob Abrams, Barry Olsen, Janet Nicol, María Teresa Bajo Molina, Robert Thompson, Alice Marwick, Paul Lukas, John Thorne, Peter Magowan, Jean Twenge, Joel Keller, Chris Baraniuk, Danah Boyd, Douglas Rushkoff, Sean Mount. Adam Grant, I'm so grateful for our correspondence. You are a giver of the first order. Richard Ryan, Michael Mohr, Silke Zimmermann, Claude Fernet, Tim Kasser, Marcia Lausen, Qi Wang, Uichol Kim, Shigehiro Oishi, Laura Miller, Michelle Nelson, Rossana Johnston, Tatyana Fertelmeyster, Sharon Shavitt, Ed Diener, Jason Barr, Paul French. Tony Ward, I'm grateful for your thoughtful conversation and insights, which led me to include actors Deirdre Madigan, Pete Bradbury, and Ray Virta in the book.

Finally, a special thanks to Invisibles Peter Canby, Marc Levitt, Herbert Seevinck, Albert Scarmato, Joseph Meltzer, and Pam Vu, for their initial interviews and repeated correspondence.

Of all the Invisibles behind this book, none were more critical than my wife, Doreen. She is my first editor, brainstormer, and most of all, supporter in my work and in life. Including a perfumer and a UN interpreter as major profiles in the book were both Doreen's suggestions. Of the countless late nights, weekends, and even vacation days when I was absent from the family toiling away under deadline, she never once complained or made me feel guilty (I had that emotion wrapped up on my own). Thanks babe, you helped make many of the challenges of this undertaking manageable. I'm honored to have you as my partner. Zev and Eliana, when you're older and you read this book I hope you are able to absorb some of the values it extols and find work that is meaningful to you.

NOTES

INTRODUCTION

2 **"arguably one of the most significant":** Aaron Liu-Rosenbaum, "The Meaning in the Mix: Tracing a Sonic Narrative in 'When the Levee Breaks,'" *Journal in the Art of Record Production*, November 2012. If your interest is piqued and you want to dig deeper, and I mean much deeper, Liu-Rosenbaum's near-ten-thousand-word exploration of the song—including charts, song maps, and sound samples—is stunningly extensive.

AMERICAN SWING

11 **"demand for technical workers":** "Problems and Solutions. We Asked HR Executives: What's Your Biggest Challenge?," Emily Glazer, *Wall Street Journal*, October 24, 2011.

11 **"odds are there are complete strangers":** Clive Thompson, "Clive Thompson on the Age of the Microcelebrity," *Wired*, November 27, 2007.

11 **"What is facebook":** Peter Stromberg, "Sex, Drugs & Boredom," *Psychology Today*, May 28, 2010.

11 **"artisanal instinct or workmanship":** Gilles Dostaler, article in *Alternatives Economiques*, June 2003.

CHAPTER 1

21 **"extrinsic" motivators:** Selfdeterminationtheory.org/theory

21 **To pick one oft-cited experiment:** This experiment has been written about in numerous places, perhaps most notably in Daniel Pink's, *Drive: The Surprising Truth About What Motivates Us* (Riverhead, 2009), 41, 59.

21 **research has shown that:** Grouzet et al., "The Structure of Goal Contents Across 15 Cultures," *Journal of Personality and Social Psychology*, 2005.

23 Car Rental Image is part of a 2003 wayfinding study prepared for Pearson International Airport by Human Factors North and Entro Communications.

26 **"Eudaimonic theories of well-being"**: Michael Steger et al., "Being Good by Doing Good: Daily Eudaimonic Activity and Well-being," *Journal of Research in Personality*, February 2008.

27 **"Look, you know,"**: Harvey Kubernik, "Engineer Andy Johns Discusses the Making of the Rolling Stones' 'Exile on Main Street,'" *Goldmine*, May 8, 2010.

30 **Neurath "argued that"**: Rayan Abdullah and Roger Hubner, *Pictograms, Icons and Signs* (Thames & Hudson, 2006), 19. The paragraph on pictogram history was derived from multiple sources, but predominantly from this text.

35 **Because people tend to flow**: Malcolm Gladwell, "The Terrazzo Jungle," *The New Yorker*, March 15, 2004.

38 **"Who are you running from?"**: Bill Rodgers and Matthew Shepatin, *Marathon Man* (Thomas Dunne Books, 2013), 118, 119, 285.

CHAPTER 2

43 **fragrance houses like Symrise**: Full disclosure: I was introduced to Apel by my wife, who also works at Symrise.

52 **"Hire the most"**: http://www.bretlsimmons.com/2011-04/leadership-traits-and-behaviors-four-evidence-based-suggestions/

52 **pink frosting**: Catherine Piercy, "Finding My Nose," *Vogue*, December 2006.

CHAPTER 3

61 **presentation he gave about the Tower**: "Gensler's Shanghai Tower: Design Development of China's Tallest Tower," video on Skyscraper.org, courtesy of the Asia Society.

62 **"ambitious strategy"**: Ibid.

66 **"forms the stability system"**: "China Central Television Headquarters construction reaches new milestone as façade is completed," *E-architect*, August 6, 2008, http://www.e-architect.co.uk/beijing/central-china-tv

66 **"an engineer is only a rudimentary"**: Interview on *Omnibus* TV Show, c. 1950s.

66 **he went ballistic:** Franklin Toker, *Fallingwater Rising: Frank Lloyd Wright, E. J. Kaufmann, and America's Most Extraordinary House* (Knopf, 2003). Letter from Wright to the client where he wrote, ". . . if I haven't your confidence—to hell with the whole thing."

66 **"the building would have collapsed":** Matthew L.Wald, "Rescuing a World-Famous but Fragile House," *The New York Times*, September 2, 2001.

67 **names are but a footnote:** (In this case it's an endnote!) There were several different engineers on the project in varying capacities and at varying stages, but the ones credited with calling for the reinforcement of the beams is the firm Metzger-Richardson.

81 **"confidence in the American economy":** President Bush's address to the joint session of Congress shortly after 9/11. This line later euphemistically (though often erroneously presented as the actual quote) was referred to as a directive to "go shopping."

82 **doesn't decrease trolling:** Gregory Ferenstein, "Surprisingly Good Evidence That Real Name Policies Fail to Improve Comments," *TechCrunch*, July 29, 2012, http://techcrunch.com/2012/07/29/surprisingly-good-evidence-that-real-name-policies-fail-to-improve-comments/

CHAPTER 4

86 **air traffic controllers:** Ingrid Kurz, "Psychological Stress During Simultaneous Interpreting: A Comparison of Experts and Novices," *The Interpreters' Newsletter*, 2003.

87 **One study showed:** Loraine Obler, "Conference Interpreting as Extreme Language Use," *International Journal of Bilingualism*, 2012.

88 **harder to interpret:** J. O. Rinne et al., "The Translating Brain: Cerebral Activation Patterns During Simultaneous Interpreting," *Neuroscience Letters*, November 17, 2000.

89 **"A simultaneous interpreter":** Nikola Krastev, "UN Interpreters Make Sure Nothing Is Lost in Translation," *Radio Free Europe Radio Liberty*, March 30, 2010.

95 **"Levels of mental and physical":** Ingrid Kurz, "Psychological Stress During Simultaneous Interpreting: A Comparison of Experts and Novices," *The Interpreters' Newsletter*, 2003.

96 **"Simultaneous interpreting is a highly complex":** J. Tommola and J. Hyona, "Mental Load in Listening, Speech Shadowing and

Simultaneous Interpreting: A Pupillometric Study," *Foreign Language Comprehension and Production*, 1990.

98 **"They have to be addicted"**: Junaid Ahmed, "How Interpreters at the UN Get The Message Across," *BBC News*, September 21, 2010.

98 **"the ego falls away"**: John Geirland, "Go with the Flow," *Wired*, September 1996.

98 **"intense feelings of enjoyment"**: Mihaly Csíkszentmihályi, "The Flow Experience and Its Significance for Human Psychology," chapter in *Optimal Experience: Psychological Studies of Flow in Consciousness*, (Cambridge University Press, 1992), 15–35.

CHAPTER 5

103 **"Baby, remember my name"**: FAME (from *Fame*), music by Michael Gore, lyrics by Dean Pitchford. © 1980 Metro-Goldwyn-Mayer Inc. All rights controlled by EMI Affiliated Catalog Inc. (Publishing) and Alfred Music Publishing Co., Inc. (Print). All Rights Reserved. Used by permission of Alfred Music.

105 **"jokes and observations about sports"**: Michele Catalano, "The Fickle Fame of Twitter," *Boingboing.net*, January 18, 2013, http://boingboing.net/2013/01/18/fickle.html. All Catalano quotes and the summary of her experience were derived from this article.

107 **shame for looking bad publicly**: E. R. Dodds, *The Greeks and the Irrational* (University of California Press, 2004).

107 **"the whole idea of the loser"**: Boris Kachka, "Has the World Finally Caught Up with Post-Punk Author Sam Lipsyte?" *New York/Vulture*, March 3, 2013.

108 **"what counted was not so much"**: Susan Cain, *Quiet* (Broadway, 2013), 21.

108 **recent research by UCLA psychologist**: Anna Mikulak, "Changes in Language and Word Use Reflect Our Shifting Values, UCLA Psychologist Reports," *UCLA Newsroom*, August 7, 2013, http://newsroom.ucla.edu/portal/ucla/changes-in-language-reflect-our-247626.aspx

109 **"I see where the Cardinals"**: Arthur Daley, "Overheard in St. Pete," *The New York Times*, March 12, 1962.

110 **Ballard got away with this**: Paul Lukas, "Is That NNOB? Or GNOB?" *Uni-Watch.com*, September 8, 2011, http://www.uni-watch.com/2011/09/08/the-real-story-behind-the-maple-leafs-1978-ghost-nameplate/

111 **In an analysis:** Jean Twenge et al, "Changes in Pronoun Use in American Books and the Rise of Individualism, 1960-2008," *Journal of Cross-Cultural Psychology*, September 2013

111 **"both studies demonstrate":** Jean Twenge and Joshua Foster, "Birth Cohort Increases in Narcissistic Personality Traits Among American College Students, 1982–2009," *Social Psychological and Personality Science*, 2010.

111 **A Pew survey:** Pew Research Center for People and the Press, "How Young People View Their Lives, Futures, and Politics," 2007.

111 **college students would rather:** Brad Bushman et al., "Sweets, Sex, or Self-Esteem? Comparing the Value of Self-Esteem Boosts with Other Pleasant Rewards," *Journal of Personality*, 2010.

111 **"the difference between *enjoying*":** Roni Caryn Rabin, "Choosing Self-Esteem Over Sex or Pizza," *The New York Times*, January 11, 2011.

111–12 **"calls attention to yourself":** Susan Cain, *Quiet* (Broadway, 2013), 77.

112 **extensions of each other:** This notion has been written about extensively by Nathan Jurgenson, social media theorist and sociologist at the University of Maryland.

112 **"Before, we had the classic panopticon":** Rob Horning, "Hi Haters!" *The New Inquiry*, November 27, 2012.

112 **A 2009 national poll:** Poll of 1,068 college students nationwide conducted by Jean Twenge, associate professor, San Diego State University and Youth Pulse LLC.

113 **In a German study:** Hanna Krasnova et al., "Envy on Facebook: A Hidden Threat to Users' Life Satisfaction?" presented at the 11th International Conference on Wirtschaftsinformatik (WI), Leipzig, Germany.

113 **"synonymous with the Internet":** Christopher Mims, "Facebook is Africa's Homepage," *The Atlantic*, July/August 2013.

114 **the size of one's audience:** "Alice Marwick on Identity," video from rdigitalife, Ryerson University.

115 **The posthumous book:** All David Foster Wallace quotes in this section are from David Lipsky's *Although of Course You End Up Becoming Yourself* (Broadway Books, 2010), 30, 74, 185, 186, 190, 192.

117 **"college students who based":** All Jennifer Crocker related quotes in this section are from "Self-Esteem That's Based on External Sources Has Mental Health Consequences, Study Says," *Monitor on Psychology*, December 2002.

118 **Pollack garners a six-figure advance:** Nathan Rabin, "Neal Pollack on Rebounding from Massive Hype and Six-Figure Deals to Online Publishing," *A.V. Club*, March 14, 2013.

120 **"A *Wired* article from 2012":** Seth Stevenson, "What Your Klout Score Really Means," *Wired*, April 24, 2012.

120 **In a piece for Forbes:** Glen Llopis, "Personal Branding Is a Leadership Requirement, Not a Self-Promotion Campaign," *Forbes*, April 8, 2013.

121 **"real goal was never fame":** Ryan Tate, "Julia Allison's Weary Morning-After Email to Wired," *Gawker*, July 18, 2008.

121 **"These things":** Danielle Sacks, "Fifty Percent of the 'Tipping Point' Is Wrong. Jonah Berger Shows You Which Half," *Fast Company*, April 2013.

122 **A 2013 corporate study:** Nicole Perlroth, "Researchers Call Out Twitter Celebrities with Suspicious Followings," *The New York Times*, April 25, 2013.

125 **"Here's to the Death of Personal Branding":** Drew Olanoff, "Here's to the Death of Personal Branding on the Internet," *TechCrunch*, October 14, 2012.

125 **One personal branding writer:** Erik Deckers, "It's Called 'Personal Branding.' Get Over It." *Problogservice*, January 4, 2012.

126 **"My recommendation is this:"** Harriet Brown, "The Boom and Bust of Ego," *Psychology Today*, January 1, 2012.

CHAPTER 6

137 **collaborate with skilled apprentices:** Adam Grant, *Give and Take* (Viking, 2013), 67, 68, 69.

137 **relationships they developed with the surgical teams:** Ibid., 70.

137 **moved alone "to a different firm":** Ibid., 72.

CHAPTER 7

150 **A study by the Stanford professor Frank Flynn:** Adam Grant, *Give and Take* (Viking, 2013), 59.

154 **The Ontario Ministry of Labor:** Jenny Yuen, "Labor Ministry Lays Charges in Downsview Radiohead Stage Collapse," *Toronto Sun*, June 7, 2013.

154 **"cutting-edge advances in sound":** Chris Jones, "Radiohead: Kid A Review," *BBC*, 2007.

154 **"layer upon layer"**: Alex Ross, "Dadrock," *The New Yorker*, September 29, 1997. (Don't let the article title fool you—it was a knock against Oasis as a point of comparison with the avant garde artistry of Radiohead.)

156 **has flown with his customized AC30**: Joe Bosso, "U2 Exclusive: The Edge's Stage Setup Revealed," *MusicRadar*, October 14, 2009.

164 **getting rejected by Michigan**: This is not meant as a slight against Michigan, Cornell, and Oberlin, all certifiably elite institutions I would have been lucky to have attended. But you know what I mean.

170 **"paradoxical mix"**: JimCollins.com, video—Level 5 Leadership.

CHAPTER 8

175 **"Only the best orchestras"**: Andrew Druckenbrod, "Rare Musikverein Residency Part of Pittsburgh Symphony Orchestra European Tour," Pittsburgh Post-Gazette, October 21, 2012.

176 **"an absolute powerhouse"**: Tim Page, "Matsuev: Muscle and Mind," *The Washington Post*, September 20, 2006.

176 **"fastest paws"**: Mark Swed, "Music Review: Young Conductor Impresses with L.A. Phil at Bowl," *Los Angeles Times*, September 5, 2012.

192 **"needs few material possessions"**: Richard O'Connor, *Happy at Last* (St. Martin's Griffin, 2009), 245.

192 **"highly autonomously motivated"**: Claude Fernet et al., "The Moderating Role of Autonomous Motivation in the Job Demands-Strain Relation," *Motivation and Emotion*, March 2013.

192 **intrinsic aspirations**: D. Coon and J. O. Mitterer, *Introduction to Psychology: Gateways to Mind and Behavior with Concept Maps* (Wadsworth, 2012).

CHAPTER 9

197 **alleged anti-semite**: I am not claiming Buchanan is or isn't anti-Semitic, only that many people, including many Jews like Zoltowsky, did/do believe this, to illustrate the psychic horror of her misdirected vote.

197 **"wouldn't sit"**: Jon Burstein and Marian Dozier, "Blizzard of Lawsuits Could Take Wing over Butterfly Ballot," *Sun Sentinel*, November 11, 2000.

198 **"All the analyses"**: Richard Smith, "A Statistical Assessment of Buchanan's Vote in Palm Beach County," *Statistical Science*, 2002.

198 **"we can state with 99.9%"**: "Who Won Florida? Are the Palm Beach Votes Irregular?" an analysis by Bruce Hansen, economics professor, University of Wisconsin.

198 **"1 in 25,000"**: "Statistical analysis of Florida voting shows 2,800 votes for Buchanan were intended for Gore," by the Indiana University political science professor Burt Monroe, an expert in multiparty elections around the world.

198 **"Do I believe these people"**: Jake Tapper, *Down & Dirty: The Plot to Steal the Presidency* (Little, Brown 2001).

198 **Additionally, a statistically outlying**: Alan Agresti and Brett Presnell, "Misvotes, Undervotes and Overvotes: The 2000 Presidential Election in Florida," *Statistical Science*, 2002.

198 **But what's not under dispute**: This is the conclusion of a multitude of analyses by academic statisticians (several of which are cited in endnotes above), and by an analysis by the *Palm Beach Post*, among others.

199 **"As far back as 1988"**: http://www.asktog.com/columns/042 ButterflyBallot.html

199 **"Maps of Election Day votes"**: Laurel Elms and Henry Brady, "Mapping the Buchanan Vote Escarpment in Palm Beach County, Florida," 2001. Paper presented at the annual meeting of the Public Choice Society.

201 **"Use lowercase letters"**: https://www.aiga.org/election-design-top-ten/

201 **"direct the voter's attention"**: Marcia Lausen, *Design for Democracy: Ballot + Election Design* (University of Chicago Press, 2007).

202 **"I joke that I have to"**: "How Does It Feel: To Be Theresa LePore," *Boca Raton*, February 2013.

204 **"I wanted to know every detail"**: Clay Tarver, "The Rock 'n' Roll Casualty Who Became a War Hero," *The New York Times*, July 2, 2013.

204 **"There was no means to"**: Judith Miller, "A Nation Challenged: Secret Sites; Iraqi Tells of Renovations at Sites for Chemical and Nuclear Arms," *The New York Times*, December 20, 2001.

205 **"Editors at several levels"**: From the Editors, "The Times and Iraq," *The New York Times*, May 26, 2004.

205 **"a lot of people"**: "Bill Keller Speaks Out on Judy Miller, Iraq War Coverage, and Fox News," *Media Matters for America*, June 3, 2011, http://mediamatters.org/blog/2011/06/03/bill-keller-speaks-out-on-judy-miller-iraq-war/180289

206 **"sites like the"**: David Zweig, "Everyone's a Fact-Checker," *The Atlantic*, August 2, 2012.

207 **"Ketchens made a mistake"**: "The Killing Towers of the US Telecom Industry," *DailyKos*, June 4, 2012.

208 **"It takes years and years of training"**: "Cell Tower Deaths," *Frontline* (transcript), May 22, 2012.

208 **"I loved the adventure"**: "The Killing Towers of the US Telecom Industry," *DailyKos*, June 4, 2012; the account of Ray Hull was culled from multiple sources, including primarily the above-referenced DailyKos and Frontline pieces.

CHAPTER 10

210 **"Westerners are the protagonists"**: Evan Osnos, "Storytelling in China and America," *The New Yorker*, September 23, 2011.

210 **"a loosely-knit social"**: The Hofstede Centre. http://geert-hofstede.com/dimensions.html

211 **"I am a wonderful"**: Qi Wang, "Culture and the Development of Self-Knowledge," *Current Directions in Psychological Science*, 2006.

211 **"People in different cultures"**: Hazel Markus, "Culture and the Self: Implications for Cognition, Emotion, and Motivation," *Psychological Review*, April 1991.

212 **"In Asian cultures"**: Susan Cain, *Quiet* (Broadway, 2013), 197.

213 **"possess, enhance, and maintain"**: Steven Heine et al., "Is There a Universal Need for Positive Self-Regard?" *Psychological Review*, October 1999.

214 Data on individualism from the Hofstede Centre, an organization tied to the work of Geert Hofstede, a highly influential Dutch researcher who pioneered global studies on individualism and collectivism.

214 **individualism and achievement**: Michelle Nelson and Sharon Shavitt, "Horizontal and Vertical Individualism and Achievement Values: A Multi-Method Examination of Denmark and the U.S.," *Journal of Cross-Cultural Psychology*, September 2002.

215 **"feel threatened by":** The Hofstede Centre. http://geert-hofstede.com

216 **In 2013 the award:** Tom Balmforth, "Vladimir Putin Presents First 'Hero of Labour' Medals Since End of Soviet Union," *The Telegraph*, May 1, 2013.

216 **everyone knows who Steve Jobs:** Steve Jobs may at first be a bit of a hyperbolic example, as by most accounts it does seem he was, at least in a supervisory role, involved in the creation of some of the most revolutionary products in the past generation, namely the iPod and iPhone. Samsung, while enormously successful, hasn't introduced products that have so altered the culture. So perhaps it's appropriate that its chief isn't as lionized. But recall the Walkman in the 1980s, a product somewhat on par with the iPod for its wow factor and near-immediate ubiquity; the head of Sony at the time wasn't mythologized the way Jobs has been.

218 **In 1995 China represented:** Harper's Index, *Harper's*, September 2013. Data via Atwood Partners.

CHAPTER 11

225 **"desperately few of us":** Douglas Rushkoff, "Learn to Code, Get a Job," CNN, January 12, 2012, http://www.cnn.com/2012/01/12/opinion/rushkoff-write-code

225 **"the way a thing gets made":** Profoundlydisconnected.com

226 **"people are using the same techniques":** "Clive Thompson on the Age of Microcelebrity: Why Everyone's a Little Brad Pitt," *Wired*, November 27, 2007.

226 **everyone will be famous to fifteen people:** This variation has several attributions, including the philosopher and writer David Weinberger, and the artist Momus, among others.

INDEX

Italic page numbers refer to illustrations.